Before You Begin:
PLEASE START HERE

The Cardinal Newman Society recommends for your consideration all of the colleges and universities in this *Guide*, because of their commitment to providing a faithful Catholic education. *The Newman Guide* is a great first step in your college search, but no guide can identify the college that is the best fit for *you*.

All of the fine institutions recommended in this *Guide* are unique, each with their own special charism, approach to education, and campus culture.

For instance, some of the colleges immerse students in every aspect of faithful Catholic life "from the classroom to the dorm room," as we like to say. The students at these colleges tend to be mostly or entirely Catholic and motivated by their faith.

On the other hand, some of the other colleges, while fully and faithfully Catholic, serve a more diverse group of students. At these institutions the Catholic culture will tend to be less intense or overt. This is typically more apparent in student activities and dorm life than in the classroom.

Also, many of the *Newman Guide* colleges are liberal arts institutions, while several others offer a wide variety of majors. Some have extensive athletics and club activities; others favor a quiet atmosphere for contemplation and study.

Some have a strong core curriculum that may run through all four years of an undergraduate program, while others offer students a choice of electives and encourage specialization.

Some allow opposite-sex visitation in student bedrooms, while others do not. This fact should be of particular interest to parents and students when considering a college.

In general, one type of institution may not be better than the other. But one type is likely better for *your* unique needs.

The editors believe this is important to highlight, because we occasionally hear from parents and students who mistakenly assume that every college in *The Newman Guide* provides the same type of experience, education and living arrangement as another.

Parents and students need to look carefully at each college to decide if what it offers is what you need and are looking for. You'll find good advice in our companion publication, *My Future, My Faith*. And we cannot recommend enough a campus visit, including an overnight stay on a Friday or Saturday night.

We are delighted in the diversity of the institutions in *The Newman Guide*, offering a number of great options for nearly every type of student who is seeking a faithful Catholic education. We pray that you successfully find the college that is the best fit for you.

Acknowledgements

Beginning last year, *The Newman Guide* became an annual publication, and this new 2014 edition reflects an update to the major redesign that occurred with the 2012-2013 edition.

Over the course of the past seven years, we have heard from countless families with requests for additional information about the Catholic colleges and universities we recommend, and this edition, *published in its most comprehensive form online*, provides that information.

The 2014 edition is comprised of three parts: this book, which includes full-color profiles of the 28 recommended institutions; our magazine, *My Future, My Faith*, which includes advice on the college search and navigating the transition from high school to college; and TheNewmanGuide.com website, which includes all of the content of the book and magazine in addition to substantially more information about each college.

Cardinal Newman Society President Patrick Reilly was responsible for making all final editorial decisions, while Executive Vice President Thomas Mead was responsible for managing the entire project.

We are grateful to the Society's Communications Director Adam Wilson, who was the managing editor for the online content, as well as our Director of External Relations David Costanzo, Marketing and Publications Assistant Kelly Conroy, and Programs Assistant Erica Szalkowksi who helped with production.

We are indebted to those who contributed articles to *My Future, My Faith*, especially Archbishop William Lori, Bishop David Ricken, Dr. Peter Kreeft, Father C. John McCloskey, Dr. Christopher Kaczor, Kathryn Lopez, Phil Lenahan, Andrew Pudewa, and the staff of FOCUS.

This *Guide* would not have been possible without the prayers and very generous support of Cardinal Newman Society members. Though too numerous to name, we realize that without their support none of this work would be possible.

Finally, we recognize that to the extent that *The Newman Guide* contributes to the renewal of Catholic higher education, it is due to the inspiration of the Holy Spirit.

Errors or omissions, if any, are the responsibility of the editors and will be corrected in the online version of the *Guide*.

Patrick Reilly, President
Tom Mead, Executive Vice President

The Newman Guide to Choosing a Catholic College

2014 Edition

Also published online at TheNewmanGuide.com with additional material

Q.ht/XqHNe

2014 Edition dedicated with grateful affection to Benedict XVI

The Cardinal Newman Society
Manassas, Virginia

The Newman Guide to Choosing a Catholic College—2014 ed.—Manassas, VA : The Cardinal Newman Society, 2013.

    p. ; cm.
    ISBN: 9780988557017 (paper)
    Library of Congress Control Number: 2013947955

1. Catholic universities and colleges—United States—Directories. 2. College choice—United States—Handbooks, manuals, etc. I. Cardinal Newman Society.

Cover photo courtesy of Christendom College

Published by: The Cardinal Newman Society
                9720 Capital Court, Suite 201
                Manassas, VA 20110
                www.CardinalNewmanSociety.org
                www.TheNewmanGuide.com
                (703) 367-0333

Printed in the United States of America

About The Cardinal Newman Society

Founded in 1993, The Cardinal Newman Society is dedicated to promoting and defending faithful Catholic education. The Society is a 501(c)(3) tax-exempt, nonprofit organization.

In addition to publishing *The Newman Guide*, the Society administers the Catholic High School Honor Roll, which recognizes high schools across America for excellence in Catholic identity, academics and civics education.

The Cardinal Newman Society's Center for the Advancement of Catholic Higher Education works to support and foster collaboration among those presidents, faculty and staff interested in strengthening and protecting their colleges' Catholic identity.

The Society's online publication and regular e-mail service, Catholic Education Daily, reports on developments on Catholic campuses and works to defend Catholic identity by shining a light on scandal.

Additionally, the Society promotes Eucharistic Adoration and is the national coordinator for the display of the Vatican's International Exposition "The Eucharistic Miracles of the World" on college campuses and at Catholic high schools.

For more information on The Cardinal Newman Society and its programs, to stand with us for faithful Catholic education as a member, or to make a donation, please visit us on the web at CardinalNewmanSociety.org.

Table of Contents

Recommended Residential Catholic Colleges

Recommended Non-Residential Colleges

Recommended International Colleges and Programs

How to Use *The Newman Guide*

The comprehensive *Newman Guide* is made up of three distinct parts: *The Newman Guide to Choosing a Catholic College* book which includes profiles of the recommended colleges; the new *My Future, My Faith* full-color magazine which includes helpful essays on how to choose a faithful college; and our comprehensive website, TheNewmanGuide.com, which includes all of the content from the book and magazine plus answers from the colleges to an in-depth questionnaire. You should look at all three resources to help you make a good choice!

1 The flagship of our program to promote and defend faithful Catholic education, the 2012-2013 edition of our *Newman Guide* is now in full color and features profiles of 28 recommended colleges, universities, and online programs. Each profile contains an overview, information on academics, residence life, student activities, and spiritual life.

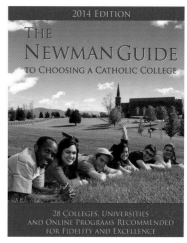

In addition, the profiles each have a "Quick Facts" box that notes the number of undergraduate students, median SAT scores and high school GPAs of admitted students, the number of majors offered, the percentage of students who are Catholic, and the cost of the college. The profiles also include a letter to parents and students from the college president and information on financial aid opportunities.

The profiles are completely updated after extensive campus visits and/or interviews with faculty, staff, administrators, students, and alumni. Don't stop here, though! The articles contained in *My Future, My Faith* really put the college search in context.

2 This new, full-color magazine features more than a dozen articles designed to help parents and students navigate the transition from high school to college. Unlike previous editions of *The Newman Guide*, we separated the essays and articles on choosing a college, because families told us they were getting lost when paired with the profiles of the recommended colleges.

Among the features are "Why Choose a Catholic College" by Baltimore Archbishop William Lori, "How to Know Which College Is Right for You," and "Fidelity Matters: Catholic Colleges Are Not All the Same."

Other topics include keys for getting into a good college, how to write an exceptional application essay, tips for making a campus visit, and how to pay for college. For the first time we also include strategies for sustaining and growing your faith on campus, suggested rules for campus dating, and an article from our friends at FOCUS on why successful and happy students pursue chastity, sobriety, and excellence.

3 Our brand new website is a content-rich, easy-to-navigate online resource that includes all of the content contained in *The Newman Guide* and *My Future, My Faith*, plus exclusive content that is only available online. The website includes promotional videos of the colleges, links to online campus photo tours, a contact form for the admissions office of each recommended college, and social media links.

In addition, we have been asked by families to provide answers to a range of questions on everything from accreditation to majors and from Mass times to student clubs. Rather than filtering this information for you, each recommended college has completed a comprehensive questionnaire on academics, student life, and institutional governance. Their answers are published online.

The additional content available on TheNewmanGuide.com is equivalent to 400+ pages of additional material for you to use to help find the right faithful college for you.

Don't forget about the important articles and essays in *My Future, My Faith*, which is available at no cost online...

Why Choose a Catholic College, by Archbishop William Lori

How to Know Which College Is Right for You

Tips for the All-Important College Visit

It's About Navigating Life: The Importance of Philosophy and Theology, by Dr. Peter Kreeft

Fidelity Matters... A Lot: Catholic Colleges Are Not All the Same, by Father C. John McCloskey

Blessings and Pitfalls of Dorm Life, by Kathryn Lopez

Getting Into a Good College: 5 Things You Need to Know, by Matthew Archbold

College Search Timeline

College Applications: Steps to an Exceptional Essay, by Andrew Pudewa

Paying for College: Big Money, Hard Choices, by Phil Lenahan

A Reminder About the Real World: Tips for Keeping Your Faith Alive in College, by Dr. Christopher Kaczor

A Checklist for Growing Your Faith, by Bishop David Ricken

The Happy and Successful Student: Pursuing Chastity, Sobriety and Excellence, by FOCUS staff

10 Rules 4 Campus Dating, by Father C. John McCloskey

www.TheNewmanGuide.com

Q.ht/zcjdG

F.A.Q.s

What is the special value of a Catholic college education?

A faithful Catholic college provides an open and healthy environment for serious consideration of ideas without the tyranny of harassment, political correctness, or enforced relativism. The same cannot be said for many secular institutions. At the colleges featured in this *Guide*, students will also find a vibrant Catholic culture on campus that respects Catholic moral teaching and offers numerous opportunities for spiritual development. Although every campus varies, differences from the typical secularized Catholic campus might include a more active Catholic campus ministry, respect for Catholic values in areas including residential life and campus programs, active pro-life and social justice efforts, community outreach programs, Catholic study groups, etc.

Can I get a good education at a Catholic college or university that is not included in this Guide?

This *Guide* presents the Catholic colleges that we recommend as placing a premium on their Catholic identity in all aspects of campus life. They also provide a good education. Among those colleges not included in the *Guide* are some with strong academic credentials but that do not have, in our opinion, the same commitment to Catholic identity. The opportunity for strengthening spiritual formation during the college years is enhanced where Catholic teachings are constantly reinforced. We believe that the best combination of spiritual and academic commitment is reflected in the colleges recommended in this *Guide*.

What is Ex corde Ecclesiae?

It is the Apostolic Constitution on Catholic higher education issued by Pope John Paul II in 1990. The document identifies what constitutes Catholic identity at Catholic colleges and universities and specifies General Norms to achieve a Catholic mission. These Norms are binding on Catholic colleges as an application of Canon Law. In 1999 the U.S. bishops approved guidelines to implement *Ex corde Ecclesiae* in the United States; these became effective in 2001. Compliance by the U.S. Catholic colleges and universities varies widely. Clearly, a Catholic institution that minimizes or subverts *Ex corde Ecclesiae*, which has the force of Canon Law, has serious problems with its Catholic identity. All colleges recommended in this *Guide* enthusiastically support and abide by *Ex corde Ecclesiae*.

How important is accreditation?

Accreditation can be very important. Problems can result down the road if a student graduates from an unaccredited college. In applying to graduate school, for example, they may find that their undergraduate work is not fully acceptable at the college to which they are applying. A few colleges in this *Guide* are not yet accredited because the process of accreditation can take several years. There is a standard process that an aspiring college must follow. The good news is that once accreditation is granted, it applies retroactively. We are impressed by the progress that the non-accredited colleges in this *Guide* have made, and we are confident that the key question is "when" not "if" they will be fully accredited. Nevertheless, students should discuss this matter with the admissions office at each college and feel comfortable with the accreditation status of the college that is finally selected.

What is a core curriculum?

General education requirements typically help ensure a foundation in the traditional liberal arts; at a Catholic college, these should include theology and philosophy. It is the mark of a good college that students learn not only specialized skills, but also how to think and communicate clearly, how to organize knowledge and thought, and how to apply the truths of the Catholic Faith in their lives. There are two common types of general education. A "core" curriculum is a set of particular courses that every student must take. It reflects a college's conviction that particular knowledge and subjects ought to be considered and shared by all students. What is labeled a "core," however, may be more properly described as a "distribution" curriculum. This allows for some flexibility in choosing electives within required disciplines, so that not every student takes the precise same courses. Interdisciplinary study, which helps students relate truth across disciplines and is encouraged in *Ex corde Ecclesiae*, is most possible in a core curriculum but may also occur within any well-designed course.

What is the mandatum?

According to the U.S. Conference of Catholic Bishops, "The *mandatum* is fundamentally an acknowledgement by church authority that a Catholic professor of a theological discipline is teaching within the full communion of the Catholic Church." According to Canon Law, every Catholic theology professor must receive the *mandatum* from his local bishop. Sadly many Catholic colleges refuse to identify theology professors who have the *mandatum*, and they may not require it as a condition of employment. Colleges in *The Newman Guide* are different; see their policies in the Q&A section for each college on our online *Guide* website at TheNewmanGuide.com.

I consider myself more a "doer" rather than a "thinker." Should I avoid colleges that place a premium on theology and philosophy courses?

No, that would be a mistake. Everyone should be concerned with "First Things"—the natural and supernatural truths that lie at the root of all knowledge and activity—and the best way to do so is to understand what they are and how to address them. You would shortchange yourself by avoiding these academic areas. For a fuller discussion of the importance of philosophy and theology, see Dr. Peter Kreeft's essay in *My Future, My Faith*.

How important is it to select a college with a vibrant spiritual life?

It is critical. While most people assume that colleges help provide a good education and prepare young people for careers, it is also a time for them to strengthen their spiritual life as they mature into adulthood. The best way to be so formed is to be in an atmosphere where the spiritual life, inside and outside the classroom, is emphasized and nurtured. A Catholic college that does this is fulfilling its role.

Is there an ideal residence hall arrangement?

In general, yes. The "hook-up culture" is real and can be a danger to students' spiritual, psychological, and physical health. Single-sex dorms help students avoid this culture and live chaste lives. Of course, the ultimate responsibility falls on the shoulders of the students, but we believe Catholic colleges have a responsibility to have living arrangements and visitation policies which help students live chaste lives. Residence halls which provide an atmosphere where chastity is expected are to be especially commended. There are some instances where colleges have males and females in the same dormitory but restrict males and females to different wings or even floors. This may reflect a college's space or financial limitations. Such an arrangement, while not ideal, might be workable provided the college maintains strict and careful supervision. These arrangements bear close inspection by parents and students.

Alcohol consumption seems to be a problem on college campuses, even at good Catholic colleges. What does this mean for a parent?

Underage and binge drinking are widespread problems and seem to reflect a general permissiveness within the broader society. It is imperative that parents discuss the issue candidly with their son or daughter. While colleges can and do address the issue through lectures and strict policies, it is ultimately the responsibility of the individual student to do the right thing.

Why are there so few larger universities in this Guide?

We recommend colleges that actively live their Catholic identity. Sometimes the larger universities, in an attempt to build a national secular reputation as a research university, feel the need to de-emphasize their Catholicism. Some call it academic freedom or even just diversity, but it often unhinges a college from its traditional Catholic moorings. A large Catholic university can be faithful to its identity if it so chooses. We are hopeful that more will begin to recognize that academic excellence, freedom of inquiry, national reputation and Catholic identity are all compatible.

Some of the colleges in this Guide are small, even very small. Should I be concerned about attending a college with a small student body?

Certainly not. Small colleges can provide great individual attention to student needs. They can help students gain confidence in classroom discussions, develop good relationships with faculty members and forge friendships with other students. But small colleges are not for everyone. Some students prefer the opportunity to interact with a wider range of students, participate in more activities and take advantage of broader course offerings. A student needs to evaluate whether he or she is comfortable with the size of the college based on such issues as his or her personality and academic needs.

I have found a few colleges in this Guide that greatly interest me. What do I do next?

Our companion publication, *My Future, My Faith*, offers helpful advice for your college search.

You should visit the online site for this *Guide* at TheNewmanGuide.com for more information about the colleges, including contact information. Next, thoroughly investigate the college's website. If you have questions, e-mail them to the appropriate college representative. Read the campus newspapers (many are online) to learn more about what's happening on campus—what are the issues, what are the problems, what do students seem to care about? When you feel you have enough information to winnow down your list, visit each campus that has made the cut. The campus visit is essential. Talk to students there, wander around the campus, explore the town, attend Mass and campus events, and speak forthrightly with college representatives. May God bless your search!

Recommended Residential Catholic Colleges

A Note About the Financial Aid and Career Services Sections

Paying for college and being able to find a job after graduation are two important considerations when choosing a college. In order to help families evaluate these two areas, the editors invited each college to submit information about them. Their submissions are printed in shaded containers within each profile.

About the Quick Facts Box

Quick Facts

Students the number of full-time undergraduate students

SATs the median SATs/ACTs for reading and math for freshmen

HS GPA the median grade point average for admitted freshmen

Majors the number of academic majors available

% Catholic the percentage of undergraduates who are Catholic

How Much? the cost of attendance for one academic year

	% Students Catholic	% Faculty Catholic	Median HS GPA	Median SATs or ACTs	# of Majors
Aquinas College	40%	67%	3.5	1210 SAT	12
Ave Maria University	84%	92%	3.5	1074 SAT 24 ACT	23
Belmont Abbey College	50%	51%	3.35	1040 SAT	14
Benedictine College	86%	65%	3.63	24 ACT	43
Catholic University of America	80%	55%	3.5	1110 SAT	73
Christendom College	99%	100%	3.7	1200 SAT	6
College of Saint Mary Magdalen	98%	93%	3.3	1210 SAT	1
Fisher More College	100%	100%	not tracked	not tracked	6
DeSales University	unknown	unknown	3.25	1090 SAT	36
Franciscan University of Steubenville	97%	94%	3.81	25.2 ACT	41
John Paul the Great Catholic University	99%	60%	3.4	1090 SAT 23 ACT	2
Mount St. Mary's University	75%	60%	3.4	1105 SAT	31
St. Gregory's University	50%	60%	3.27	900 SAT 21.25 ACT	32
Thomas Aquinas College	98%	96%	3.8	1280 SAT	1
Thomas More College of Liberal Arts	87%	100%	3.75	1200 SAT	1
University of Dallas	83%	not available	3.65	1204 SAT	29
University of Mary	52%	not available	3.39	23 ACT	54
University of St. Thomas	64%	70%	3.61	1128 SAT 25 ACT	38
Walsh University	43%	52%	3.35	1050 SAT 22.57 ACT	53
Wyoming Catholic College	98%	100%	not available	1160 SAT	1

	Extraordinary Form of the Mass? * denotes if offered every Sunday	# of days confessions scheduled (per week)	# of days Adoration scheduled (per week)	All on-campus students in single-sex dorms?	Opposite sex visiting hours in student bedrooms?
Aquinas College	No	5	1	No (temporary dorms)	No
Ave Maria University	Yes*	5	perpetual	Yes	Yes (open door policy)
Belmont Abbey College	No	7	7	Yes	Yes
Benedictine College	No	7	perpetual	Yes	Yes
Catholic University of America	No	2	2	No (97% in single-sex)	Yes
Christendom College	Yes	7	5	Yes	No
College of Saint Mary Magdalen	Yes	6	varied	Yes	No
Fisher More College	Yes*	7	1	Yes	No
DeSales University	No	1	1	No (60% in single-sex)	Yes
Franciscan University of Steubenville	Yes	4	perpetual	Yes	Yes (open door policy)
John Paul the Great Catholic University	No	4	4	Yes	No
Mount St. Mary's University	No	7	6	No (3% in single-sex)	Yes
St. Gregory's University	No	3	1	Yes	Yes
Thomas Aquinas College	Yes*	7	7	Yes	No
Thomas More College of Liberal Arts	Yes	5	1	Yes	No
University of Dallas	No	4	5	No (50% in single-sex)	Yes (open bolt policy)
University of Mary	No	3	5	No (76% in single-sex)	Yes
University of St. Thomas	Yes	3	2	No (0% in single-sex)	Yes
Walsh University	No	6	6	No (0% in single-sex)	Yes
Wyoming Catholic College	Yes*	7	5	Yes	No

AQUINAS COLLEGE

Nashville, Tennessee

411

For more information on Aquinas, visit their website at:

www.aquinascollege.edu

Admissions contact:

800/649-9956
admissions@aquinascollege.edu

Overview

The Dominican Sisters of St. Cecilia (the "Nashville Dominicans") celebrated the 50th anniversary of Aquinas College in Nashville, Tennessee, in 2011. Since then, the College has welcomed a new president, Sister Mary Sarah Galbraith, O.P., opened its first housing for resident students, and launched graduate programs in teacher education and nursing education.

Begun in 1928 as a teacher-training school for Dominican sisters, Aquinas became a junior college in 1961 and a four-year college in 1994. Its education program is the training ground for lay people as well as the Dominican sisters who teach in 41 Catholic schools in 23 dioceses in the United States. And the Sisters belong to one of the few congregations of women religious in the United States that today enjoy significant growth—nearly 50 percent in the last 15 years.

The small College has an exciting future with the launch of a long-desired residential program for its 83-acre campus, just five miles from downtown Nashville. Limited housing opened in 2012, and permanent campus residences are

scheduled to be completed by 2014. By the next year, the College expects undergraduate enrollment to increase 40 percent to 1,000 students. That should lead to expanded academic programs and an increasing percentage of full-time and Catholic students.

Aquinas has managed to remain a faithfully Catholic institution surrounded by a largely Protestant and Evangelical Christian population. Because the previously non-residential college has drawn from the local community, only about a third of the lay students are Catholic, but devotion to Christ and traditional morals nevertheless pervade the campus. The presence of the Dominican Sisters and a faithful faculty and staff ensure the strong Catholic identity of the College.

"What Aquinas is today is clearly a result of careful thought and prayer," Sister Mary Sarah told Aquinas College magazine, citing several examples of the Sisters' foresight and Catholic inspiration. "They set in place a liberal arts core but attached practical programs to it. To address the battle of the mind, they founded the School of Education. To address the battle for human life and dignity, they founded the School of Nursing. To address the battle for humane growth in the marketplace, they instituted the School of Business."

Unlike many Catholic colleges that are now legally independent of the religious congregations that founded them, the Dominican Sisters of St. Cecilia have never ceded control of Aquinas. They are the sole owners of the College, with a mixed lay-religious board of trustees. Sister Mary Sarah entered the Congregation in 1988, has advanced degrees in education administration and history, and has worked as a teacher, professor, principal, and dean in various Catholic schools and colleges.

The undergraduate tuition remains far below the average private college tuition in the country.

Quick Facts

2013-2014 Academic Year

Students 550

SATs 1210

HS GPA 3.5

Majors 12

% Catholic 40%

How Much? $29,250
tuition, room and board

Academics

Aquinas integrates the liberal arts and Catholic teaching into the undergraduate programs for each of its four schools: nursing, education, business, and arts and sciences. According to one administrator, the College strives to teach "what theology and philosophy have to say about other disciplines."

Course requirements vary according to degree program. All students with majors in the School of Arts and Sciences—including theology, philosophy, history, English, and liberal arts—take three Catholic theology courses in  fundamental theology, moral theology, and Scripture and three philosophy courses in logic, ethics, and philosophy of the human person. They also study English composition and speech, and choose among electives in history, literature, math, science, fine arts, and a foreign language. More than half the credits Professorrequired for a bachelor's degree come from the core and distribution requirements.

Nursing, education, and business students take fewer theology and philosophy courses, but still at least 40 percent of total credits come from the liberal arts.

The theology professors have all received the *mandatum* from Nashville Bishop David Choby, who attended Aquinas in the 1960s before moving on to the seminary. He has taught moral theology at the College and is a strong supporter of the College and the Congregation.

Brother Ignatius Perkins, O.P., former dean and nursing professor at Spalding University, directs the Aquinas School of Nursing and has done much to raise its national profile. "We give students the tools to help their patients make the right moral decisions," said one nursing professor.

Support for a free-market economy is complemented by a desire for "Christian moral constraints" in the business program. The College boasts, "The primary goal of the Bachelor of Business Administration (BBA) Program is training competent business leaders who are conscious of their broader responsibilities to society."

Ten Dominican sisters teach at Aquinas, joined by more than 70 other full- and part-time professors. Most full-time, non-nursing faculty members hold doctorates or equivalent terminal degrees.

The College makes an effort to ease the challenge of the first year for students through its Aquinas College Cares about Every Student's Success (ACCESS) program and a freshman formation retreat launched in the 2011-2012 academic year. ACCESS is a required program of mentoring, tutoring, and advising for first-year and other new students. The freshman retreat introduces students to classic Dominican spirituality and education.

Students also benefit from the College's Write Reason Center, which aims to strengthen student writing across the curriculum and provides mentors to assist students. The unique program is rooted in the classical Trivium, emphasizing habits of mind (logic) and habits of expression (grammar and rhetoric) so that students learn to write and think logically and with concern for objective truth.

Spiritual Life

ChapelThe center of the campus' spiritual life is St. Jude's Chapel. Aquinas offers many spiritual programs including weekly Adoration of the Blessed Sacra-

Financial Aid Office Info

The mission of the Office of Financial Aid at Aquinas College is to ensure each student receives the best financial aid package for which he or she qualifies.

A variety of assistance is available including: Federal Pell Grants, Federal Supplemental Educational Opportunity Grants, Federal Stafford Subsidized/Unsubsidized/PLUS Loans, Federal Work-Study, Tennessee State Grants, Tennessee Education Lottery Scholarships, Private Alternative Loans and Aquinas College Grants and Scholarships. There is also financial aid available to eligible Graduate Students.

For information about which scholarships and grants you may qualify for and how to apply for them, visit the Office of Financial Aid or call (615) 297-7545 ext. 442.

ment, weekday confessions, daily Mass, Lenten Stations of the Cross, an annual Eucharistic Procession, and numerous other opportunities for group prayer.

The campus ministry is heavily involved in pro-life activities. Students pray at abortion clinics and each January erect a "Cemetery of the Innocents" on the front lawn of campus next to busy Harding Pike to memorialize aborted children.

Campus ministry also sponsors Bible study groups, social activities, inquiry sessions for non-Catholics, and retreats for student leaders.

Residential Life

Perhaps the most exciting recent development at Aquinas has been the launch of its residential program, which is likely to transform the college as many more full-time students from around the country find it easier to come to Aquinas.

In 2012, Aquinas announced a partner-

Student Activities

A Student Activities Board sponsors speakers and other events, and student organizations include groups for student nurses and prospective teachers, a business fraternity, a classical literature reading group, a theology club, and a philosophy club.

Sister and studentsThe Frassati Society encourages students to conform their lives according to the Beatitudes and sponsors pro-life and social activities. There also is a weekly student discussion group that is similar to the popular "Theology on Tap" programs around the country.

The student chapter of the Association for Supervision and Curriculum Development provides professional development opportunities for teacher education students and allows them to attend the Association's national conferences. Other honor and service organizations, such as Sigma Beta Delta (business honor society), Alpha Beta Nu (nursing honor society), and Delta Epsilon Sigma (academic honor society) are active at Aquinas College.

Known as the "Athens of the South," Nashville offers many cultural, social, and entertainment opportunities. There is, of course, the venerable Grand Ole Opry with its internationally broadcast Saturday night performances, a growing Christian music community, and also National Football League (Tennessee Titans) and National Hockey League (Nashville Predators) teams to follow. Cultural attractions include the Frist Center for the Visual Arts, the Ryman Theater, the Bridgestone Arena and the Schermer-

ship with St. Thomas Hospital, which is adjacent to the campus, to house students in a portion of the hospital's Seton Lodge. Students have access to the medical services and health club at St. Thomas Hospital. The hotel-like residence, which is single-sex by floor, will accommodate only a small number of students for the first year, but the College hopes to greatly increase the number of residents for the 2013-2014 academic year. Residents for the 2012-2013 year hail from ten states: Washington, New Mexico, Texas, Minnesota, Ohio, Maryland, Delaware, Virginia, Tennessee, and Alabama.

The College expects the number of residential students to triple in 2013-14, even as it begins construction of on-campus residences. These will all be single-sex residences with visitation restricted to common areas. While campus housing is under development, Aquinas assists students looking for off-campus houses or apartments.

Aquinas promotes the "house system" with students, faculty, staff, and alumni joining together voluntarily to support each other and organize joint activities. Four houses each for men and women are named for patron saints who represent the ideals and morals toward which the students strive.

Nashville is the capital city of Tennessee with a population of more than 630,000 people. In addition to famous and historical ties to the country music industry, Nashville has a vast health care sector and a growing automobile manufacturing industry.

Nashville is a transportation hub, which includes the Nashville International Airport, a hub for Southwest Airlines and host to other major carriers easily accessible from the College. Due to its central location and the numerous interstate highways converging in the city, Nashville is within a day's drive of two-thirds of the nation's population. Despite being located in such a busy urban area, the campus has a very low crime rate.

horn Symphony Center, which hosts the Nashville Symphony.

The Bottom Line

Aquinas College is a growing Catholic college that has carved out an important niche in the Bible Belt with its nursing, education, and business programs, as well as a strong emphasis on the liberal arts for all students. It is significantly expanding its campus and both its undergraduate and graduate programs.

This has long been an obvious choice for students in the Nashville region and those who are interested in nursing and education. But especially with the new residential options, affordability, solid liberal arts foundation, and careful attention and dynamic spirit that the Dominican Sisters and dedicated faculty and staff provide to faithful education, Aquinas will be increasingly attractive to Catholic families both regionally and nationally.

Letter from the President

Dear parents and students,

Aquinas College in Nashville, Tennessee, is privileged to bear the name of one of the greatest Catholic educators, St. Thomas Aquinas; and we are dedicated to the Church's mission of imparting to others the beauty and majesty of the Catholic faith through the nearly eight hundred year old tradition of Dominican prayer, study, and teaching.

Much like the medieval university, Aquinas College finds itself happily at the crossroad where culture and faith meet. Our strategic plan is already bearing fruit. In the fall of 2012 we began our first Residential Program and our first Graduate Studies in Nursing Education and Teacher Education. All have had wonderful success, and we foresee a flourishing of other programs that will enable our students to be true witnesses to the hope of Christ.

We welcome you to our campus and invite you to be a part of Aquinas College's commitment to this great endeavor.

Sincerely,

Sister Mary Sarah, O.P.

Aquinas College
Frequently Asked Questions

We get questions from Catholic families on a regular basis about the colleges we recommend. Rather than filter the answers, we asked Aquinas officials nearly 100 questions in categories such as academics, curriculum, programs of study, campus ministry, residence life, student activities, the make up of the study body, and institutional identity. The answers to some of the most asked questions are provided below and the rest are available on the Aquinas profile page at TheNewmanGuide.com.

Majors

List the major, minor and special program areas that students may choose for specialization while pursuing an undergraduate degree:

Nursing (ASN, BSN); Liberal Arts (AA, BA); English, History, Philosophy and Theology (BA); Interdisciplinary Studies (K-6 Teacher certification) or English (7-12 certification) (BA); Management, Finance (BBA)

What are the three most popular majors or specialty disciplines for undergraduate students, and about what percentage of undergraduate students specialize in these disciplines?

ASN, 50%

Teacher Ed., 12%

Liberal Arts, 6%

Spiritual Life

Please list the schedule of Masses, noting the following for each Mass: the day and time, the Form or Rite of the Mass, and the style of music, if any (chant, traditional, contemporary, etc.):

Mo 12:20 p.m. Traditional, Ordinary Form

Tu 12:20 p.m. Traditional, Ordinary Form

We 12:20 p.m. Traditional, Ordinary Form

Th 12:20 p.m. Traditional, Ordinary Form

Fr 12:20 p.m. Traditional, Ordinary Form

Sa N/A

Su 6:30 p.m. Traditional, Ordinary Form

List the schedule for Confession by day and time:

Mo 11:30 - 12:10 p.m.

Tu 11:30 - 12:10 p.m.

We 11:30 - 12:10 p.m.

Th 11:30 - 12:10 p.m.

Fr 11:30 - 12:10 p.m.

Sa

Su

Other: Always by appointment

List the schedule for Adoration of the Blessed Sacrament by day and time:

Wednesdays 9:30 a.m. - 12:10 p.m.

Please identify regularly scheduled devotions on campus for students such as the Rosary and prayer groups:

Rosary, Eucharistic processions, Stations of the Cross, Frassati Prayer Group, Advent and Lenten Retreats, Vigil night of prayer

Residence Life

Please describe options for students to reside on and off campus:

Aquinas recently launched a campus-wide house system and a Residential Life Program to accommodate on-campus residents. Current resident students live on single-sex floors, in a temporary residence at St. Thomas' Seton Lodge adjacent to campus. Current housing is available to all qualifying freshmen, 21 or younger. The Student Affairs office keeps both a bulletin board with off-campus housing information and a binder of local apartment complexes for students looking for off-campus houses or apartments. Student Affairs also assists students who are looking for roommates to share a house or apartment.

The College has plans to offer additional single-sex residence halls within the next two years. Within these halls, we plan to foster a wholesome environment conducive to personal growth that will bring students closer to God and promote and support chastity. Students of the opposite sex will not be allowed to visit student's room. There will be convenient and comfortable common areas where students can meet for study, prayer and other social activities.

Does your institution offer only single-sex residence halls?

No

What percentage of students living on campus live in single-sex residence halls?

0%. Our current, temporary residence hall offers single-sex floors with restricted access. Planned future housing will be single-sex residence halls.

Are students of the opposite sex permitted to visit students' bedrooms?

No.

How does your institution foster sobriety and respond to substance abuse on campus, particularly in campus residences?

The institution fosters sobriety by sponsoring Social Norms events , displaying posters around campus with published sobriety statistics from a core survey. Students of any age are not permitted to have alcohol anywhere on campus.

How does your institution foster a student living environment that promotes and supports chastity, particularly in campus residences?

The institution promotes and supports chastity, especially in campus residences by only offering single-sex residence floors, promoting residence community mass and dinner on Sunday evenings, RA-led prayer groups, 24 hour chapel access and weekly adoration.

Student Body

Describe the makeup of your institution's undergraduate student body with regard to sex, religion, home state/country and type of high school (public, private, homeschool):

Total number of undergraduates: 600
Male: 15% Female: 85%

Catholic: 35% Other Christian: 55%
Jewish: 1% Muslim: 1% Other: 10%

Number of states represented: 11
Top three states: Tennessee, Texas, Mississippi
Students from top three states: 96%

Catholic HS: 27% Homeschool: 11%
Private HS: 11% Public HS: 42%

AVE MARIA UNIVERSITY

Ave Maria, Florida

Overview

Ave Maria University (AMU) was founded by former Domino's Pizza owner Tom Monaghan as a direct response to Blessed Pope John Paul II's call for a new evangelization.

"Ave Maria's Catholic identity is palpable in every aspect of its campus life from academics to student activities," said Michael Dauphinais, dean of the faculty. "The faculty and students enjoy being at a university where they possess the freedom to be Catholic."

AMU has quickly built a national reputation for its strong Catholic identity, largely because of the notoriety and devotion of its founder. What is less known is AMU's academic quality, which is quite good.

Built from the ground up on a tract of farmland, AMU moved from Michigan to its permanent site in 2007, adjacent to the new town of Ave Maria and approximately 25 miles east of Naples, Florida. "It was the easiest place to attract students and faculty to, and I wanted to be close to Latin America," said Monaghan, who has donated much of his wealth to the University and owns a half-interest in the town and its development, upon

which AMU's future partly depends.

AMU now has 940 undergraduate students, most of them Catholic. The decline of the real estate market in recent years has delayed plans for a much larger university and community. Nevertheless, relative to other new institutions, AMU and its surroundings have experienced dramatic growth and construction. This includes all of the Frank Lloyd Wright-inspired campus buildings, the massive Oratory, and the town's bright-colored retail shops and condominiums. Even Oil Well Road, the primary route to AMU, expanded from a two-lane road making it easier to get to the campus.

In February 2011, AMU welcomed its second president H. James Towey, who had been president of St. Vincent College in Pennsylvania and also a federal government official responsible for grants to faith-based programs. With Towey the presidency assumed the typical role of chief executive, which had previously been held by Monaghan in a supervisory role over the president.

The University is governed by a 21-member board of trustees consisting of both laity and clergy, but all must be Catholic. Bishop Frank Dewane of Venice, Florida, is an ex officio board member. He officially recognized AMU as Catholic in 2011, following a period of review.

Catholicism is exhibited throughout the University's architecture, art, and curriculum. The centrality of the Oratory and the availability of the Sacraments highlight the school's focus. Beautiful religious art is found throughout the 400,000-volume Canizaro Library.

Academics

Both students and faculty speak of the academically rigorous coursework at Ave Maria. "If you're not coming here for academics, you'll have four years of suffering, and the teachers will have no

Quick Facts

2013-2014 Academic Year

Students 941

SATs 1074 (ACT 24)

HS GPA 3.5

Majors 23

% Catholic 84%

How Much? $32,286
tuition, room and board

leniency," said graduate Daniel Montgomery. But among the students we have spoken to, they simply love the quality of their classes.

Half of the 128 undergraduate credits required for graduation must be within the core curriculum. All students take 16 core courses, including three in each of history/politics, philosophy, and theology, as well as math, literature, a foreign language, and the natural sciences. These are intensive four-credit courses, instead of the typical three-credit courses at many institutions.

Currently, the University offers 23 undergraduate majors. In addition to majors such as theology, biology, business, and psychology, students can emphasize interdisciplinary majors including Catholic studies, biochemistry, global affairs, and managerial economics. The most popular majors are biology, business, theology, and literature. Minors are available in many of the same subjects as well as catechetics, ecology and conservation biology, and family and society.

All of the theology faculty take the Oath of Fidelity and have the *mandatum* from the local bishop. Notably, the theology and philosophy Graduatesfaculty includes three members of the Pontifical Academy of St. Thomas Aquinas: Dr. Michael Waldstein, an expert on the Theology of the Body; Dr. Michael Pakaluk, translator and interpreter of Aristotle's Ethics; and Dr. Stephen Long, a Thomist and moral theologian.

Students can attend lectures integrating Catholic theology with particular disciplines as a series of panels including faculty from various departments, titled "Honors Integrated Colloquia." They can also study at the University's program in Rome.

Spiritual Life

Five priests serve the campus. Several Dominican religious sisters also assist the campus and the nearby private K-12 Catholic school.

AMU offers various liturgical styles. In addition to an Extraordinary Form Mass each Sunday and twice during the week, a variety of daily and Sunday Masses are offered in Ordinary Form Latin and English, including one featuring charismatic praise and worship music. The Sacrament of Reconciliation is available four days a week.

According to Father Robert McTeigue, S.J., "The motto of the Office of Campus Ministry, 'Christus mundo—mundus Christo' ('Bringing Christ to the world and the world to Christ'), epitomizes our mission of evangelization, catechesis, discipleship, fellowship, and worship. The overwhelming majority of Catholic students attend Sunday Mass and many students attend daily Masses and receive the Sacrament of Reconciliation."

Students describe a strong spiritual life that includes various devotional groups, approximately 18 voluntary "households" of students supporting each other in prayer and service, and student activity clubs such as the Knights of Columbus, Communion and Liberation, Peer Ministry Team, and Marian consecration. Students impressively maintain perpetual Eucharistic Adoration in the University chapel as well as a daily rosary walk. Students also have joined mission trips to Calcutta, Ecuador and Nicaragua.

At least 20 men and as many women who have attended AMU are now discerning religious life.

The dean of students conducts a senior exit interview with each student. The

Financial Aid Office Info

A college degree is an important investment in your future, but figuring out the financial aid process can seem overwhelming at times. At Ave Maria, we are committed to helping you through the process and making the University affordable for you and your family. We offer both need-based aid and merit scholarships for eligible students, so be sure to complete your FAFSA. We look forward to working with you to help you access one of the greatest values in Catholic higher education in the country!

When you compare Ave Maria University to other colleges, we're one of the best values for higher education. Our education is founded in truth and based on the timeless liberal arts tradition. Therefore, the knowledge you acquire at Ave Maria University is never obsolete or outdated.

The faculty works diligently to build an outstanding academic program, and to raise the standard of authentic Catholic higher education to a new level. We take great pride in making a high quality education affordable.

Aid available to students includes: federal and state grants, including Florida Bright Futures; Federal Work Study and Florida Work Experience, which allow you to earn money while attending college; low interest loan opportunities; and academic, leadership and athletic institutional scholarships.

For more information visit www.avemaria.edu or call Anne Hart at (239) 280-1669.

one comment heard most often is, "I came here with my parents' faith, but am leaving here with a deeper faith of my own."

Residential Life

With exceptions for students over 23 years of age or whose families reside in Ave Maria, it is university policy for all

students to live on campus.

Residence halls are separated by gender, but the University recently loosened its restrictions on visiting dorm rooms. Whereas visitation was previously not allowed, students may now visit the rooms of the opposite sex—with doors propped open—on Friday and Saturday evenings until midnight and on Sunday afternoons. In common areas, visiting hours are until 1:00 a.m. and extended to 2:00 a.m. on Friday and Saturday.

AMU desires to give students "true freedoms." Students are encouraged to dress "with modesty and prudence," and the student handbook offers guidelines regarding dressing with dignity. The University sponsors discussions and classes to promote chastity and teach the Theology of the Body. Movies and television programs viewed on campus "should be in good taste and not offensive to Catholic morals and values."

Alcohol is allowed with limitations, and there is no campus curfew. Those who violate the alcohol policy are sanctioned with community hours and/or fines, plus seminars and counseling for repeat violations.

The town of Ave Maria provides a number of convenient stores and services including a large grocery store, a few restaurants, and a pub. Due to the size, everyone tends to know everyone, and students and faculty often travel around campus and town by bike.

However, there are some inconveniences: the nearest hotel is 26 miles away, and the nearest hospital is about 20 miles northwest of the campus. Southwest Florida International Airport in Fort Myers is approximately 45 minutes away. Off-campus employment is limited.

Student Activities

More than 55 student clubs, organizations, ministries, outreach efforts, and households offer an abundance of activities that include athletic clubs (such as running, ice skating, swing dance, rugby, and fishing) and academic clubs (such as newspaper, writing, film, and business).

The University's 17 varsity teams compete in the National Association of Intercollegiate Athletics (NAIA) in baseball, basketball, cheerleading/dance, cross country, football, golf, soccer, softball, tennis, and volleyball. Students can also participate in a variety of club and intramural sports.

Much of the student body is engaged in some form of service work. The nearby Hispanic farming community of Immokalee is one of the poorest regions in the country and affords students numerous opportunities for service, including a food and clothing bank, soup kitchen, Christmas toy and shoe collection, Habitat for Humanity, and youth ministry.

Every Saturday, students travel to Naples and Fort Myers to pray and minister outside an abortion business. The pro-life and chastity clubs are popular, and more than 150 students attend the March for Life in Washington, D.C., each year.

The Bottom Line

AMU is a new institution that has been under intense scrutiny from both the media and the Church, largely because of Monaghan's high profile as the multimillionaire who built and sold Domino's Pizza. But there has also been a lot of interest in the grand vision for a major Catholic university that will one day rival the University of Notre Dame.

Now responsible for fulfilling a somewhat more practical vision in a tough economy, President Towey says the University has survived "the pains of childbirth," and it has emerged a quite attractive university for students. Hoping one day for an enrollment of 5,000, the University today enjoys a close-knit community in a small campus town, where it is common to run into professors at the Smoothie shop or the supermarket. The European-style town with education, faith, and art at its center is something of an oasis.

When you take into account the un-

From the Career Services Office

The Ave Maria University Career Services Department offers a wide array of resources and tools to assist our students and alumni in their professional development, including the following: career coaching to help students implement their personal four-year career development plan, job-search training, internship advisor, career fairs, graduate school fairs, Ave Maria JobsOnline site where students and alumni post resumes and view employer job opportunities, extensive online career planning library including career advice podcasts and career exploration assessments, and Career Services Newsletter.

swerving promotion of Catholic values, the strong core curriculum, and the presence of an impressive and faithful faculty, Ave Maria stands as an exciting new option available to American Catholics today.

"They've raised something up for the glory of God, and the good of students," says President Towey of his predecessors. "Ave Maria is a prototype of what Catholic education in the 21st century can be."

Letter from the President

Dear Prospective Students and Parents:

I am excited to introduce you to Ave Maria University!

We offer a classical liberal arts education that is authentically Catholic and academically rigorous. The class sizes are small and 96% of our full-time faculty have PhDs, providing students the tools they need to become critical thinkers, competent writers, and lovers of learning. Ave Maria offers 21 majors, including new ones in business and psychology, and also three pre-professional programs.

Graduates of the Class of 2012 were admitted to top law schools and other graduate programs of distinction, including Dartmouth College and Creighton University School of Medicine. Indeed, despite our young history, an Ave Maria education has been a springboard for many to promising careers and vocations. A number of our graduates have entered the seminary or religious life. Others have discovered their calling to the married life – many with a fellow Ave classmate! We believe that university life should provide an environment for young men and women to mature into responsible adults who celebrate their faith in Jesus Christ and apply their knowledge to the challenges of the 21st century. While attendance at Mass on Sunday is not mandatory on our campus, it is expected, and the moral climate in our dorms allows our students to maintain the values instilled in them by their parents.

It is clear to me that what our founder, Tom Monaghan, envisioned is coming to fruition, and that the Lord is honoring His holy Mother by blessing us with another year of record enrollment this fall. Put simply, Ave Maria is unique, affordable and authentic.

I hope you will visit our campus and see for yourselves why Ave Maria University is attracting some of our country's finest scholars and students.

Kind regards,

H. James Towey

Ave Maria University
Frequently Asked Questions

We get questions from Catholic families on a regular basis about the colleges we recommend. Rather than filter the answers, we asked Ave Maria officials nearly 100 questions in categories such as academics, curriculum, programs of study, campus ministry, residence life, student activities, the make up of the study body, and institutional identity. The answers to some of the most asked questions are provided below and the rest are available on the Ave profile page at TheNewmanGuide.com.

Majors

List the major, minor and special program areas that students may choose for specialization while pursuing an undergraduate degree:

MAJORS: Accounting; American Studies; Biology; Biochemistry; Business; Catholic Studies; Classics; Economics; Education; Global Affairs & International Business; Greek; History; Humanities & Liberal Studies; Literature; Managerial Economics & Strategic Analysis; Mathematics; Music; Philosophy; Physics; Political Economy & Government; Politics; Psychology; Theology.

MINORS: Biology; Business; Catechetics; Chemistry; Ecology & Conversation Biology; Economics; Education; Family & Society; Greek; History; Latin; Litertaure; Mathematics; Music; Philosophy; Physics; Politics; Psychology; Theology.

PRE-PROFESSIONAL PROGRAMS: Pre-Law; Pre-Medicine.

What are the three most popular majors or specialty disciplines for undergraduate students, and about what percentage of undergraduate students specialize in these disciplines?

Theology, 13%

Economics/Business, 12%

Biology, 10%

Spiritual Life

Please list the schedule of Masses, noting the following for each Mass: the day and time, the Form or Rite of the Mass, and the style of music, if any (chant, traditional, contemporary, etc.):

Mo 7:30 a.m., noon, 5:00 p.m.

Tu 7:30 a.m. (Extraordinary Form), noon, 5:00 p.m.

We 7:30 a.m., noon (Ordinary Form Latin), 5:00 p.m.

Th 7:30 a.m. (Extraordinary Form), noon, 5:00 p.m.

Fr 7:30 a.m., noon, 5:00 p.m.

Sa 9:00 a.m., 5:00 p.m.

Su 8:00 a.m. (Extraordinary Form, chant), 10:00 a.m. (Ordi-

nary Form, contemporary), 12:30 p.m. (Ordinary Form, traditional), 7:00 p.m. (Ordinary Form, contemporary)

All daily Masses are Ordinary Form except where noted.

List the schedule for Confession by day and time:

Mo 2:45-3:45 p.m., 6:00 p.m.

Tu

We 2:45-3:45 p.m., 6:00 p.m.

Th 6:00 p.m.

Fr 2:45-3:45 p.m., 6:00 p.m.

Sa 9:30-10:30 a.m.

Su

Other: Any time by request or appointment and at the High School on Tuesday and Thursday following the 8:00 a.m. daily Mass at the High School.

List the schedule for Adoration of the Blessed Sacrament by day and time:

Perpetual Adoration 24/7/365

Please identify regularly scheduled devotions on campus for students such as the Rosary and prayer groups:

9:00 p.m. nightly Rosary Walk, Weekly Praise and Worship, Weekly Divine and Mercy Chaplet

Residence Life

Please describe options for students to reside on and off campus:

Ave Maria University provides students with five single-sex residence halls, each of which is staffed by four or more Resident Assistants and one professional Residence Director. All residence hall rooms are furnished to accommodate two or more students and offer a private or adjoining bathroom.

Men's Residence Halls:
Saint Sebastian Hall and Saint Goretti Hall both have a capacity for 190 students each. Standard rooms and suites are available

and all have bathrooms. Common areas include a computer lab, a TV lounge, a kitchenette, a chapel and laundry facilities.

Saint Joseph Hall has a capacity for 234 male students. Standard rooms and suites are available and all have bathrooms. Common areas include a computer lab, a TV lounge, a chapel and laundry facilities.

Women's Residence Halls:
Mother Teresa Hall has a capacity for 420 students. Double rooms with an adjoining bathroom are available. Common areas include a computer lab, a TV lounge, a chapel and laundry facilities.

Pope John Paul II Hall has a capacity for 408 students. Double rooms with an adjoining bathroom are available. Common areas include a computer lab, a TV lounge, a chapel and laundry facilities.

It is Ave Maria University's policy that all students live in the residence halls. The Office of Housing and Residence Life does not provide options for off-campus living.

Does your institution offer only single-sex residence halls?

Yes

Are students of the opposite sex permitted to visit students' bedrooms?

Yes. Friday from 6pm - midnight, Saturday from 6pm - midnight, Sunday from 2pm - 8pm. Open door policy: the doors of the residence hall rooms where members of the opposite sex are visiting must be propped open, sufficient to allow a person to walk through the doorway normally.

How does your institution foster sobriety and respond to substance abuse on campus, particularly in campus residences?

Although the number of alcohol policy violations remains low at AMU, the decision was made to purchase an online alcohol education module that provides basic alcohol education information to students who do violate the alcohol policy. Through a review of topics related to safe consumption, characteristics of high risk drinking, positives and negatives of consumption, and social norms, students gain a better understanding of how irresponsible alcohol use can negatively impact their academics and personal lives. The anticipated outcome is that students will make better decisions in the future related to alcohol use. There are also a number of counseling options available to the students, both through the University Counseling Office as well as local meetings for independent support groups like Alcoholics Anonymous.

How does your institution foster a student living environment that promotes and supports chastity, particularly in campus residences?

Ave Maria University encourages and fosters healthy Christian relationships within the residence halls. The Residence Life Staff provides programming that draws attention to the dignity of each human person. All of the residence halls have common rooms with "common hours" for the students to freely and responsibly develop friendships and deepen in their understanding and appreciation for the masculine and feminine dynamics experienced with the occurrence of positive human interaction. Ave Maria University sponsors discussions, preaching and teaching sessions, and Theology of the Body classes. The University has a number of active student organizations on campus, such as households, that foster a chaste lifestyle along with residence hall programming that encourage chastity. Student Activities Board, Student Government Association, Office of Student Life, Campus Ministry, and Office of Housing and Residence Life all collaborate and form a united front, in establishing effective initiatives to support and promote a culture of chastity.

Student Body

Describe the makeup of your institution's undergraduate student body with regard to sex, religion, home state/country and type of high school (public, private, homeschool):

Total number of undergraduates: 941
Male: 52% Female: 48%

Catholic: 84% Other Christian: 6%
Jewish: 0% Muslim: 0% Other: 1%
Not Reported: 9%

Number of states represented: 47
Top three states: Florida, Illinois, California
Students from top three states: 69%

Catholic HS: 30% Homeschool: 10%
Private HS: 11% Public HS: 47%

BELMONT ABBEY COLLEGE

Belmont, North Carolina

411

For more information on Belmont Abbey, visit their website at:

www.bac.edu

Admissions contact:

704/461-6665
admissions@bac.edu

Overview

In 1876, Benedictine monks planted their roots in North Carolina, which was then the nation's least Catholic state, and built the first and only abbey cathedral in the history of the United States. Partially as a result of the monks' efforts and example, Roman Catholics are today the largest Christian body in the neighboring city of Charlotte.

The monks' faith and perseverance remain evident at Belmont Abbey College, which is under the direct ownership of the Benedictine monastery. Today the College enjoys a dramatic increase in enrollment, an outstanding faculty, a quality core curriculum, and a national reputation for tenacity on behalf of Catholic principles.

In recent years, Belmont Abbey has championed religious liberty in disputes with the federal government. When the Equal Employment Opportunity Commission ruled that the College had to include coverage for contraception in its employee health insurance plan, the College's leaders refused to compromise the College's Catholic mission. In 2011, the College was the first of many religious organizations to sue the Obama administration over its health insurance mandate affecting both employees and students. President Bill Thierfelder has testified before Congress on religious freedom concerns.

The leadership of Abbot Placid Solari, O.S.B., and Dr. Thierfelder has been inspiring. Abbot Solari has led the monastery since 1999, and is a former president and dean of the College. Dr. Thierfelder has been president since 2004, bringing a wide range of experiences as a businessman, sports psychologist, former college All-American high jumper, and Olympian.

"As a small community, we have an intentional focus of trying to have monks directly involved in the College," said Abbot Solari. "The presence of the monks in the school is the best way to impart the image we want for the College."

Belmont Abbey provides a strong witness to the Catholic faith, even though only about half the faculty are Catholic. The remainder are primarily Protestant and Evangelical Christians, as are a significant minority of students. The president and all the vice presidents are practicing Catholics.

The curriculum, policies, and leadership are all clearly directed toward a serious and authentically Catholic education. The recently revised core curriculum offers a thorough grounding in the liberal arts and Western thought. Campus life features frequent opportunities for the sacraments and prayer, single-sex residences, and a variety of activities including NCAA Division II athletics.

Academics

Somewhat more than half (896) of the Abbey's students are of traditional college age; the rest are adults taking evening and weekend classes.

For traditional students, a new core curriculum was introduced in 2011, with heavy emphasis on the liberal arts, the

Quick Facts

		2013-2014 Academic Year
Students 896		*Majors* 14
SATs 1040		*% Catholic* 79%
HS GPA 3.35		*How Much?* $28,594 tuition, room and board

Catholic intellectual tradition, and Western thought. Of the 120 credit hours required for graduation, 53 are in the core curriculum. Students become acclimated to Benedictine values through a First-Year Symposium and take required courses in rhetoric, logic, grammar, and writing; Western civilization; literary classics; political philosophy; scripture study; and theology.

Theology faculty members have received, or applied to, the local bishop for the *mandatum*, as is required by college policy, and the courses provide sound Catholic theology.

Belmont Abbey offers 14 majors, a balance between liberal arts and career-oriented programs. More than half the full-time students concentrate in business or education. Sports management is also a very popular major, in part because of the nearby NASCAR headquarters. The College has a reputation for its strong biology department, which has a 100 percent placement rate for graduates into medical, dental, and veterinary schools.

The Honors Institute has an emphasis on Great Books. In addition to the 15-course program, Honors students have the opportunity to attend an array of extracurricular lectures and programs, are eligible for generous grants, and travel to Rome during the summer between their junior and senior years.

The College also features the Felix Hintemeyer Catholic Leadership Program, which selects students who have earned exceptional academic records, a strong involvement in parish or Church activities, and evidence strong leadership qualities. Those selected receive a generous grant and travel to Rome in the summer after their junior year.

The Saint Thomas More Scholarship

program provides scholars with a series of seminars, two public lectures, several social events each year, and an opportunity for a values-oriented internship.

Spiritual Life

Spiritual life at Belmont Abbey is centered at the historic Abbey Basilica of Mary, Help of Christians, constructed with financial support from St. Katharine Drexel. The brick structure features Bavarian painted-glass windows. A granite platform where slaves were once sold has been carved out as a baptismal font, with a plaque that reads: "Upon this rock, men once were sold into slavery. Now upon this rock, through the waters of baptism, men become free children of God."

Three Masses are celebrated each weekend. Sunday Mass at 7 p.m. features student-led readings and music. The monastic community's Mass is celebrated at 5 p.m. on weekdays when school is in session and 11 a.m. daily during school breaks. Confession is offered 30 minutes before each weekday Mass. Students can join the monks for the Divine Office prayers of Lauds, Midday Prayer, and evening sung Vespers.

The Blessed Sacrament is exposed 15 hours a day in the St. Joseph Adoration Chapel. Regarding the chapel's construction in 2008, Dr. Thierfelder told The Catholic News & Herald, "I wanted this to be the first thing that we broke ground on, because I thought that it communicated, more powerfully than I possibly could, what we actually value and what we think is at the core and root of Belmont Abbey College." Mass is celebrated every Tuesday morning in the chapel. The chapel is also used frequently by student groups for various purposes, including weekly praise and worship on Wednesday nights and com-

Financial Aid Office Info

By coming to a college begun by Benedictine monks – an order founded by St. Benedict 1,500 years ago – you will become part of a long tradition guided by the Benedictine charism of hospitality.

In the fall 0f 2013, Belmont Abbey took a bold step to make an authentically Catholic education more accessible: we reset tuition from $27,622 down to $18,500, and will freeze tuition at these same rates for the 2013-2014 and 2014-2015 academic years. This is part of the Abbey's proactive effort to counter the trend of ever increasing tuition rates across the country. Belmont Abbey College remains steadfast in its commitment to providing an outstanding, affordable education to students, while remaining focused on the most important aspect of learning: the powerful relationship between student and professor.

In addition to the lower price, the College provides many scholarship opportunities that will further make a great education accessible for students and their families. If you are strong academically, and are interested in a program inspired by Pope John Paul II, you may want to apply for an Honors Fellowship. If you have the courage of moral conviction and consider yourself a Renaissance Man or Woman, you may be interested in the Saint Thomas More Scholarship. If you are interested in becoming a Catholic leader, you may be eligible for a Felix Hintemeyer Catholic Leadership Scholarship. If you are talented in drama, you may be a "natural" for our John Oetgen Excellence in Theatre Scholarship. If you are athletically gifted, you may be eligible for an athletic grant.

We also offer many other generous merit packages. More than 90 percent of our students receive financial aid.

munal prayer by the men's and women's households.

A Lourdes Grotto in the center of

campus was dedicated in 1891 and has been given special status as a Pilgrimage Shrine for religious vocations. There is a special program of prayer at the Shrine each May.

There are many other opportunities for spiritual enrichment: "United by Praise" nights of praise and worship, confession and adoration; Rosary in the Quad; breakfast reflections on the Rule of St. Benedict and daily life led by Abbey faculty and staff; and mountain hiking and day retreats with Abbot Placid. A team of four missionaries from the Fellowship of Catholic University Students (FOCUS) provide mentoring and discipleship training and teach students to lead weekly Bible studies, which currently include about 120 students.

Despite a substantial number of non-Catholic students, ministry activities are distinctly Catholic. For those who are not Catholic, the College provides an active R.C.I.A. program.

Residential Life

With the addition of two new residence halls in 2013, campus housing accommodates about 732 students in single-gender buildings. Overnight visitation by members of the opposite sex is prohibited. Students over 21 are allowed to possess and drink alcohol in moderation in the apartments for upper-class students, but only if no person under the age of 21 is present. Students under the age of 21 are not allowed to drink alcohol or even be in the presence of alcohol.

The "household" system was introduced to the College more than a decade ago, which enables students to form voluntary associations of residents to socialize and encourage spiritual growth. At present there are two households, one for men and another for women.

The residence halls recently underwent a major renovation, bringing Internet access, electrical upgrades and new lighting, heating and air conditioning. In 2012, the College completed a new 13,000-square foot, state-of-the-art dining center, doubling the serving capacity and enabling continuous service throughout the day. The former dining hall has been converted into a new

24-hour Student Center. Student mailboxes and the campus post office are also located there. The Student Center is located in the midst of the residence halls and only 50 feet from freshman residences. Students also enjoy Holy Grounds Coffee Shop and Cafe, which has a piano and large-screen television, and The Catholic Shoppe, a religious book and goods store on campus.

The town of Belmont is quaint, with several boutiques, restaurants and shops and an old-fashioned hardware store—but also many new restaurants and retail businesses. Belmont is 10 minutes west of Charlotte, which offers numerous activities and events. The Residence Life office often makes tickets available for concerts, sporting events, and theater. Charlotte is home to some of the nation's largest banks and several museums, as well as NASCAR, the NFL, NBA, and the U.S. National Whitewater Olympic Training Center.

Students have access to a Wellness Center for routine medical issues. Gaston Memorial Hospital is located about eight miles west of the campus.

The Charlotte Douglas International Airport is an easy 10-minute drive from Belmont and is a major hub for U.S. Airways.

Student Activities

Students have access to about 30 student clubs and organizations. There is a student-run newspaper, The Crusader, and a literary magazine, Agora. The 129-year-old Abbey Players perform in the College's historic Haid Theater and may be eligible for the Father John Oetgen, O.S.B., Excellence in Theatre Scholarship. Three sororities and two fraternities are also available. Greek life

From the Career Services Office

The Office of Career Services and Internships (OCSI) at Belmont Abbey College serves students, alumni, faculty, and staff, enabling them to cultivate the skills and attitudes that will help them to develop professionally and find good jobs. OCSI provides an impressive array of internship opportunities to ensure that our students are able to apply the lessons from the classroom to everyday work experiences. The Office coordinates about 165 internships each year, which include placement for Theology majors in local Catholic parish ministry and with the diocesan newspaper, the *Charlotte Catholic News & Herald*. The Office of Career Services and Internships also offers the opportunity to participate in mock interviews and in on-campus job interviews with employers, as well as an annual career and graduate school fair. Information on full-time and part-time jobs and current internship opportunities is available at: careerservices@bac.edu | 704-461-6873.

is committed to community service and the mission of the College, organized according to the Benedictine Hallmarks, and involved with FOCUS Bible study.

One popular student group is Crusaders for Life. Members help support the work of the maternity home, Room at the Inn; pray two Saturdays a month at a Charlotte abortion business; and organize and travel in buses to the annual March for Life in Washington, D.C.

Students enjoy concerts sponsored by the Arts at the Abbey series while earning "cultural events credits." Belmont Abbey encourages all students to attend several cultural events each year.

Among the options available for community service are working with maternity homes or crisis pregnancy centers, helping needy and homeless people in the area, teaching religion to young people at local parishes, and mentoring and coaching at local schools.

President Thierfelder takes sports seriously, and the athletic director works directly under his supervision.

"I believe sport is a means of developing virtue," says Dr. Thierfelder. "The athletic director's role is to make certain that sports and a virtuous life are fully integrated in the athletic department."

Belmont Abbey has 21 sports teams—19 varsity and two junior varsity. Of these, 11 men's and nine women's teams compete in NCAA Division II through the 12-team Conference Carolinas. The sports teams have enjoyed great success, at both the regional and national levels. There is an active intramural sports program.

The college's athletic facilities include a fitness center, a basketball court, a wrestling area with mats, a baseball stadium, and a softball, baseball, lacrosse, and soccer field. In addition to these amenities, students have free access to the Belmont YMCA facility, which features a weight room, cardio machines, basketball courts, a pool, and exercise classes. In 2012, a new fitness center was opened which everyone associated with the College can use six to eight hours a day.

Letter from the President

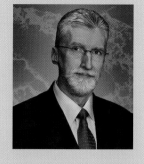

Dear Parents and Prospective Students:

It brings me great joy to introduce Belmont Abbey College to you.

In coming to a college founded by Benedictine monks over 135 years ago, you would be part of a long tradition of learning and holiness that I hope you will make your own. Blessed John Henry Newman captured the essence of our college in these words: "It is all, and does all, which is implied in the name of home. Youths, who have left the paternal roof, and traveled some hundred miles for the acquisition of knowledge, find an 'altera Troja' and 'simulata Pergama' at the end of their journey and in their place of temporary sojourn.

"…Moreover, it [the College] is the shrine of our best affections, the bosom of our fondest recollections, a spell upon our after life, a stay for world-weary mind and soul, wherever we are cast, till the end comes. Such are the attributes or offices of home, and like these, in one or other sense and measure, are the attributes and offices of a college in a University." It is in a home, such as this, that a student can fully experience the blessing of a liberal arts education.

I don't believe in accidents. I believe in Divine Providence. If you're reading my words right now, it's no accident. God is calling you to look and discern and pray and to say, "Maybe I'm supposed to be here. Maybe I'm supposed to be contributing in some way to what God is calling this place to be!" And I'm hoping that you're going to come and join us!

I look forward to personally welcoming you to our beautiful campus sometime soon.

Sincerely in Christ,

Dr. William K. Thierfelder

Soccer, baseball, and softball fields are available on-campus. At the nearby U.S. National Whitewater Center and Olympic Training Center, students take advantage of the public park's custom-made whitewater river.

The Bottom Line

Belmont Abbey College is a growing institution that has set an exciting course. After more than a century of providing a liberal arts education to students in the region, many of them not Catholic, the College is attracting Catholic students from around the country, highlighting its religious identity and educational mission.

"The campus is 130 years old," a student commented. "It has a stability from the monks, yet there's an excitement of growth. The college still feels young."

And Belmont Abbey's Catholic identity has a unique quality, since the College is a bastion of Benedictine spirituality in a largely Protestant region of the country. It is a college that offers much to Catholic students who choose to live out their faith, just as Belmont Abbey has chosen to live out its Catholic mission and Benedictine charism with resolve and enthusiasm.

Belmont Abbey College
Frequently Asked Questions

We get questions from Catholic families on a regular basis about the colleges we recommend. Rather than filter the answers, we asked Belmont officials nearly 100 questions in categories such as academics, curriculum, programs of study, campus ministry, residence life, student activities, the make up of the study body, and institutional identity. The answers to some of the most asked questions are provided below and the rest are available on the Belmont profile page at TheNewmanGuide.com.

Majors

List the major, minor and special program areas that students may choose for specialization while pursuing an undergraduate degree:

Majors: Accounting, Biology, Business Management, Criminal Justice, Educational Studies, Elementary Education, English, Government and Political Philosophy, History, Mathematics, Psychology, Sport Management, and Theology.

Note: Students majoring in Biology, Business Management, and Mathematics may select specific concentrations within the major.

Minors: Accounting, Biology, Business Management, Chemistry, Computer Studies, Criminal Justice, Education, English, Government and Political Philosophy, History, Mathematics, Psychology, Sport Management, Theatre Arts, and Theology.

What are the three most popular majors or specialty disciplines for undergraduate students, and about what percentage of undergraduate students specialize in these disciplines?

Business Management, 15%

Elementary Education, 11%

Sport Management, 10%

Spiritual Life

Please list the schedule of Masses, noting the following for each Mass: the day and time, the Form or Rite of the Mass, and the style of music, if any (chant, traditional, contemporary, etc.):

Mo 5:00 p.m., Ordinary Form, traditional music

Tu 10:00 a.m., Ordinary Form, no music;
    5:00 p.m., Ordinary Form, traditional music,

We 5:00 p.m., Ordinary Form, traditional music

Th 5:00 p.m., Ordinary Form, traditional music

Fr 5:00 p.m., Ordinary Form, traditional music

Sa 11:00 a.m., Ordinary Form, traditional music

Su 11:00 a.m., Ordinary Form, traditional music w/organ;
    7:00 p.m., Ordinary Form, chant and traditional music

List the schedule for Confession by day and time:

Mo 1:00-3:00 and 4:30-5:00 p.m.

Tu 1:00-3:00 and 4:30-5:00 p.m.

We 1:00-3:00 and 4:30-5:00 p.m.

Th 1:00-3:00 and 4:30-5:00 p.m.

Fr 1:00-3:00 and 4:30-5:00 p.m.

Sa 10:30-11:00 a.m.

Su 10:30-11:00 a.m.

Other: Spiritual Direction and Confession are regularly available by appointment with members of the monastic community.

List the schedule for Adoration of the Blessed Sacrament by day and time:

We have an Adoration Chapel that is open 24 hours a day, with Exposition from 6:00 a.m. - 10:00 p.m. daily.

Please identify regularly scheduled devotions on campus for students such as the Rosary and prayer groups:

All students are invited to join the monks in praying Lauds, Mid-Day Prayer, and Vespers; Men's Household has a weekly "Man Rosary;" Wednesday evenings, after Reposition, there is Praise & Worship in the Adoration Chapel; FOCUS runs 20+ Bible Study groups on a weekly basis; Women's Household has weekly meetings on Sunday evenings; students are invited to communally pray the Stations of the Cross each Friday in Lent; and students organize an annual Total Consecration to Mary as well as a May crowning.

Residence Life

Please describe options for students to reside on and off campus:

O'Connell and Poellath Halls are suite style halls with 4 double occupancy rooms sharing one bath. These buildings are 50%

sophomores and 50% freshmen. Raphael Arthur is an upper-classmen hall with four private rooms sharing a bath. Cuthbert Allan Apartments house four upper-class students sharing an efficiency apartment. The residential population will increase to 732 students starting in the fall 2013 semester. Two new residence halls will come on line that will house 110 students (one building for men and one for women). Each hall will contain a chapel, lobby, kitchen, and lounge areas. The bedrooms are suites with 2 private bedrooms, a small common area, and a shared bath.

Does your institution offer only single-sex residence halls?

Yes

Are students of the opposite sex permitted to visit students' bedrooms?

Yes. Students in O'Connell and Poellath Halls, as well as the New Residence Hall (schedule to open the Fall 2013,) are allowed visitation until 12:00 a.m. 7 days a week. Those residing in the Cuthbert Allan Apartments and Raphael Arthur Hall have visitation until 12:00 a.m. Sunday-Thursday and 2 a.m. Friday and Saturday evenings.

How does your institution foster sobriety and respond to substance abuse on campus, particularly in campus residences?

Students of the age of majority may consume in moderation in Cuthbert Allan Apartments and Raphael Arthur Hall only, and not in the presence of those under 21. Alcohol use is framed within the perspective of moderation and the virtue of stewardship. We are stewards of our bodies and are accountable for what we do with them. Underage drinking is taken very seriously as is abuse of alcohol by those of age. The Residence Life staff works closely with other key departments to provide a proactive approach to alcohol education.

How does your institution foster a student living environment that promotes and supports chastity, particularly in campus residences?

We have an explicit policy on Christian Sexual Morality. In keeping with John Paul II's Theology of the Body, we make clear that sex is a gift from God to be enjoyed by those who have received the Sacrament of Marriage and for the purpose of the mutual good of the spouses and for bringing children into the world as a gift from God, in accord with Catholic teaching and Canon Law.

The Residence Life staff educates students about respect for the Abbey's Christian Sexuality Statement in all aspects of the students' lives. This includes dress, inappropriate posters and daily respect for the opposite sex. Students who do not abide by this policy face the possibility of suspension or expulsion.

Student Body

Describe the makeup of your institution's undergraduate student body with regard to sex, religion, home state/country and type of high school (public, private, homeschool):

Total number of traditional undergraduates: 896
Male: 55% Female: 46%

63% of traditional students report a religious affiliation. Of those, the percentages are as follows:

Catholic: 79% Other Christian: 20%
Jewish: <1% Muslim: 1% Other: 1%

Number of states represented: 45
Top three states: North Carolina, New York and South Carolina
Students from top three states: 58%

Catholic HS: 30% Homeschool: 10%
Private HS: 15% Public HS: 45%

BENEDICTINE COLLEGE

Atchison, Kansas

411

For more information on Benedictine, visit their website at:

www.benedictine.edu

Admissions contact:

800/467-5340 ext. 7476
bcadmiss@benedictine.edu

Overview

The Abbey tower and cross rise above the trees as you approach Benedictine College, set on the Kansas bluffs overlooking the Missouri River. Although these sure signs of a Catholic community have dominated the landscape for generations, the College has more recently found a renewed strength in its Catholic identity—with very exciting results.

Students describe the Abbey as "The Rock," referencing the limestone blocks that make up its imposing Church. But there is also a deeper meaning: the Abbey tower sits precisely above the Tabernacle at the center of the 100-acre campus, a reminder that Christ and His Church are the true foundation of the monastic community and the College.

What was originally St. Benedict's College was founded in 1858—a men's college before its merger with the all-female Mount St. Scholastica College in 1971. Despite efforts to maintain a strong Catholic identity—for instance, the Abbey leased its land to the College on the condition that all students take nine credit hours of theology—the College became something of a "party school" from the 1970s to the early 1990s. Suffering financially, Benedictine almost closed on more than one occasion.

But Benedictine's recent turnaround is a remarkable example of what can happen when a college embraces its Catholic identity with passion. Today Benedictine routinely refers to its four "pillars": Catholic, Benedictine, liberal arts, and residential. As a result, Benedictine has experienced tremendous success, and the School's enrollment has doubled within the past 10 years.

Stephen Minnis has been the College's president for much of that period. A former prosecuting attorney and corporate lawyer, Minnis is a Benedictine College alumnus. His wife Amy is also a graduate and teaches math and computer science at the College, as well as serving as one of the caretakers for the Marian Grotto.

The board of directors is composed of 43 lay members and College personnel, including four priests, the prior of the Abbey, and three religious sisters.

Academics

As a liberal arts College, Benedictine requires every student to complete 58 credits in foundational courses. These include core courses in English composition, a foreign language, theology, logic and nature, wellness for life, physical fitness, and the Benedictine College Experience. The latter course introduces first-year students to the value and qualities of a Catholic liberal arts education.

In addition, students have a variety of choices from various disciplines to fulfill the Foundations requirements in areas such as faith, aesthetics, philosophical inquiry, and understanding the natural world. Likewise, Skills and Perspectives courses are required in broad areas such as global perspective, communication, and scientific method.

The College offers more than 40 tradi-

Quick Facts
2013-2014 Academic Year

Students	1,716	Majors	43
ACTs	24	% Catholic	86%
HS GPA	3.63	How Much?	$30,000 tuition, room and board

tional majors. Business, education, biology, and theology are popular majors, and Benedictine is one of few Catholic liberal arts colleges to offer engineering and astronomy.

Benedictine is careful when hiring theology professors. It wants only "candidates who will seek the *mandatum* from the local ordinary in accordance with *Ex corde Ecclesiae*," according to Dr. Richard White, associate professor and chair of the Theology Department.

Benedictine recently expanded its engineering physics major to a complete engineering program that offers accredited chemical, civil, mechanical, and electrical engineering degrees through a partnership with the University of North Dakota. Also, Benedictine's nursing program was approved by the Kansas State Board of Nursing in 2010.

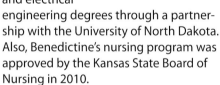

The Education Department has been nationally recognized by the National Council for the Accreditation of Teacher Education.

About 70 percent of students majoring in natural sciences continue in graduate and professional schools, nearly twice the national average.

Benedictine offers a study abroad semester at its Florence campus in Italy for up to 40 students per semester. They reside at Villa Morghen, a former monastery located approximately three miles from the historic center of Florence. In addition to courses in Italian, Florentine history and culture, and the saints and mystics of Italy, students visit Subiaco, Monte Cassino, Assisi, Perugia, Pisa, and Livorno. The final week of the program is spent in Rome.

The College is also part of an exchange program that allows students to study in Australia, Ireland, or anywhere in a network of 275 colleges and universities in 39 different countries. Students major-ing in French or Spanish are required to complete one semester abroad.

Spiritual Life

The presence of the Benedictine monks on campus is a blessing. Not only are five chaplains available to celebrate Mass and hear confessions, but several also provide spiritual direction.

Four Ordinary Form Masses are available daily at the various chapels and churches on campus, with five Masses on Sunday. In total, daily Masses are attended by approximately 600 students, more than one-third of the student body. Father Brendan Rolling, OSB, college chaplain, estimated that 80 percent of Benedictine students worship weekly.

"You have your options from a very conservative Mass [at the Abbey] to a more charismatic Mass with praise and worship," said one student. "There is nothing irreverent and you can find one that fits your spirituality."

Confession is available 30 minutes prior to each Mass, and Perpetual Eucharistic Adoration is offered at St. Benedict's Parish Church adjacent to Ferrell Hall. A variety of retreats are regularly made available to students as well.

The St. Gregory the Great vocational discernment group is active on campus, and over the past few years, 60 students have announced their intention to discern the priesthood or religious life.

At least half of Benedictine's college ministry programs are dedicated to social justice and human rights. One group of students is engaged in prison ministry. Past mission trips have gone to Belize, El Salvador, India, Tanzania, and Indian reservations in North Dakota.

Students are also involved in serving the poor through Simple House, an outreach program in Kansas City. Each

Financial Aid Office Info

In addition to any federal and state grants and loans, Benedictine College offers a wide range of institutional scholarships for academics, athletics, music and theatre, and other skills and honors you might bring to the school. First and foremost among the offerings are the Presidential Scholarships. Each year in February, top students come to campus for the exciting Presidential Scholarship Weekend. Anyone with a minimum 27 ACT/1210 SAT and a 3.5 GPA is invited. Based on an essay and an interview session, five students are selected to receive full tuition, Presidential Scholarships ($21,475 per year) and another five are selected to receive ¾ tuition, Dean's Scholarships ($16,106 per year). These scholarships are renewable for the four years.

There are many other academic scholarships available and they are awarded based simply on ACT/SAT scores and high school GPA. They range from $4,000-$12,000 and are renewable for four years. In this instance, your application for admission to the college serves as your application for scholarships. The Financial Aid Office will award you everything for which you qualify. National Merit Finalists are eligible to receive an additional one-time award of $2,500.

Music and Theatre scholarships are available for $500-$1,000 to students interested in vocal/instrumental music or theatre participation. An audition is required. These scholarships are renewable based on active participation.

The coaching staff determines eligibility for an athletic scholarship. Contact the head coach for your sport to inquire about availability. For more information, please contact Mr. Tony Tanking, Financial Aid Director, at ttanking@benedictine.edu or call 913.360.7485.

week, more than 400 students skip a meal and donate the food to the poor. In addition, students have sponsored a Christmas giving tree for foster children,

adopted poor families in Kansas City, visited local senior citizens, volunteered at a soup kitchen, and participated in Habitat for Humanity.

Residential Life

Benedictine has 15 residence halls, eight for women and seven for men. Each of the residence halls has a different style and houses students depending upon their class. One hall features lofts, suites, and apartment-style rooms for upper-class women. Another has single rooms for men and has been described as a mini-seminary. There are also newer two and four bedroom apartment-style residences for upper-class men and children of alumni.

Each hall is staffed by a residence director and multiple student resident assistants. "All resident directors study the virtues, *Ex corde Ecclesiae*, the Rule of St. Benedict, the Pope's Theology of the Body, and the documents on the dignity of the human person and the vocation of women," said Father Rolling. Residence Life structures fellowship around a "family model" that promotes wholesome community.

The College maintains a strict visitation policy for each of its halls: between 12 p.m. and 12 a.m. on weekdays and between 10 a.m. and 2 a.m. on weekends.

Benedictine has a household program, called the School of the Lord's Service, where students live together and act and pray as a community. This is a joint initiative of the College, the Archdiocese of Kansas City's Office of Evangelization, and the Minnesota-based St. Paul's Outreach.

The campus has a strict no-smoking policy that allows students to smoke only in designated areas. But there is no dress code, and moderate drinking is permitted by students of legal age. Whereas the party atmosphere was prevalent in earlier decades, it has diminished in recent years, and underage drinking and partying takes place largely off-campus.

Situated along the Missouri River, Atchison is quintessential small-town Midwest. There is a main street with local businesses located just blocks away from campus and larger retailers located a bit farther near the edge of town. The town boasts of more than 20 sites on the National Register of Historic Places and is the birthplace of famed pilot Amelia Earhart.

In addition to Kansas City, students can easily reach St. Joseph, Missouri, which is

From the Career Services Office

Benedictine College recognizes that what sets our school apart is that we are a premier liberal arts college with a strong focus on students' post-graduate and professional success. Our ad campaign, "Real College, Real Faith, Real Results" features alumni who are part of our network of success, including, since the year 2000: 13 bank CEOs, seven university presidents, 88 priestly and religious vocations, four bishops, and one Nobel Peace Prize winner.

We are proud of alumni who are successful and faithful, both. We have featured: a young graduate who coaches in the NFL and has started Bible study groups at the Chicago Bears and Cleveland Browns; the Vice Chairman of the FDIC lauded for the fiscal responsibility he learned from our monks; the president of Hallmark, Canada, who is active in his parish and wrote a book on happiness for his children; three presidents of *Newman Guide* schools are Benedictine College graduates; many successful Catholic school teachers, administrators and principals are alumni, including members of the School Sisters of Christ the King, the Marian Sisters of Lincoln, Nebraska, and the Franciscan Sisters of the Martyr Saint George.

We have launched two programs to capitalize on employers' interest in our graduates and our unique position as "the cradle of college presidents."

HireBenedictine.com. After regional companies expressed interest in the writing, team-building and critical thinking skills that our liberal arts curriculum provides, we rebranded our career center "HireBenedictine.com" and provided employers more opportunities to meet Benedictine students to fill their internships.

PostGraduate Success Center. Susan (Orr) Traffas, who advanced pro-life principles in leadership positions in Washington, D.C., heads our center to prepare students for graduate school via the courses and tests they need and by competing for the grants, awards and opportunities that will enrich their education.

about 20 miles across the state border.

Student Activities

Benedictine has more than 35 student groups, clubs, and organizations, including academic clubs, sports clubs, and others. The most popular student organization is Ravens Respect Life, which takes large numbers of students to the annual March for Life. In addition, the University has a Theology of the Body club, a Knights of Columbus group, the BC Nun Run (for women considering a religious vocation), a Swing and Social Dance club, Pipe and Cigar Enthusiasts Club, and many others.

The Fellowship of Catholic University Students (FOCUS) was founded at Benedictine, and the local campus-based team maintains an office on campus. Seventy percent of new students sign up for the 72 FOCUS Bible studies taking place on campus, and nearly a quarter of the student body attends the FOCUS national conference.

Benedictine has seven different student choirs. Among them, the Chamber Singers have traveled to Italy several times, performing in Venice, Rome, and even for the Pope. Other active groups on campus are the Communion and Liberation group that meets weekly, and a Hunger Coalition that serves approximately 400 meals to the Atchison community each week.

The College is a member of the National Association of Intercollegiate Athletics and offers 16 varsity athletic programs including women's basketball, cross country, soccer, softball, Spirit squad (cheer and dance), indoor and outdoor track and field, and volleyball; and men's baseball, basketball, cross country, football, soccer, and indoor and outdoor track and field. There is also an intramural and club sports program that includes rugby and ice hockey.

The Student Union and the Haverty Center, including the Monte Cassino Inn restaurant and pub, are popular stu-

Letter from the President

Dear Parents and Prospective Students,

At Benedictine College we are building one of America's great Catholic colleges through our mission of community, faith and scholarship.

There are so many exciting new developments at Benedictine College, it is hard to know where to start.

Our students can now earn ABET-accredited Chemical, Mechanical, Electrical and Civil Engineering degrees. The chairman of our Engineering department is a great promoter of our Catholic identity.

We launched our Mother Teresa Center for Nursing and Health Education on Mother Teresa's 100th birthday, with help from the Missionaries of Charity and our first nursing majors.

Benedictine 2020: A Vision for Greatness is our bold, visionary plan to build one of America's great college Catholic faculties to attract and prepare students who will transform the world.

We consider Benedictine College a primary example of the power of *Ex corde Ecclesiae*. The college traces its renaissance to our efforts to strengthen our Catholic identity. The U.S. bishops and the Vatican have invited us to share our lessons with the Church.

We do all of this in addition to a great varsity sports program — from football to volleyball — more than 40 majors and a campus in Florence, Italy. It's a great time to be a Raven!

Yours in Christ,

Dr. Stephen D. Minnis

dent social hangouts. The Center also features a student lounge area, a coffee shop, and a bookstore. The Student Union includes athletic coach offices, the office of student life, some classrooms, the mailroom, an auditorium, a gymnasium, campus ministry offices, and a deli.

The Bottom Line

In many ways, Benedictine College is the "new Steubenville," with an equally compelling story to tell. The Franciscan University of Steubenville is well-known for its transformation from a wayward party school into a vibrant, Catholic institution. At Benedictine, the transfor-

mation can be attributed to remarkable students and faculty as well as inspiring leaders. The results are impressive.

Benedictine is a growing college located in a small town, where the president still tries to learn all of the incoming students' names. Because of the wide range of opportunities at Benedictine, nearly any type of student should be able to fit in and have a successful college experience.

Students seeking a solid Catholic college offering a host of majors and a family-like environment—all with the excitement and confidence of newfound success—will find much that is attractive about Benedictine.

Benedictine College
Frequently Asked Questions

We get questions from Catholic families on a regular basis about the colleges we recommend. Rather than filter the answers, we asked Benedictine officials nearly 100 questions in categories such as academics, curriculum, programs of study, campus ministry, residence life, student activities, the make up of the study body, and institutional identity. The answers to some of the most asked questions are provided below and the rest are available on the college profile page at TheNewmanGuide.com.

Majors

List the major, minor and special program areas that students may choose for specialization while pursuing an undergraduate degree:

Accounting, Art, Art Education, Astronomy, Athletic Training, Biochemistry, Biology, Business, Chemical Engineering, Chemistry, Civil Engineering, Classics, Computer Science, Criminology, Dance, Economics, Education, Electrical Engineering, Elementary & Secondary Education, Engineering Physics, English, English Literature, Entrepreneurship, Finance, Foreign Language, French, History, International Business, International Studies, Journalism, Journalism & Mass Communications, Latin, Liberal Studies, Management, Marketing, Mass Communications, Mathematics, Mechanical Engineering, Music, Music Education, Natural Science, Nursing, Philosophy, Physical Education, Physics, Political Science, Psychology, Social Science, Sociology, Spanish, Special Education, Theatre Arts, Theatre Arts Management, Theology, Youth Ministry

PRE-PROFESSION: Dentistry, Law, Medical Technology, Medicine, Occupational Therapy, Optometry, Pharmacy, Physical Therapy

What are the three most popular majors or specialty disciplines for undergraduate students, and about what percentage of undergraduate students specialize in these disciplines?

Business, 20.4%

Education, 16.3%

Theology, 9.2%

Spiritual Life

Please list the schedule of Masses, noting the following for each Mass: the day and time, the Form or Rite of the Mass, and the style of music, if any (chant, traditional, contemporary, etc.):

Mo 8:15 a.m., Ordinary Form, hymn;
  Noon, Ordinary Form, spoken antiphons;
  5:15 p.m., Ordinary Form, hymn;
  9:30 p.m., Ordinary Form, hymn

Tu 8:15 a.m., Ordinary Form, hymn;
  Noon, Ordinary Form, spoken antiphons;
  5:15 p.m., Ordinary Form, hymn;
  9:30 p.m., Ordinary Form, hymn

We 8:15 a.m., Ordinary Form, hymn;
  Noon, Ordinary Form, spoken antiphons;
  5:15 p.m., Ordinary Form, hymn;
  9:30 p.m., Ordinary Form, traditional, poliphany

Th 8:15 a.m., Ordinary Form, hymn;
  Noon, Ordinary Form, spoken antiphons;
  5:15 p.m., Ordinary Form, hymn;
  9:30 p.m., Ordinary Form, praise

Fr 8:15 a.m., Ordinary Form, hymn;
  Noon, Ordinary Form, spoken antiphons;
  5:15 p.m., Ordinary Form, hymn

Sa 8:15 a.m., Ordinary Form, hymn;
  Noon, Ordinary Form, spoken antiphons;
  5:15 p.m., Ordinary Form, hymn

Su 8:30 a.m., Ordinary Form, hymn;
  10:00 a.m., Ordinary Form, chant, poliphany, hymn, organ;
  10:30 a.m., Ordinary Form, chant, poliphany, hymn, piano;
  6:30 p.m., Ordinary Form, hymn;
  9:00 p.m., Ordinary Form, hymn, praise, piano, guitar

List the schedule for Confession by day and time:

Mo 12:30 p.m., 4:00-5:00 p.m., 9:00-9:30 p.m.

Tu 12:30 p.m., 4:00-5:00 p.m., 9:00-9:30 p.m.

We 12:30 p.m., 4:00-5:00 p.m., 9:00-9:30 p.m.

Th 12:30 p.m., 4:00-5:00 p.m., 9:00-9:30 p.m.

Fr 12:30 p.m., 4:00-5:00 p.m.

Sa 10:00-11:00 a.m., 4:00-5:00 p.m.

Su 9:00-10:00 a.m., 7:00-8:00 p.m.

Other: All retreats, at spiritual direction, before All-School Masses, before Baccalaureate Mass and by appointment with chaplains

List the schedule for Adoration of the Blessed Sacrament by day and time:

Perpetual Adoration on campus; Wed-Thurs Memorial Chapel Adoration, 12:00-9:00 p.m.; Wednesday Morning Eucharistic Hour for the College, Abbey Crypt; Saturday Holy Hour for Vocations, Abbey Crypt, 8:00-9:00 p.m.

Please identify regularly scheduled devotions on campus for students such as the Rosary and prayer groups:

7:00 a.m., Liturgy of the Hours, Residence Halls

3:00 p.m., M-F, Divine Mercy Chaplet, Church

9:00 p.m., M-Th, Rosary, Chapel

11:00 p.m., M-F, Rosary, Men's and Women's Halls

7:00 a.m., W, Student Leader Eucharistic Holy Hour

7:30 a.m., W, President's Rosary

Total Consecration to Mary, Fall Semester

All School Masses, Holy Days of Obligation

70 Bible Studies, Weekly

Lord's Day, Men's and Women's Households

Weekly Prayer Meetings, Households

Novenas: Various Saints

Residence Life

Please describe options for students to reside on and off campus:

All of our residence halls are single-sex and residents are grouped primarily by academic class standing. Throughout their four years living on campus, students have a variety of residence hall configurations to live in. Our freshmen live in traditional style residence halls in which two residents live in a room and the hall has community lounges aimed at building community and facilitating friendships. Upperclassmen residence halls vary from suite style rooms with shared common spaces and bathrooms to apartment style residence halls where residents have their own kitchen. Residence life at Benedictine College ultimately strives to develop the whole person in a safe living and learning environment that fosters growth in virtue as residents develop into men and women of character who respect the dignity of the human person.

Does your institution offer only single-sex residence halls?

Yes

Are students of the opposite sex permitted to visit students' bedrooms?

Yes. Between 12 noon and 12 midnight Sun.-Thurs; Friday and Sat from 12 noon to 1:30 am.

How does your institution foster sobriety and respond to substance abuse on campus, particularly in campus residences?

Benedictine College strives to cultivate the virtue of sobriety in our student body as well as a moderate drinking culture for our students who can legally consume alcohol. To accomplish this, we have both proactive and reactive initiatives in place. Proactively, we provide healthy alcohol-free programs for our students throughout the year in the residence halls. This is highlighted with our Alcohol Free competition each year. During the competition each residence hall puts on an alcohol-free event which both serves as a model for how to engage in healthy activities without the use of alcohol and disseminates information about the dangers of abusing alcohol. Last year our alcohol-free competition reached 1,500 students. (See the Benedictine profile page at TheNewmanGuide.com for more information.)

How does your institution foster a student living environment that promotes and supports chastity, particularly in campus residences?

We have many initiatives in residence life that promote a healthy view of the human person and appropriate human relationships. First and foremost providing single-sex residence halls across campus naturally supports and promotes chastity on campus. Our 50 resident assistants on campus receive instruction in Theology of the Body as a part of their RA training. The incoming freshman class is required to attend chastity talks as a part of their orientation weekend that promote both physical and emotional chastity.

The policies in the residence halls promote chastity through educational initiatives and assigned community service when visitation hours are violated. We also distinguish a period of night in which the violation of visitation hours is considered "cohabitation." In these cases we will assign more in-depth education initiatives or have the students involved meet with one of our counselors. Students in this situation will also lose the right to visitation for a specified period of time.

Student Body

Describe the makeup of your institution's undergraduate student body with regard to sex, religion, home state/country and type of high school (public, private, homeschool):

Total number of undergraduates: 1,716
Male: 46.5% Female: 53.5%

Catholic: 86% Other Christian: 0%
Jewish: 0% Muslim: 0% Other: 14%

Number of states represented: 39
Top three states: Kansas, Missouri
Students from top three states: 54%

Catholic HS: 41% Homeschool: 13%
Private HS: 2% Public HS: 41%

GIBBONS HALL

THE CATHOLIC UNIVERSITY OF AMERICA

Washington, District of Columbia

411

For more information on Catholic U, visit their website at:

www.cua.edu

Admissions contact:

202/319-5305
cua-admissions@cua.edu

Q.ht/3sJJg

Overview

The Catholic University of America (CUA) is the only pontifical university in the United States that serves primarily lay students. With the support of Pope Leo XIII, the American bishops founded CUA in 1887 for the initial purpose of graduate studies in theology, philosophy, and canon law.

Today CUA has about equal numbers of undergraduate and graduate students, with an undergraduate program that is distinctly and reliably Catholic. The largely Catholic student body has a wide variety of schools and majors from which to choose—unique features for a comprehensive university that embraces a strong Catholic identity.

The CUA mission statement reads in part: "As the national university of the Catholic Church in the United States, founded and sponsored by the bishops of the country and with the approval of the Holy See, The Catholic University of America is committed to being a comprehensive Catholic and American institution of higher learning, faithful to the teachings of Jesus Christ as handed on by the Church."

John Garvey became CUA's 15th president in 2010, after several years as dean of Boston College Law School. The Harvard-educated legal expert has earned much respect with his public defense of Catholic institutions from the Obama administration's violations of religious liberty. In addition, he made CUA a standard-bearer for other institutions to follow with his announcement in 2011 that student residence halls would no longer be co-ed.

CUA's Catholic identity has also been enhanced by strengthening the campus ministry and by hiring professors and staff members who reflect Catholic iden-

tity. More than 110 former CUA students have entered religious life over the past decade.

CUA is governed by a 50-member board of trustees: 48 elected and two members—the president and the chancellor, who is always the archbishop of Washington, D.C—by virtue of their position. Half of the elected members must be clerics, with at least 18 of them members of the U.S. Conference of Catholic Bishops.

Located in Northeast Washington, D.C., in the inner-city residential Brookland neighborhood, CUA is about three miles north of the U.S. Capitol. Students must beware of crime in the neighboring area, but they also will find numerous seminaries and other religious institutions in the area, which has earned the nickname "little Rome." At its nucleus is the Basilica of the National Shrine of the Immaculate Conception, the nation's largest Catholic Church, adjacent to CUA's 180-acre campus.

Academics

Garvey has been forthright about hiring faculty who support the University's mission: "The universities themselves will only be distinctive and distinctively

Quick Facts

2013-2014 Academic Year

Students 3,694

SATs 1110

HS GPA 3.5

Majors 73

% Catholic 80%

How Much? $52,852
tuition, room and board

Catholic if they hire people who want to make them that, and to do that you have to count, and not just count people who have a baptismal certificate, but those who really care about putting those things together. In hiring non-Catholics, you need to pay attention to what they will contribute to the culture of the institution."

Currently, about 55 percent of the faculty is Catholic. More than half of the theology faculty members are clerics or religious, including Benedictines, Dominicans, Franciscans, and Jesuits. At present, 63 faculty members have a canonical mission, which substitutes for the *mandatum* at pontifical institutions. Six non-Catholics in the School of Theology and Religious Studies have received the venia docendi, or permission to teach in the name of the Church.

Among CUA's 12 schools are: architecture and planning, arts and sciences, business and economics, canon law, engineering, law, music, nursing, philosophy, professional studies, social service, theology and religious studies, and the university seminary, Theological College.

As with any large university, several departments have surfaced in our interviews that require prudence when pursuing courses there. These include anthropology, modern languages, history, and The National Catholic School of Social Service. And at such a large university, students should be diligent in seeking out professors in every discipline who embrace the university's Catholic mission.

For students who qualify, there is an honors program that includes a core curriculum organized into a number of four-course sequences. Those successfully completing one or more sequences are honored at graduation. Graduation requirements vary according to the school to which the student is admitted.

CUA offers a variety of scholarships to students, such as the $1,000 alumni grant awarded to a freshman nominated by a graduate, and the Parish Scholarship whereby parish priests can nominate students for a $3,000 annual renewable scholarship.

CUA has a number of institutes and centers. Students have abundant opportunities for international enrichment, choosing from over 20 education abroad programs to locations such as Spain, Ireland, Australia, China, and CUA's premiere program in Rome.

One ongoing concern at CUA is the low retention rates in the undergraduate program; about 30 percent of students leave before their junior year. To enhance undergraduate education, CUA now includes a freshman "First Year Experience" program that creates learning communities integrating five specific courses. CUA's proximity to Washington, D.C., offers unparalleled opportunities for internships with more than 2,000 organizations, including political parties, radio and television networks, museums, social service and government agencies, The White House, and many more.

Spiritual Life

Four Conventual Franciscan Friars and four lay people staff the campus ministry office. With the help of priests from CUA's faculty, the friars offer four daily Masses in St. Paul's Chapel in Caldwell Hall, the law school chapel, and St. Vincent's Chapel. There are also two Sunday Masses in St. Vincent's Chapel. There are six daily Masses and seven Sunday Masses at the Basilica—one offered on Sunday afternoon for the University community.

Two new chapels have opened in student residence halls, one in Flather Hall (Sacred Heart Chapel), the other in

Financial Aid Office Info

The Catholic University of America offers several forms of financial assistance to qualifying students. Our focus is helping as many eligible students as possible achieve their goal of obtaining a high-quality academic and values-based education.

Eight out of every 10 full-time students at Catholic University receive some level of financial aid, based on demonstrated financial need, academic potential, or both.

Catholic University offers university and federal need-based grants, low-interest loans, and work-study opportunities to students based on their eligibility as determined by the Free Application for Federal Student Aid.

The Catholic University of America provides a range of scholarships, including the CUA Alumni Scholarship, CUA Parish Scholarship, and the CUA Scholarship, which recognize and reward students for outstanding academic performance in high school as well as exceptional leadership and service in school, church, and community. The CUA Alumni and Parish scholarships require a separate application at the time of application for admission. All students are automatically considered for the CUA Scholarship based on their high school career; no additional application is required. All admission scholarships are renewable for up to eight semesters.

The university participates in the Tuition Exchange Program and Veteran Administration's Yellow Ribbon Program. Our Office of Financial Aid maintains a "counselor on call" initiative to help students and their parents make practical decisions for financing their education. Student and parents may also schedule an appointment to speak to a financial aid counselor. For more information, visit our website at http://financialaid.cua.edu, call toll free at 888-635-7788, or e-mail cua-finaid@cua.edu.

Opus Hall (Blessed Sacrament Chapel). Both provide students with the opportunity to make private visits to the Blessed Sacrament. Each Monday at 9 p.m., Mass is celebrated in the Sacred Heart Chapel.

Daily Masses frequently attract 40 to 50 students, with as many as 300 participating in the Sunday evening Mass. About half the undergraduate students are weekly communicants. The Sacrament of Reconciliation is offered twice a week during the academic year, in each residence hall during Advent and Lent, on every CUA retreat, and by appointment.

CUA holds four special Masses during the academic year at the Basilica: the Freshman Orientation Mass, the Mass of the Holy Spirit, the Mass in Honor of St. Thomas Aquinas, and the Baccalaureate Mass.

A Holy Hour with Benediction is celebrated on campus twice a week: Wednesday night Praise and Worship Adoration, and Thursday evening Solemn Adoration. Daily Eucharistic adoration marks the Lenten weekdays between the 12:15 p.m. and 5:10 p.m. Masses.

During the first month of every academic year, friars visit every residence hall on campus, blessing the rooms of all who express interest.

Other opportunities for spiritual growth include nine annual class-based and student-run retreats, the priest-led "Going Deeper" retreat series, and days of recollection for specific student

organizations. Campus Ministers sponsor student organizations dedicated to men and women's spiritual growth, the Church's teachings on social justice, and her intellectual tradition. CUA also has an online "Prayernet" site, a R.C.I.A. program, and a Renew program.

Campus ministry coordinates all community service for CUA. During the 2011-12 academic year students performed more than 125,000 hours of community service. Campus Ministry also sponsors mission trips, and students have gone to Guatemala, Jamaica, Panama, Belize, Honduras, Tanzania, and Costa Rica. In fall 2012 the University expanded its Religious in Residence program, with three sisters living in two residence halls for women and one priest living in a residence hall for men.

Residential Life

CUA is largely a residential campus, with more than 2,200 students living in 17 residence halls and 25 modular units grouped into five "neighborhoods" or clusters. About two-thirds of undergraduates live on campus. Access to residence halls is secure.

The University is in the final stages of transitioning to all single-sex housing, a process that began in 2011. In 2013-14, 97 percent of students will live in single-sex housing, including all freshmen . The campus has a visitation policy, allow-

From the Career Services Office

The programs and services offered by the Office of Career Services are available to Catholic University undergraduate students, graduate students, and alumni. Through face-to-face appointments (scheduled and walk-in) and distance service (emailed and dropped-off resume and cover letter critiques), career services counselors assist students with a range of career development concerns, most notably choosing a career, searching for jobs and internships, writing résumés and cover letters, interviewing, and applying to graduate and professional school.

Career Services Programs and Initiatives: 1) Assists students in clarifying their career identity through direct counseling supplemented by career interest assessment tools and an online career information resource library; 2) Collaborates with faculty to provide information on career options and graduate school preparation; 3) Provides students with opportunities to explore and test out potential career options through experiential opportunities such as internships, part-time jobs, and summer jobs; 4) Holds career fairs for part-time jobs, internships, summer jobs, and full-time employment; 5) Prepares students to be successful job seekers through individual coaching on job search strategies; networking; resume, curriculum vitae and cover letter writing; and interview skills development; 6) Provides students with opportunities for employer information sessions and on-campus interviews.

It also engages employers and alumni in educational programs related to job searching, and coordinates and markets an on-campus student employment system to provide students with opportunities to gain experience while earning money for school expenses. The Career Services office manages the federal work-study employment system and researches student job and internship opportunities to assist students in targeting jobs and internships.

ing visitors until midnight during the week and later on weekends. Overnight opposite-sex visitation is not permitted.

Students over the age of 21 are free to have alcohol in their rooms, but they may not have it in common areas or provide it to others; 52 resident assistants are responsible for enforcement.

The campus health clinic is located in the Student Health and Fitness Center. It is open weekdays for routine services as well as physical examinations, and is staffed by a physician, a nurse practitioner, a physician assistant, and a nurse. There are a number of urgent care clinics in the area, and Providence Hospital is nearby.

Washington is easily accessible from everywhere. Ronald Reagan Washington National Airport is across the river from the city, while the Baltimore/Washington International Thurgood Marshall and Washington Dulles International airports are about 45 minutes away. Amtrak has a broad network that uses Union Station, and the Metro subway system has a station adjacent to the campus.

Student Activities

Reflecting the scope of a larger university, CUA offers more than 100 student organizations covering a wide range of professional, social, community service, and advocacy areas.

The pro-life group is very active, expanding its work beyond abortion and addressing lifestyle issues and chastity. In addition to praying and sidewalk counseling outside abortion businesses, it also sponsors Theology of the Body student/reading groups. Surrounding the March for Life, students provide extensive hospitality in housing out-of-town marchers and pro-lifers on campus and at the Basilica.

A separate Live Out Love chastity group speaks to local middle-school and high-school students. In addition, the University has a chapter of Catholic Athletes for Christ, the organization's first college chapter. There are no pro-abortion or homosexual rights groups.

The music school sponsors about 200 recitals a year, and students have given concerts at the Vatican, Washington's Kennedy Center for the Performing Arts, in a number of U.S. cities, and abroad.

The Hartke Theatre features five or six performances annually by the nationally recognized drama department.

In addition to all these organizations and cultural opportunities, CUA has a rich array of intercollegiate, club, and intramural athletic programs. The CUA Cardinals compete in the NCAA Division III with 21 varsity sports teams; club sports exist in 12 areas.

Washington offers a wide variety of social, cultural, and entertainment opportunities, such as the Kennedy Center for the Performing Arts, a large array of museums within the Smithsonian system, and prominent art museums. Next to the university is the Blessed John Paul II Shrine. Washington is also home to several professional sports teams.

The Bottom Line

CUA has greatly strengthened its Catholic identity and academic prowess over the past several years, with changes ushered in since 1998 during the presidencies of Bishop David O'Connell and John Garvey. Today the undergraduate program can be an excellent choice for students seeking a mid-sized university in an urban environment.

"There's a level of professionalism that comes with being in D.C. that can't be matched," said Christine Mica, dean of university admissions. "Students are given opportunities they wouldn't have anywhere else."

Across the spectrum, CUA is on the move. Most importantly, the "bishops' university" has confidently embraced a well-rounded Catholic approach to higher education. It is exciting that Catholic families today, many who are not seeking a liberal arts college, have the option of an authentically Catholic, comprehensive university located in our nation's capital.

Catholic University of America Frequently Asked Questions

We get questions from Catholic families on a regular basis about the colleges we recommend. Rather than filter the answers, we asked CUA officials nearly 100 questions in categories such as academics, curriculum, programs of study, campus ministry, residence life, student activities, the make up of the study body, and institutional identity. The answers to some of the most asked questions are provided below and the rest are available on the CUA profile page at TheNewmanGuide.com.

Majors

List the major, minor and special program areas that students may choose for specialization while pursuing an undergraduate degree:

School of Architecture and Planning: Four-Year Bachelor of Science in Architecture, Dual Degree Program with Civil Engineering. *School of Arts and Sciences*: Anthropology, Art History, Art: Studio, Biochemistry, Biology, Chemical Physics, Chemistry, Classical Civilization, Classical Humanities, Classics-Greek and Latin, Drama, Education (Early Childhood, Elementary, Secondary), Education Studies (non-teaching), English Language and Literature*, Environmental Chemistry, French, German, History*, Mathematics*, Media Studies, Medical Technology, Medieval and Byzantine Studies, Philosophy, Philosophy concentration, Pre-Law concentration, Physics, Politics, Psychology, Sociology, Spanish, Spanish for International Service, Theology and Religious Studies, Undecided/Exploratory. *Indicates areas of study that are also offered with Secondary Education Minor. *School of Business and Economics*: Accounting, Economics, Finance, International Business, International Economics and Finance, Management, Marketing. *School of Engineering*: Biomedical, Civil (Construction, Dual Degree with Architecture), Computer Science, Electrical (Alternative and Renewable Energy), Mechanical (Environmental). *Benjamin T. Rome School of Music*: Bachelor of Art, Music (General, Performance, Music History and Literature), Bachelor of Music, Collaborative Piano, Composition, Music Education (General-Choral Music Education, Instrumental Music Education, Combined General-Choral and Instrumental Music Education), Instrumental Music Education/Orchestral, Instruments (dual degree), Musical Theater, Performance (Orchestral Instruments, Organ, Piano, Voice), Piano Pedagogy. *School of Nursing*: Four-Year Bachelor of Science. *School of Philosophy*: Philosophy Program of Concentration, Pre-Law Program of Concentration. *National Catholic School of Social Service*: Social Work. *Pre-Professional Studies*: Dental, Law, Medicine, Veterinary. Note: Students interested in Pre-Professional Studies must also select an official major, such as biology, biomedical engineering or politics. *Metropolitan School of Professional Studies*: Information Technology, Interdisciplinary Studies, Management.

What are the three most popular majors or specialty disciplines for undergraduate students, and about what percentage of undergraduate students specialize in these disciplines?

Business and Economics, 10%

Politics, 10%

Engineering, 9%

Spiritual Life

Please list the schedule of Masses, noting the following for each Mass: the day and time, the Form or Rite of the Mass, and the style of music, if any (chant, traditional, contemporary, etc.):

Mo 12:10 p.m., 12:30 p.m., 10:30 p.m

Tu 12:10 p.m., 12:30 p.m., 8 p.m., 10:30 p.m.

We 12:10 p.m., 12:30 p.m., 10:30 p.m.

Th 12:10 p.m., 12:30 p.m., 9 p.m., 10:30 p.m.

Fr 12:10 p.m., 12:30 p.m., 5:10 p.m.

Su 11:00 a.m., schola and traditional hymn
4:00 p.m., schola and traditional hymns

Basilica Crypt Church
9:00 p.m., choir, contemporary sacred music

All are Ordinary Form. For Sunday Masses, the 11 a.m. features traditional hymns, the 4 p.m. features traditional hymns and schola; the 9 p.m. is contemporary Church music.

List the schedule for Confession by day and time:

Mo

Tu

We 10:00 p.m.

Th

Fr

Sa

Su 10:00 p.m.

List the schedule for Adoration of the Blessed Sacrament by day and time:

We 9:00-10:00 p.m., Th 9:00-10:00 p.m.

Please identify regularly scheduled devotions on campus for students such as the Rosary and prayer groups:

Our prayer group meets each week on Monday nights. Rosary is prayed Monday afternoon. Compline (night prayer) is prayed every night of the week in multiple campus locations. During Lent we pray weekly the Stations of the Cross.

Residence Life

Please describe options for students to reside on and off campus:

CUA is largely a residential campus, with more than 2,200 students living in 17 residence halls and 25 modular units grouped into five "neighborhoods" or clusters. On-campus housing options include traditional-style rooms, suites, and apartments.

About two-thirds of undergraduates live on campus.

CUA strongly believes in the benefits that on-campus living has to offer to our first- and second-year students in terms of academic success, personal development, and involvement within the CUA campus community. As such, CUA requires all first- and second-year undergraduate students to live in on-campus housing (an exception is made for students whose families live in the D.C. area and who wish to commute from home to campus).

Does your institution offer only single-sex residence halls?

No, we have one building single-sex by floor or wing designated for graduate students and a small number of upper-class undergraduates. 97% of students living on campus are in single-sex residence halls.

Are students of the opposite sex permitted to visit students' bedrooms?

Yes. Students may visit in student rooms from 9:00 a.m. to midnight, Sunday through Thursday, and 9:00 a.m. to 2:00 a.m., Friday and Saturday.

How does your institution foster sobriety and respond to substance abuse on campus, particularly in campus residences?

Residence Life staff actively monitor residential communities and enforce all policies related to alcohol. Students documented for alleged violation of alcohol polices are referred to the Office of Student Conduct and Ethical Development for disciplinary interventions.

Alcohol 101 workshops are offered in each first-year student residence hall within the first six weeks of the fall semester as part of new student orientation. The University recognizes National Collegiate Alcohol Awareness Week, National Drunk and Drugged Driving Prevention Month, and Safe Spring Break

Week with information distribution and campus-wide programming. Alcohol education and training are provided for Resident Assistants, Orientation Advisers, and Resident Ministers each summer. These programs are coordinated by the Office of the Dean of Students and are supported by the Department of Athletics, the Kane Fitness Center, Office of Residence Life, Student Health Services, and the Counseling Center. (See the CUA profile page at TheNewmanGuide.com for more extensive information.)

How does your institution foster a student living environment that promotes and supports chastity, particularly in campus residences?

Catholic University, in both policy and action, reinforces the dignity of the body. The University affirms, in our Code of Student Conduct, that sexual relationships are designed by God to be expressed solely within a marriage between husband and wife. Sexual acts of any kind outside the confines of marriage are inconsistent with the teachings and moral values of the Catholic Church and are prohibited.

Residential staff are expected to confront disruptive and unhealthy behaviors including those related to sexual activity. Students alleged to have violated University standards in this regard meet with professional staff within the Division of Student Life for intervention and consequences within the student conduct system.

The University encourages conversations about sex, relationships, and marriage, and supports a number of student organizations whose missions involve these topics specifically. Student organizations such as Live Out Love, *Vitae Familia*, Students for Life, and the peer education group CUAlternative bring speakers to campus and host events that focus on love and relationships with emphasis on the Church's teachings on marriage and family life. Ultimately, the messages students receive is to never settle for less than lives of purity and true love.

Student Body

Describe the makeup of your institution's undergraduate student body with regard to sex, religion, home state/country and type of high school (public, private, homeschool):

Number of undergraduates: 3,694
Male: 45% Female: 55%

Roman Catholic: 80% Protestant: 2%
Muslim: 3% Other: 15%

Number of states represented: 50
Top three states: Maryland (21%), New Jersey (14%), New York (11%)

Catholic HS: 46% Homeschool: 1%
Public HS: 3% Unspecified: 50%

CHRISTENDOM COLLEGE

Front Royal, Virginia

Overview

The two words that best describe Christendom College are Catholic and traditional, in the very best sense of both words. The College was founded in 1977 by the late historian, Warren Carroll, to counter harmful trends in American higher education and return to an emphasis on serious study and student development. Today Christendom sets a standard for fidelity and traditional education against which other Catholic liberal arts colleges are measured.

"The College has a very clear vision," says President Timothy O'Donnell. "We stress academics and Catholicism. …We end up attracting a person who hungers for what we are providing."

Proudly proclaiming that Catholicism is "the air that we breathe," the College's vision statement proclaims, "Only an education which integrates the truths of the Catholic Faith throughout the curriculum is a fully Catholic education." All professors are Catholic and teach all classes with a clear Catholic worldview. They annually make a Profession of Faith and take the Oath of Fidelity before the Bishop of Arlington. The 15-member governing board, including one priest and Dr. O'Donnell, also takes an annual Oath of Fidelity.

Nestled in Virginia's Shenandoah Valley, Christendom is intentionally small, with an undergraduate program at Front Royal, Virginia, and a graduate theology program in Alexandria, Virginia. The College is designed to reach a maximum number of 450 residential undergraduates, only about 30 above its current enrollment.

Christendom undergraduates choose among six major areas of study, with a traditional emphasis on the liberal arts. The 86-credit core curriculum constitutes about two-thirds of the four-year program, with emphasis on Catholic theology and philosophy. The study-abroad semester in Rome is popular among third-year students.

Dr. O'Donnell has taught at Christendom since 1985 and was named its third president seven years later. He has a doctoral-level degree in theology from the Angelicum in Rome, has been a Consultor to the Pontifical Council for the Family since 2002, authored two books, and is host of numerous television programs for the Eternal Word Television Network (EWTN).

Christendom has been on a path of steady growth, building, and expansion. Upcoming planned expansions will include a piazza, two academic buildings, the expansion of St. Lawrence Commons, and a cruciform Gothic Church with a 100-foot tower.

The tuition rate is below the average private college cost in Virginia, and the typical financial aid package at Christendom is generous. The College is wary of government entanglements and so does not participate in the federal student aid programs, but it provides scholarships and loans from its own resources, as well as helping students obtain funds from private sources.

Quick Facts

2013-2014 Academic Year

Students 420

SATs 1200

HS GPA 3.7

Majors 6

% Catholic 99%

How Much? $31,000
tuition, room and board

Academics

All courses in the freshman and sophomore years are prescribed and include four theology courses and four philosophy courses. Juniors and seniors must take two more theology courses and two additional philosophy courses. Two years of a foreign language—Latin, Greek, or French—are required as are courses in English, history, math, science, and political science.

Students can select from six majors and begin work in a concentration in the third and fourth years. The majors are classical studies, English

language and literature, history, philosophy, political science and economics, and theology. Students can also choose to minor in mathematics, economics, or liturgical music. An 86-credit hour Associate of Arts degree is given to undergraduates who choose to transfer elsewhere to major in disciplines other than the six at Christendom.

Students have the opportunity to attend the Junior Semester in Rome either in the fall or spring. It is a rigorous semester that includes one course each in theology, art and architecture, Italian, and interdisciplinary studies. Dr. O'Donnell said that in their senior exit interviews, most students talk about the transformative power of the Rome experience. There also is a shorter summer program available in Ireland.

As a helpful complement to its academic program, Christendom has recently hired a full-time career development officer and has rolled out a series of classes and workshops to help students discern career vocations and prepare for job interviews.

Spiritual Life

The Chapel of Christ the King is at the center of the campus and of campus life. The chapel bells ring several times each day, calling students to Mass and prayer. Time is set aside daily for Mass, which about 70 percent of the students attend. Masses are reverently celebrated, and a more solemn Ordinary Form liturgy is celebrated in Latin on Sundays, Tuesdays, and Fridays, with one of the daily Masses each week offered in the Extraordinary Form. The liturgies are traditional with traditional music. On Sundays, some students attend the 12:30 p.m. Extraordinary Form Mass at St. John the Baptist parish in Front Royal.

Confessions are available daily, normally twice a day throughout the week and once a day on the weekends. There is adoration of the Blessed Sacrament most mornings and recitation of the Rosary and Evening Prayer. On the first Thursday of each month, a special holy hour is offered in reparation to the Sacred Heart, followed by all-night adoration ending at the 7:30 a.m. Mass on Friday.

All religious ministries at Christendom are specifically Catholic.

Emphasis is placed on both religious and married vocations. A vocational discernment weekend is held annually, and Christendom offers a debt forgiveness program for graduates entering religious life who take a vow of poverty. In a given year, about five percent of graduating students choose a religious vocation, with more than 140 men and women as priests and religious, or in seminary formation, and Christendom has had more than 350 alumnus-to-alumna marriages.

Residential Life

Campus housing is provided for full-time students. About 90 percent of students live on campus, while others may live at home and commute to campus.

There are five female and six male resi-

Financial Aid Office Info

We deliver a high-quality education at an affordable price. That's why *Kiplinger's Personal Finance* magazine ranks us in the top 100 schools in the nation that provide both academic quality and affordability.

You're not going to find our caliber of education and personal formation anywhere in the country—especially at our price. If you want to come to Christendom, we'll try our hardest to make it happen. We'll also help you graduate with as little debt as possible.

Over 70% of our students receive some form of financial assistance every year. We have a strong commitment to providing a comprehensive financial assistance program to our students. We offer financial assistance through our need-based aid and merit-based academic scholarships. Need-based aid consists of loans and grants. Merit-based scholarships are granted automatically upon acceptance and are based on your SAT or ACT score. Additionally, all students may apply for employment with the College through the College's Student Employment Website.

The Financial Aid Program is funded through private gifts and grants from many generous donors and the College's growing endowment. While Christendom accepts no direct federal aid, nor does it participate in indirect programs of federal aid such as the Student Guaranteed Loan, the College maintains a robust financial assistance program that matches and mirrors support received through federal aid programs.

The Financial Aid Office stands ready to work with students and parents on paying and financing a college education. Please contact Ms. Alisa Polk anytime with your questions: 800-877-5456 ext. 1214 or apolk@christendom.edu. She is here to help you! Christendom.edu/aid.

dence halls. Freshmen males are mixed with upper classmen. Inter-visitation is

Front Royal is easily reachable. Dulles International Airport is about an hour east of the campus, and Ronald Reagan Washington National Airport offers flights closer to the nation's capital.

Student Activities

A professional dress code is maintained in the classroom—as well as at Mass, lunch, and special events. Usually this includes a dress shirt and necktie for men and a dress or blouse with skirt or dress slacks for women. A jacket is also required for men at Sunday Mass and for speakers' presentations.

For a small school, Christendom offers many activities, with approximately 20 different clubs and organizations. The St. Lawrence Commons, where students dine, is the scene for dances and performances sponsored by the Student Activities Council. There are a variety of college activities, as well as Catholic cultural festivities and lectures.

Students in the Shield of Roses pray the Rosary and offer sidewalk counseling in front of Planned Parenthood in Washington, D.C., each Saturday morning. Participation in the annual March for Life, also in the nation's capital, includes nearly the entire student body, with the College cancelling classes on that day.

The Corporal Works of Mercy group ministers to the poor in the Front Royal area by helping at soup kitchens, delivering

prohibited.

Every floor in every hall has a resident assistant whose job it is to promote community life, enforce college behavior policy, and assist students. There are weekly room inspections. Neither television nor Internet access are available within the residence halls but are provided in campus centers. Freshmen and Sophomores under the age of 21 have a curfew of midnight during the week and 1:00 a.m. on weekends.

Students eat all their meals at the St. Lawrence Commons. It is common to see professors and staff eating and talking with students during lunch time.

Drinking is prohibited in the college residences, but at some campus events, students over the age of 21 are allowed

to consume a moderated number of alcoholic beverages. There is also a restriction on public romantic displays of affection.

The College has a part-time nurse for student medical care. If needed, Warren County Memorial Hospital is a 196-bed facility in Front Royal about ten minutes from campus. There are also medical specialists and hospitals in Washington, D.C.

The small town of Front Royal has a population of about 14,500. Downtown has quaint shops including a Catholic book and gift store, coffee shop, laundromat, antique shop, boutiques, restaurants, and a three-screen movie theater. There are newer hotels, restaurants, and retail stores nearby.

From the Career Services Office

The Career Development Office at Christendom College provides career counseling and orientation for students about potential career choices; provides information on deadlines for GRE and LSAT examinations, graduate fellowships, etc.; and assists students with résumé writing, mock job interviews, and graduate and law school applications.

Every student participates in the Education for a Lifetime Program, which focuses on enhancing the student learning environment by integrating students' career discernment into their liberal arts education. The program consists of two one-credit courses, one spanning the Freshman through Sophomore years and the other spanning the Junior through Senior years. In the program, students are not only able to discern occupations, but also are equipped with the basic 21st century research, computer communication, and job search competencies. (http://www.christendom.edu/academics/elp.php)

The Career Development office also maintains a listing of job opportunities for seniors and Christendom College graduates and acts as a clearinghouse for graduate job seekers and employment opportunities. Liberal arts graduates are in great demand because they possess the high moral values, communication skills, and habits of problem solving and "high level thinking" sorely lacking in graduates of so many of the modern universities.

A liberal arts education is an excellent preparation for the professions, and Christendom counselors can guide students so that they can complete programs in nursing, engineering, accounting, and the like quickly and efficiently, should they be called to those fields.

meals, and visiting nursing homes.

The St. Juan Diego Confraternity assists in the formation of student missionary workers who participate in the college mission programs to such places as Honduras, the Dominican Republic, and the streets of New York City. Members pray for the Catholic evangelization of the Americas and participate in trips within the region.

The College has a student schola that provides music and Gregorian chant for Mass. There is also an active drama contingent on campus, called the Christendom Players, and there many opportunities for students to participate in musical events, such as the annual St. Cecilia's Eve, Coffee House, Piano Night, and various Pub Nights.

Cultural opportunities and lectures also exist through the Major Speakers Program and the Beato Fra Angelico Arts Program. In addition, the Chester-Belloc Debate Society helps students hone their argumentation and rhetorical skills. They can also write for the student journal, The Rambler, or for The Chronicler, a weekly synopsis of life at Christendom.

The John Paul the Great Student Center is the locus for student activity after class. It houses the Student Life office, Career Development, a lounge, and student post office boxes, as well as St. Kilian's Café, which often becomes a working pub. The lower level features a large-screen television, ping pong, foosball, pool, and air hockey tables. The St. Louis the Crusader Gym is also available for student use, which has a full-size basketball court, a weight room, an exercise room, and two racquetball courts, as well as a student lounge area.

Christendom is a member of the United States Collegiate Athletic Association and the Shenandoah-Chesapeake Conference and has seven varsity teams and various intramural sports.

The Blue Ridge Mountains provide a beautiful backdrop for Christendom, and outdoor opportunities include the Shenandoah River for canoeing, tubing, and fishing. Hiking is available at Shenandoah National Park and mountains. In addition, the nation's capital is about 70 miles away and presents historical, cultural, artistic, and political opportunities for students.

The Bottom Line

For more than 35 years, Christendom College has made a vital contribution to American Catholic life through its solid spiritual formation and its liberal arts curriculum. What was once a tiny holdout against the decline of higher education is today a model for Catholic liberal arts colleges, with a well-de-

served reputation even in Rome.

"It is refreshing to see a Catholic college where the parents can send their children and not get worried whether they will get serious Catholic education—without discount—just as it is," said Cardinal Francis Arinze, then-Prefect of the Vatican Congregation for Divine Worship and the Discipline of the Sacraments, while visiting Christendom in 2008.

Students seem to appreciate Christendom's commitment to the Catholic faith and its small size, friendliness, and close-knit community. On the key measures of Catholic identity and liberal arts education, few American colleges can compare.

Christendom College
Frequently Asked Questions

We get questions from Catholic families on a regular basis about the colleges we recommend. Rather than filter the answers, we asked Christendom officials nearly 100 questions in categories such as academics, curriculum, programs of study, campus ministry, residence life, student activities, the make up of the study body, and institutional identity. The answers to some of the most asked questions are provided below and the rest are available on the college profile page at TheNewmanGuide.com.

Majors

List the major, minor and special program areas that students may choose for specialization while pursuing an undergraduate degree:

Theology, Philosophy, History, English Language and Literature, Early and Classical Christian Studies, Political Science & Economics. Students may minor in Math, Liturgical Music, Economics or any of the above-listed majors.

What are the three most popular majors or specialty disciplines for undergraduate students, and about what percentage of undergraduate students specialize in these disciplines?

Philosophy, 26%

History, 25%

Political Science, 16%

Spiritual Life

Please list the schedule of Masses, noting the following for each Mass: the day and time, the Form or Rite of the Mass, and the style of music, if any (chant, traditional, contemporary, etc.):

Mo 7:30 a.m., 11:30 a.m., both Ordinary Form

Tu 7:30 a.m., Extraordinary Form; 11:30 a.m., Ordinary Form

We 7:30 a.m., 11:30 a.m., both Ordinary Form

Th 7:30 a.m., 11:30 a.m., both Ordinary Form

Fr 7:30 a.m., 11:30 a.m., both Ordinary Form

Sa 7:30 a.m., 9:00 a.m., both Ordinary Form

Su 10:00 a.m. Ordinary Form

All Masses are traditional liturgies, some with chant, others with pipe organ and choir, some celebrated in Latin, others in English.

St. John the Baptist Roman Catholic Church is the local Catholic parish (4 miles away) and offers additional Masses on Sunday and throughout the week, including a 12:30 p.m. Sunday Mass, offered in the Extraordinary Form each week.

List the schedule for Confession by day and time:

Mo 11:00-11:30 a.m., 6:00-6:30 p.m.

Tu 11:00-11:30 a.m., 6:00-6:30 p.m.

We 11:00-11:30 a.m., 6:00-6:30 p.m.

Th 11:00-11:30 a.m., 6:00-6:30 p.m.

Fr 11:00-11:30 a.m., 6:00-6:30 p.m.

Sa 11:00-11:15 a.m.

Su 9:15-9:45 a.m.

Other: Anytime by appointment

List the schedule for Adoration of the Blessed Sacrament by day and time:

Monday-Friday 8:00 - 11:20 a.m. (Benediction at 11:20 a.m.) and also for First Fridays a 9:30 p.m. Holy Hour on First Thursdays followed by all-night Adoration.

Please identify regularly scheduled devotions on campus for students such as the Rosary and prayer groups:

Daily Rosary at 6:00 p.m., Adoration of the Most Blessed Sacrament each weekday, daily Liturgy of the Hours include vespers at 6:30 p.m. and night prayer at 10:00 p.m.

The OREMUS prayer group offers *lectio divina* (a guided meditation of Sacred Scripture), open prayer and sacred song on Wednesdays at 8:00 p.m. One Wednesday a month, OREMUS offers a Holy Hour of praise and worship of the Most Blessed Sacrament from 8:00 to 9:00 p.m. in Christ the King Chapel.

Residence Life

Please describe options for students to reside on and off campus:

90% of full-time students reside on campus in the college's residence halls, which are separated by gender. Only students who are living at home, with parents, or who have special needs, may live off campus. These students must get permission from the Dean of Students.

Does your institution offer only single-sex residence halls?

Yes.

Are students of the opposite sex permitted to visit students' bedrooms?

No.

How does your institution foster sobriety and respond to substance abuse on campus, particularly in campus residences?

Christendom College takes a pro-active approach in fostering sobriety on campus. While students are not allowed to possess or store alcohol in the residence halls or on campus, alcohol is provided to students of legal drinking age at certain school sponsored events. In this way, alcohol consumption happens in a social capacity with limits and accountability to encourage a balanced and moderated approach to drinking. Christendom is also proactive in providing alternatives to the common College "drinking scene". With College-sponsored and student-organized events every weekend night students have fun, safe, and positive opportunities and outlets during their college years.

Christendom works hard to promote sobriety on campus, but substance abuse is a personal struggle that a few students may encounter. Understanding that a number of factors may contribute to substance abuse the Office of Student Life works hard to provide pastoral care to these students. Spiritual direction is available on campus and references to Catholic counselors are available. In the residence halls, Resident Assistants are trained to recognize the signs of substance abuse and provide residents with the resources and references they need to overcome these struggles. RAs are encouraged to build personal relationships with each resident and foster a strong community in the halls so that they can assist a struggling resident in a truly fraternal matter.

How does your institution foster a student living environment that promotes and supports chastity, particularly in campus residences?

Through both policy and formation we strive to develop student's sense of chastity and respect for the distinction and dignity of the genders. College is a natural time to begin pursuing a vocation, and while many students pursue romantic relationships during their time here they are asked to refrain from any physical romantic interaction on campus. Unlike many colleges, living a life of chastity and respect for dignity of each gender is the prevailing attitude by students on campus and infrequently needs to be addressed by staff. Lastly, students are also required to comply with a modest dress code that is in place at all times.

While the College recognizes the academic benefits of the internet, we also recognize that it can be an intrusive source of temptation and so internet access is not provided in the residence halls. Men and women are housed separately on campus, which allows for specialized formation events and healthy relationships be fostered throughout the year. In these ways we hope to provide the boundaries and education necessary for students to grow in appreciation of their own dignity and the dignity of others.

Student Body

Describe the makeup of your institution's undergraduate student body with regard to sex, religion, home state/country and type of high school (public, private, homeschool):

Total number of undergraduates: 420
Male: 41% Female: 59%

Catholic: 99% Other Christian: 1%
Jewish: % Muslim: % Other: %

Number of states represented: 45
Top three states: VA, TX, CA
Students from top three states: 35%

Catholic HS: 25% Homeschool: 55%
Private HS: 10% Public HS: 10%

COLLEGE OF SAINT MARY MAGDALEN

Warner, New Hampshire

411

For more information on Magdalen, visit their website at:

www.magdalen.edu

Admissions contact:

877/498-1723
admissions@magdalen.edu

Overview

The College of Saint Mary Magdalen is a small residential Catholic liberal arts college founded in 1973, as part of the new wave of renewal in American Catholic higher education. Now the College is undergoing its own internal renewal, with a new name, an expanded curriculum focused on the Great Books, and an emphasis on student development in virtue.

In 2010 the board of trustees changed the name from Magdalen College to more clearly honor its patroness, Saint Mary Magdalen, more strongly affirm its Catholic identity, and indicate a somewhat new direction. In 2011, the trustees selected the College's fourth and current president, Dr. George Harne, who has both a background in the Great Books—having received a Master's degree from St. John's College—and a doctorate in musicology from Princeton University.

"We want our graduates to be part of the 'creative minority'... the creative force that will transform the West," says Dr. Harne.

The College's recently revised curriculum integrates Socratic study of the Great Books with the classical seven liberal arts. The study of theology and an eight-semester series of seminars in philosophy and humanities are at the center of the integrated curriculum. In their junior and senior years, students complement these studies with concentrations in theology, philosophy, literature, or politics. Students also study in Rome during the spring semester of their sophomore year.

The College offers a Vatican-approved Apostolic Catechetical Diploma following the completion of six semesters of theology and catechesis that covers the entire Catechism of the Catholic Church, as well as pivotal Church documents and key texts by the Church Fathers and Doctors of the Church. Through this program, students are prepared to be effective communicators of the Faith in their homes, parishes, and communities.

The faculty, chaplain, and student life staff annually take the Oath of Fidelity, and theologians have received the *mandatum*.

The College of Saint Mary Magdalen rests on the 3,500-foot Mount Kearsarge in Warner, New Hampshire, a quaint town of 2,800 residents in the Lakes Region. But students are also just 90 minutes from Boston, with numerous educational, cultural, and social opportunities.

Students come from across the United States and other countries, and over 95 percent are Catholic. A significant number of the students have gone on to graduate study, and about 10 percent of the graduates have become priests or other religious.

With the assistance of an investment by the Catholic Order of Foresters, the College was able to double its freshmen class for the 2012-2013 academic year. Accredited by the American Academy

Quick Facts

2013-2014 Academic Year

Students 61

SATs 1210

HS GPA 3.3

Majors 1

% Catholic 98%

How Much? $27,200
tuition, room and board

for Liberal Education, the College is seeking regional accreditation from the New England Association of Schools and Colleges.

The tuition is less than half the typical private-college tuition in New Hampshire, and the College strives to help families who need financial aid.

Academics

The College of Saint Mary Magdalen's liberal arts education is built upon the careful reading, study, and discussion of the Great Books of the West, covering key texts from ancient Greece, Rome, the Church Fathers, medieval authors, modernity, and post-modernity. The College orders its curriculum according to the traditional seven liberal arts, combined with a strong emphasis on theology, philosophy, and the fine arts—the latter being rather unique by comparison to most other colleges, with a strong emphasis on music.

With the exception of two concentration courses per semester in the junior and senior years, all students follow the same Great Books curriculum. The course of studies includes a four-year philosophy and humanities sequence of seminars, a summer course of studies in Rome and Norcia, three years of theology leading to an Apostolic Catechetical Diploma, four years of music and art, two years of Greek or Latin, three years of science, and courses in logic, geometry, grammar, rhetoric, and non-Western cultures. Students complete a junior project based in their concentration and as seniors complete comprehensive exams and write a senior thesis.

Freshmen and sophomores take a writing workshop each semester in which they prepare one paper each week on a topic related to the humanities. Class meetings include oral presentation of those papers and practice in writing and editing.

The College's authority to award the Apostolic Catechetical Diploma, granted by the Vatican to the College in 1983, is unique. Historically, this diploma has only been available through graduate programs. Students must demonstrate their mastery of the fundamental teachings of the Church by completing six semesters of theology based on the Catechism of the Catholic Church and other key theological documents. The diploma is presented to students upon completion of their bachelor's degree.

Students may elect to participate in the Honors Program, which was launched by Dr. Harne in his previous role as academic dean. With form and content similar to graduate seminars, the honors colloquia explore a variety of topics such as modern cinema, Dante's Divine Comedy, a Catholic understanding of gender, the operas of Mozart, and phenomenology. Honors students must maintain a grade point average of 3.25 or higher and complete six honors colloquia, 16 credit hours of honors-level courses, and an honors thesis.

Spiritual Life

Our Lady, Queen of Apostles Chapel is the center of campus spiritual life. The chaplain offers Mass and Confession daily, marking Holy days and the liturgical seasons with special observances. No classes are held during Mass times. Students also gather for Lauds and Vespers in the chapel.

On important feast days such as the Immaculate Conception, the College of Saint Mary Magdalen closes its offices and marks the feast with Mass, special meals, speakers, and other activities.

The Rosary is prayed daily in the chapel or residence halls, and adoration and Benediction are available on a regular

Financial Aid Office Info

Over 90% of the students at The College of Saint Mary Magdalen receive some form of financial aid. The college makes it possible for every eligible student to finance his or her education through a variety of need and merit-based awards, as well as private loans. Need-based financial aid is based on a review of the Magdalen Aid Application, along with supporting documents, and is offered to worthy students who would otherwise be unable to attend a private college. Merit scholarships are based on academic achievement, talent, leadership skills, and other criteria. They are offered to first-time, full-time students, with the exception of the Achievement Award, which is open to both new and returning students. These awards are renewable each year, for a maximum of four years.

The Presidential Scholarship is a full tuition scholarship awarded in honor of Pope Benedict XVI. This is awarded to an incoming freshman who has written a compelling essay in response to one of Pope Benedict's encyclicals—*Deus caritas est*, *Spe salvi*, or *Caritas in veritate*—demonstrating his or her close reading of the text.

Students receive valuable work experience as well as additional financial assistance by participating in campus work study. Work study grants are calculated and awarded based on financial need. Students are assigned to various departments on campus and receive awards which are deducted from tuition fees.

Please contact Marie Lasher at mlasher@magdalen.edu or call 603.456.2656 for more information.

basis. Both the men's and women's residences have chapels in which the Blessed Sacrament is reserved.

The College places a special emphasis on reverence and beauty in campus liturgy, with a strong commitment to

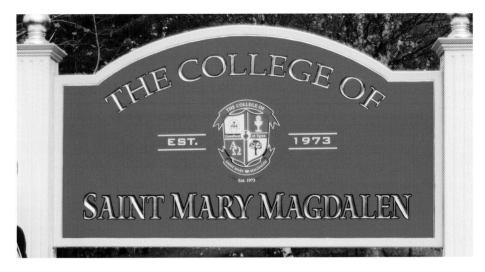

liturgical renewal. Dr. Harne says it was the beauty of the liturgy that initiated his conversion to the Catholic Church, entering "through the door of the beautiful." The student choir sings chant, motets, polyphony, and traditional hymns.

In 2011, Magdalen announced that students would chant the Propers of the Mass in newly composed English settings. Dr. Harne explained: "The introit, offertory, and communion chants of the *Graduale Romanum* have largely disappeared from the celebration of Mass. These chants have remained the ideal, being advocated in all magisterial documents concerning the liturgy in the past one hundred years, including those following the Second Vatican Council. Restoring the singing of these chants to our celebration of the Mass is another step toward fulfilling the Holy Father's call for a reform of the reform."

All Masses are celebrated ad orientem, facing East as was traditional for much of the Church's history, and students kneel to receive the Eucharist. Mass is celebrated in both the Ordinary and Extraordinary (or Tridentine) Forms.

Residential Life

Built with clapboard siding, brick, and shuttered windows, the residences are a "home away from home" for students enrolled at the College. Both residences—St. Mary's for the women and St. Joseph's for the men—have a large living room, a chapel where Christ resides in the Blessed Sacrament, study areas, and laundry facilities. Each bedroom accommodates several students with bunk beds, wardrobes, storage spaces, and a bathroom.

In past decades, Magdalen was known for its unusually strict policies governing student behavior, including mandatory Mass attendance, rigorous room inspections, and dating restrictions. But today the College's policies are similar to other faithful Catholic colleges, allowing students independence while strongly encouraging moral development and growth in the virtues. Opposite-sex visitation is not permitted in the campus residences.

All students participate in the Campus Service Program by working in the library, serving in the administrative offices, or helping maintain campus facilities. This program helps defray the cost of tuition and promotes responsible stewardship of the campus buildings and grounds.

Student Activities

The College of Saint Mary Magdalen concurs with the German Catholic philosopher Josef Pieper that "leisure is the basis of culture," and believes that student activities can be more than idle diversions. Students may choose from a variety of on-campus activities, and the College's location in beautiful New Hampshire offers students access to Boston (with its historical, cultural, and athletic attractions), the beauty of the Atlantic Coast, and nearby slopes for skiing and snowboarding in the winter.

On campus, the initiative of the students and the efforts of the student life staff combine to provide activities for students year-round. These include a film series, concerts, student run clubs (such as Spes Vitae, the pro-life club), an intramural sports program, the Outdoors Club, the St. Joseph's Confraternity, the Sodality of Mary, a Knights of Columbus council, a New Evangelization Group, the Art Club and the Cooking Club. The basketball and soccer teams have hosted other collegiate teams in recent years.

The St. Genesius Players, the College's drama club, has performed works by Shakespeare, Tennessee Williams' The Glass Menagerie, Thornton Wilder's Our Town, Oscar Wilde's An Ideal Husband, as well as popular musicals.

Members of the college choir sing at daily Mass, and the full College Choir sings at each Sunday Mass and on Feast Days. Smaller ensembles, such as the Performance Choir, Polyphony Choir, and the chant schola, require an audition. The choirs of the College sing at St. Joseph's Cathedral in Manchester, in the procession for the Boston Eucharistic Conference, and at various other venues. Music also finds a prominent place around campus in more informal settings, such as the Academic Convoca-

From the Career Services Office

Beginning in the academic year 2012-2013, the College of Saint Mary Magdalen launched an internship program for their students that includes opportunities in wide variety of fields locally, in New England, and across the country. The College also actively encourages and assists students seeking admission to graduate school and professional programs. Please see the College's website for details.

tion, parents' weekend, and the annual Advent celebration (following the "Lessons and Carols" service.).

Pro-life activities are another important component of student life, with over half the student body participating in the annual March for Life in Washington, D.C. Many students also participate in local pro-life activities, attending marches and vigils in Concord, and supporting the national "40 Days for Life."

Annual traditions include the elegant and formal dance known as the Winter Ball, a men's and women's retreat weekend, the Fall Festival, and special meals hosted by each class.

The locale provides ample opportunities for outdoor and winter activities both on and off campus.

The Bottom Line

The College of Saint Mary Magdalen offers an education of the whole person—both in and beyond the classroom. With joy, theCollege proudly proclaims its fidelity to the Church, its commitment to intellectual excellence, and its determination to prepare Catholic leaders who will fearlessly renew the culture for Christ.

Students attending Magdalen find themselves in a small community that is intensely serious about the liberal arts and the Catholic faith, finding expression in the beautiful and reverent liturgies and music. Even so, the College has worked to ensure that campus policies balance expectations with students' need for independence.

Today Magdalen offers students an idyllic setting and the opportunity to freely participate in a small community seeking to know the Truth, love the Faith, and transform the world.

Letter from the President

Dear Parents and Prospective Students:

At the College of Saint Mary Magdalen, we believe that a faithful, Catholic, Great Books education is a danger—a danger to the forces of secularization and moral relativism that threaten to overtake our nation. We believe that the education we offer prepares our graduates to embody and communicate the divine gifts of truth, goodness, and beauty that will renew and transform our nation and the world.

But what makes the College of Saint Mary Magdalen unique?

We combine fidelity to the Magisterium with a rigorous Great Books curriculum (with concentrations in Theology, Philosophy, Literature, and Politics) that draws its strength and coherence from the Catholic intellectual tradition as it has developed over two millennia.

We cultivate a collegiate culture rooted in traditional Catholic piety and liturgical practice—featuring Gregorian chant and *ad orientem* celebration of the Mass in both the Ordinary and Extraordinary forms—through which our students can respond freely to Christ's call to radical discipleship.

Our students can spend a semester in Rome, the Eternal City, exploring its classical and sacred treasures. By successfully completing our required six semesters of theology that comprehensively treat the Deposit of Faith—as it is articulated in the *Catechism of the Catholic Church*—our students can earn an Apostolic Catechetical Diploma.

Our beautiful New England setting—with plentiful opportunities for hiking and skiing—and our proximity to Boston and other urban areas give students the chance to experience and enjoy the full range of natural and cultural riches of the region.

We not only liberally educate our students but also prepare them, through career planning and internships, for their postgraduate lives.

The complete education we offer at the College is not for the faint of heart: the journey to freedom—intellectual and spiritual freedom—is arduous. But no one at the College undertakes this journey alone. The students, the faculty, and the larger community of the College support one another within and outside the classroom, seeking to become fully human and fully free, thriving in the light of Truth.

We invite all who wish to know the Truth, love the Faith, and transform the world, to come and join us.

In the hearts of Jesus and Mary,

George A. Harne

George Harne

College of Saint Mary Magdalen
Frequently Asked Questions

We get questions from Catholic families on a regular basis about the colleges we recommend. Rather than filter the answers, we asked Magdalen officials nearly 100 questions in categories such as academics, curriculum, programs of study, campus ministry, residence life, student activities, the make up of the study body, and institutional identity. The answers to some of the most asked questions are provided below and the rest are available on the college profile page at TheNewmanGuide.com.

Majors

List the major, minor and special program areas that students may choose for specialization while pursuing an undergraduate degree:

All students follow a single Great Books curriculum for four years. In their junior and senior years, students may select a concentration in Theology, Philosophy, Literature, or Politics that supplements and extends the Great Books curriculum.

What are the three most popular majors or specialty disciplines for undergraduate students, and about what percentage of undergraduate students specialize in these disciplines?

Great books, 100%

Spiritual Life

Please list the schedule of Masses, noting the following for each Mass: the day and time, the Form or Rite of the Mass, and the style of music, if any (chant, traditional, contemporary, etc.):

Mo 11:15 a.m., Ordinary Form English, chant

Tu 11:15 a.m., Ordinary Form English, chant

We 11:15 a.m., Ordinary Form English, chant

Th 11:15 a.m., Ordinary Form English, chant

Fr 11:15 a.m., Ordinary Form Latin, chant

Sa 9:00 a.m., Ordinary Form English, chant

Su 10:00 a.m., Ordinary Form English, chant

Mass is always celebrated ad orientem. Communion is received kneeling and on the tongue.

Once per week, depending on the Feast day, our chaplain celebrates Mass in the Extraordinary Form.

List the schedule for Confession by day and time:

Mo 10:45 a.m.

Tu 10:45 a.m.

We 10:45 a.m.

Th 10:45 a.m.

Fr 10:45 a.m.

Sa 8:45 a.m.

Su

Other: Confession and spiritual direction are also available by appointment

List the schedule for Adoration of the Blessed Sacrament by day and time:

Adoration is available and encouraged throughout the year. Days and times vary each semester.

Please identify regularly scheduled devotions on campus for students such as the Rosary and prayer groups:

The Rosary and the Divine Office are prayed in the College chapel daily. Compline is prayed in the residence chapels daily. The Angelus is prayed following Mass each day and at 6:00 p.m. each evening. Novenas are prayed throughout the year. The College chaplain also leads processions on campus on special feast days and provides the opportunity for the veneration of relics. Each class begins and ends with prayer. The Stations of the Cross and Advent prayers are also part of community life.

Residence Life

Please describe options for students to reside on and off campus:

Students normally reside on campus in one of the single-sex residences.

Does your institution offer only single-sex residence halls?

Yes.

Are students of the opposite sex permitted to visit students' bedrooms?

No.

How does your institution foster sobriety and respond to substance abuse on campus, particularly in campus residences?

We have a "dry campus." At the College, sobriety is the cultural norm that is expected and maintained on campus. If such a problem does arise, the situation is immediately addressed.

How does your institution foster a student living environment that promotes and supports chastity, particularly in campus residences?

For the 2013-2014 academic year, the College of Saint Mary Magdalen will invite various speakers to campus to give chastity talksto both male and female students.

Student Body

Describe the makeup of your institution's undergraduate student body with regard to sex, religion, home state/country and type of high school (public, private, homeschool):

Total number of undergraduates: 61
Male: 44% Female: 56%

Catholic: 98% Other Christian: 2%
Jewish: % Muslim: % Other: %

Number of states represented: 20
Top three states: NH, AZ, TX
Students from top three states: 21%

Catholic HS: 34% Homeschool: 48%
Private HS: 8% Public HS: 10%

The College of Saints John Fisher and Thomas More

Fort Worth, Texas

411

For more information on Fisher More, visit their website at:

www.fishermore.edu

Admissions contact:

817/923-8459 ext. 1
Peter.Capani@fishermore.edu

Overview

The College of Saints John Fisher and Thomas More—which also goes by the nickname Fisher More College—has recently undergone a significant transformation, including an emphasis on traditional Catholicism and the Extraordinary Form of the Mass, as well as accredited online courses that can be applied toward an undergraduate degree.

The small College, founded in 1981, had 40 students in 2013-2014, all of them Catholic. Now President Michael King is trying to enlarge the College, beginning with a new campus and a long-term goal of 250 students.

The recent addition of St. John Fisher as a patron signals a greater emphasis on spirituality, including the development of a residential campus where students are encouraged to immerse themselves in the Extraordinary Form of the Mass and traditional prayer.

The orientation is unique among Catholic colleges, and it has led to some disagreements about tradition and contemporary Catholicism; a professor's criticisms of the Second Vatican Council

last academic year provoked internal debate, and concerns prompted the chancellor and a professor to resign.

But Dr. King says the College does not question the validity of the Ordinary Form Mass and eagerly submits "with mind and will to the infallible teachings of the Church and Her ordinary and universal Magisterium."

The curriculum still includes the classical liberal arts and the Great Books, but with much greater emphasis on philosophy and theology. The core requirements account for three-quarters of the credits required for graduation, including eight courses in theology and seven in philos-

ophy. Students take a series of seminars on the interior life to support their spiritual development.

Also, whereas the College formerly awarded only degrees in liberal arts, now the College also offers concentrations and degree programs in classical studies, history, literature, philosophy, and theology. Fisher More is also seeking accreditation to award a degree in finance and economics.

The College is governed by an entirely lay board of trustees. President King was formerly at Benedictine College (Kansas) for 10 years as professor of finance and chairman of the business school, following several years as an entrepreneur, investment banker, and employee for the U.S. Senate Commerce Committee.

Tuition is far below average private college tuition in Texas—and after scholarships, the average student pays even less. The College deliberately does not participate in the federal loan program, but it also is committed to helping students avoid private debt by providing generous scholarships and a work-study program.

Academics

All students study for a bachelor of arts

Quick Facts

2013-2014 Academic Year

Students 40

SATs SATs are not required

HS GPA Does not track

Majors 6

% Catholic 100%

How Much? $10,000
tuition, room and board

in the liberal arts, but beyond the core required courses, students can opt for a general liberal arts degree (requiring eight additional courses approved by the dean) or a concentration. The requirements vary from five additional courses for theology, philosophy and literature, and six courses for history and classical studies.

The substantial core curriculum has a Catholic emphasis throughout, with eight foundational theology courses. The last required theology course is Catholic Social Teaching, which begins with the French Revolution and the papal teachings of that time, not the 1960s.

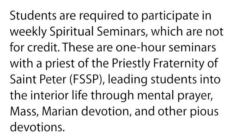

Theology electives include Mariology and Theology of the Roman Rite. This latter course studies the theology of traditional Roman liturgical prayers and structures—not only the Extraordinary Form Mass, but also the Breviary and papal liturgies.

Although Fisher More's theology is faithfully Catholic, theology professors do not currently have the mandatum to teach. The College hopes that all theology professors will have the mandatum soon after a new bishop is installed in the Fort Worth diocese. The president of the College and all faculty take the Profession of Faith and Oath of Fidelity, as well as the Oath Against Modernism issued by Pope St. Pius X in 1910.

The seven required philosophy courses emphasize Thomistic philosophy. Fisher More does not begin theology courses until the sophomore year, following the traditional scholastic order of philosophy before theology. The sequence in the core curriculum is based on the tradition that theology presumes philosophy.

Whereas the College previously required four years of both Greek and Latin, Greek is no longer required but offered. Students have two semesters of Latin requirements, but those who do not pass the Latin placement exam may be required to take an additional two semesters of introductory and intermediate Latin.

Other core courses include six in literature, four in history, and one each in art, math, music, natural science, and rhetoric. Some courses are scheduled with an interdisciplinary approach; for instance, Ancient Greek and Roman History is taken at the same time as the literature course Epic 1, featuring Homer and Virgil. The Art and Civilization course looks not simply at paintings, but also architecture, churches, cities, and music. The course emphasizes the roots of art in all of the humanities, including theology, and in Western culture and Catholic Christendom.

Students are required to participate in weekly Spiritual Seminars, which are not for credit. These are one-hour seminars with a priest of the Priestly Fraternity of Saint Peter (FSSP), leading students into the interior life through mental prayer, Mass, Marian devotion, and other pious devotions.

Socratic dialogue is an important part of classes and seminars. The core curriculum begins for freshmen with Logic and Rhetoric, which prepares students for engaging in Socratic dialogue responsibly. In addition to the College, Fisher More operates its own classical high school on campus. It is considering opening an elementary school in the near future.

The College has a relatively strict dress code. For classes and in the chapel, men wear long pants (no jeans) and collared shirts with ties; women wear dresses or blouses with skirts, but no pants or shorts. Suits and dresses are worn at occasional formal college events. Leisure wear includes shirts with sleeves, and no shorts for the women.

College courses in the new Fisher More

Financial Aid Office Info

Fisher More College is committed to providing an affordable opportunity to students and their families. We endeavor to find a workable financial package for every student who gains admission to the College.

The College does not participate in the Title IV program of the federal government, does not participate in any student loan programs, and strongly discourages students from taking out private loans in order to cover the cost of attendance.

Instead, we offer students financial aid opportunities through scholarships and work-study programs. Scholarships, often substantial, are available based on both need and academic promise. We do, however, expect families to make a serious effort, and we try to devise a financial package adjusted to the needs of each individual student.

Online program are accredited and can be transferred to another institution or applied to a Fisher More degree. Students usually meet with their instructor and classmates for two live, interactive sessions each week. Students must have access to computers with Internet, voice and video capability. The 2013-14 courses cover subjects in literature, philosophy, history, math, science, Latin and music.

Spiritual Life

Fisher More says that campus life is "centered around the Sacred Liturgy," and the liturgy is very traditional.

"The College's first goal is to foster true devotion and piety in our students through the liturgy and tradition of the Catholic Church," explains the College. "All graces, even intellectual graces, flow to us from Christ our Lord and thus through the Holy Sacrifice of the Mass. Hence, Fisher More is a place of spiritual formation and scholastic excellence."

There is one Mass each day, including Sunday, and they are always celebrated

in the Extraordinary Form. Nearly all the resident students attend Sunday Mass on campus, and nearly all attend daily Mass.

Confession is available 20 minutes before and after each Mass, except for the full hour allowed on Mondays. Students gather for communal prayer including daily morning prayer (Sext) chanted in Latin, a daily Rosary, the Angelus at noon, and the Chaplet of Divine Mercy and Eucharistic Adoration each Friday.

The College has one full-time chaplain, Fr. Joseph Orlowski, FSSP. Masses are celebrated daily in a chapel located inside the College building that was built in 1907. After restoring the chapel to its original beauty—it hasn't been used as a chapel for 25 years—the capacity should be about 250 people, with a choir loft and confessional.

Residential Life

Beginning with the 2013-2014 academic year, Fisher More is located in a new campus at the very large former Our Lady of Victory building in Fort Worth.

The five-story, 76,000 square-foot building was built in 1909 and served as the provincial house for the Sisters of St. Mary of Namur. The College plans to house 60 students immediately and up to 120 students within two years. Students will live in the top two floors, with men and women separated by east and west wings.

The building includes a chapel, classrooms, offices, a library, a refectory, and high school facilities. Initially the campus will occupy three acres, but the College hopes to acquire additional acres and build new facilities in the future.

Students who do not live locally with their parents are expected to live on campus. Visitation by students of the opposite sex is never allowed in the residences. Currently a coed student lounge is available from 9 a.m. until midnight for socialization.

The College does not allow alcohol on campus.

Fisher More is located in a residential neighborhood of southeast Fort Worth

near Texas Christian University and near a few other small colleges. The city of 658,000 people has more than doubled its population since 1950, with a crime rate significantly above the national average but relatively low among large U.S. cities.

The Dallas/Fort Worth International Airport is between the two cities, about 15 miles east. The Baylor All Saints Medical Center is two miles from campus.

Student Activities

The College has not in the past devoted substantial attention to student life outside the classroom, but that is changing. Fisher More has hired a Director of Student Life who organizes campouts, weekend outings, events, and spiritual activities such as Eucharistic Adoration.

Students, faculty, and staff gather together for a communal lunch each weekday. It often includes a spiritual reading.

There are no formal clubs, but some students work with the Franciscan Friars of the Renewal to help the poor and there are plans to begin a Legion of Mary apostolate for students. In addition, students help with teaching and organizing catechism classes, children's choir, and training for altar servers.

The College sponsors occasional lectures and events, such as the 2012-2013 Year of Faith Lecture Series. It featured such speakers as Christopher Check of Catholic Answers, speaking on the Battle of Lepanto, and Dominican Father Thomas Joseph White on Marian theology. Actor and director Chuck Chalberg presented his biographical play on G.K. Chesterton.

The Fisher & More College Institute of Apologetics offers lectures to help

From the Career Services Office

The College's size allows it to offer individualized guidance regarding opportunities available to graduates as well as those seeking summer intern positions. Additionally, a major goal of the College is to have graduates leave with as little debt as possible, so that they can have a much wider range of options upon graduation. Too often, large amounts of debt translate into having to make career decisions based solely on compensation.

The individualized guidance from our faculty and staff, combined with the freedom to choose from a wide range of options allows our graduates, the freedom to pursue a wide range of options based on non-economic considerations. Our approach allows graduates to consider donating a year to Catholic-affiliated groups, travel, the exploration of various career interests that might not be high-paying initially and continuing on with higher-degree programs.

Catholics to defend the Faith and expose error in other religions and world views. All lectures are presented by theology professor Karl Strauch.

Fort Worth boasts a number of cultural attractions, including theater, music, sports, a zoo, and a science center. The Kimball Art Museum is regarded as having one of the best collections in the world, including examples of modern architecture, and the Amon Carter Museum is noted for its displays of American art. There are many employment opportunities, including the headquarters of Lockheed Martin, American Airlines and Radio Shack. The city is home to several other colleges including Texas Christian University and Texas Wesleyan University. Dallas is 30 minutes east and offers a number of additional activities and opportunities.

Bottom Line

The College of Saints John Fisher and Thomas More is on the move with a revised curriculum, new campus, and plans for substantial growth. The College trusts in Divine Providence in all things, but it hopes to possess all the ingredients of success.

Fisher More's attraction is clearly its strong curriculum with heavy emphasis on philosophy and theology. But Catholic families will also find a highly traditional liturgical and prayer life that is uncommon even among *Newman Guide* colleges. The academics and spiritual life combine to provide a thoroughly Catholic experience that aspires to the higher things.

Letter from the President

Dear Parents and Prospective Students:

The faculty and staff of Fisher More College feel obligated to an apostolate toward one another as well as toward our students in order to form them in the love and imitation of Our Savior. We use the word "apostolate" here knowingly, as it captures our resolve to remain faithful to the intellectual, moral, spiritual, and liturgical traditions of the Roman Catholic Church.

The liturgical life is the source of the apostolate, allowing all members of our community to enter into an active participation in the Holy Mysteries and to pursue a fruitful interior life. This liturgical life, which Pope St. Pius X called the "prime and indispensable source of the true Christian spirit," orders all activities of the College toward achieving our mission of "guiding the souls committed to our care toward the purpose for which God created them: to know, to love, and to serve Him."

The College understands its role is to assist the Church and families in the continued formation of young men and women, a complete formation of intellect and will, of body and soul. We invite you to become part of a vibrant, joyful Catholic culture, one that enables students to develop the virtues necessary for their state in life, to grow in service and charity toward God and neighbor, to answer Christ's call to be the salt of the earth and the light of the world.

Ad Jesum per Mariam,

Michael King

Fisher More College
Frequently Asked Questions

We get questions from Catholic families on a regular basis about the colleges we recommend. Rather than filter the answers, we asked Fisher More officials nearly 100 questions in categories such as academics, curriculum, programs of study, campus ministry, residence life, student activities, the make up of the study body, and institutional identity. The answers to some of the most asked questions are provided below and the rest are available on the college profile page at TheNewmanGuide.com.

Majors

List the major, minor and special program areas that students may choose for specialization while pursuing an undergraduate degree:

Theology, Philosophy, Literature, History, Classical Studies, Liberal Arts, and Finance/Economics (in process of seeking accreditation approval).

What are the three most popular majors or specialty disciplines for undergraduate students, and about what percentage of undergraduate students specialize in these disciplines?

Editor's note: Not answered.

Spiritual Life

Please list the schedule of Masses, noting the following for each Mass: the day and time, the Form or Rite of the Mass, and the style of music, if any (chant, traditional, contemporary, etc.):

Mo 7:30 a.m., Latin Extraordinary Form

Tu 7:30 a.m., Latin Extraordinary Form

We 7:30 a.m., Latin Extraordinary Form

Th 7:30 a.m., Latin Extraordinary Form

Fr 7:30 a.m., Latin Extraordinary Form

Sa 9:00 a.m., Latin Extraordinary Form

Su 10:00 a.m., Latin Extraordinary Form

List the schedule for Confession by day and time:

Mo 60 minutes before and after every Mass

Tu 20 minutes before and after every Mass

We 20 minutes before and after every Mass

Th 20 minutes before and after every Mass

Fr 20 minutes before and after every Mass

Sa 20 minutes before and after every Mass

Su 20 minutes before and after every Mass

List the schedule for Adoration of the Blessed Sacrament by day and time:

Friday 1:00-3:00 p.m.

Please identify regularly scheduled devotions on campus for students such as the Rosary and prayer groups:

Sext (chant in Latin) daily at 11:45 a.m., Angelus daily at noon followed by the Rosary, Chaplet of Divine Mercy at 3:00 p.m. on Friday.

Residence Life

Please describe options for students to reside on and off campus:

Students live on campus unless they live locally or with parents.

Does your institution offer only single-sex residence halls?

Yes. We have moved into a single campus facility where the students live on two floors (4th and 5th) in different "wings" (girls on east and boys on west) of the building. The wings that are divided and not passable except if the security/fire doors open. If these doors would ever open without the fire alarms going off, they will trigger a security alarm. We have adult staff live in each wing.

Are students of the opposite sex permitted to visit students' bedrooms?

No.

How does your institution foster sobriety and respond to substance abuse on campus, particularly in campus residences?

Alcohol is banned entirely on campus except during specific college-sponsored events when faculty and staff are present.

How does your institution foster a student living environment that promotes and supports chastity, particularly in campus residences?

There is no visitation. Also, the College enforces a "three-person rule" which requires that two students of the opposite sex cannot be alone on campus without a third person present.

Student Body

Describe the makeup of your institution's undergraduate student body with regard to sex, religion, home state/country and type of high school (public, private, homeschool):

Total number of undergraduates: 40
Male: 50% Female: 50%

Catholic: 100% Other Christian: %
Jewish: % Muslim: % Other: %

Number of states represented: 10
Top three states: Not reported.
Students from top three states: 70%

Catholic HS: % Homeschool: 80%
Private HS: % Public HS: %
Other not reported: 20%

DESALES UNIVERSITY

Center Valley, Pennsylvania

Overview

In 1964 at the request of the Bishop of Allentown, Pennsylvania, the Oblates of St. Francis de Sales founded Allentown College. The nation's only Oblate college took on the name DeSales University in 2001 to more succinctly affirm its patron and its Catholic identity, as well as its expanding graduate programs.

Since then, DeSales has continued to strengthen its Catholic identity, looking to *Ex corde Ecclesiae* for its guiding principles. The University's statement of philosophy says it plainly, "DeSales University is firmly and publicly committed to the principles of Roman Catholic doctrine and morality."

That commitment is notable at a regional university like DeSales, which does not have the uniformly Catholic student body found at some smaller Catholic colleges. DeSales serves about 1,600 undergraduates and 1,000 graduate students, most of them from Pennsylvania, Delaware, and New Jersey. The University does not track the percentage of Catholic students, but only about a third attended Catholic high schools, while 60 percent attended public schools.

The sprawling campus is located on 480 acres near the city of Allentown, Pennsylvania's fastest-growing city and its third-largest after Philadelphia and Pittsburgh.

DeSales offers a wide variety of 36 majors, ranging from the traditional liberal arts to forensics, pharmaceutical marketing, and physician assistant programs. The most popular majors are nursing, medical studies, and theatre.

Undergraduates choose up to 16 courses in the general education program, which includes courses in communications, Western civilization, theology, and other liberal arts subjects.

The Oblate religious have a strong presence at DeSales in leadership and faculty positions. The Salesian Center for Faith and Culture promotes the congregation's spirituality through research, dialogue, and community partnerships that involve both faculty and students. Student opportunities include an honors program, leadership training, writing awards, and participation in Center lectures and events.

The 34 members of the board of trustees include Father Bernard O'Connor, O.S.F.S., president since 1999, and 11 other Oblate priests. In Father O'Connor's 35 years at DeSales, he has served as chairman of the theology and philosophy departments, academic dean, and vice president for academic affairs. He still teaches at least one philosophy course every year, saying he wants to "have his finger on the pulse" of what students are thinking.

DeSales' tuition, room and board, and student fees total $41,420 in 2013-14, well below the state average for private colleges. About 90 percent of the students receive financial aid, including scholarships and federal aid.

Academics

The undergraduate programs at DeSales combine a liberal arts program

Quick Facts

Students 1,597

SATs 1090

HS GPA 3.25

2013-2014 Academic Year

Majors 36

% Catholic Unknown

How Much? $41,420
tuition, room and board

with career-focused specialization. The University is large enough to support more than 30 different majors, honors programs, study abroad opportunities, professional internships, and advanced study programs.

The required 16 courses that satisfy the University's general education requirements span the usual liberal arts disciplines, allowing students discretion in choosing among a range of options. But the program aims for much more than a random buffet of subject matter. Some of the courses are interdisciplinary, and all follow a sequence designed to help students develop intellectually

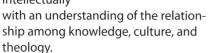

with an understanding of the relationship among knowledge, culture, and theology.

Other courses include two that develop written and oral communications skills, and three courses or activities in physical health—both uncommon requirements that reflect the Oblates' interest in graduating students who are prepared for careers and for life outside the classroom.

The "cultural literacy" sequence of six courses, taught by either history or political science professors, teaches students about human culture with an emphasis on Western civilization. The unique "modes of thinking" courses help students understand the similarities and differences of learning in literature, mathematics, natural science, philosophy, and social science.

All students are required to take the introductory Catholic theology course, one intermediate theology course, and a Values Seminar. The seminar applies theology and ethics to the student's chosen major field of study. Although philosophy and theology are combined in a single department, the theology courses are identifiable and faithfully Catholic, and theology professors must have the

mandatum to teach. The department offers a unique interdisciplinary major in marriage and family studies, which draws from the works of Blessed Pope John Paul II.

Many DeSales students choose "marketable majors," and these include a highly regarded undergraduate degree in medicine and a five year master of science in physician assistant studies. Graduates of the physician assistant program have achieved a near-perfect passing rate on the National Certifying Examination—10 percent higher than the national average—and the 200-plus graduates have been employed in this growing field.

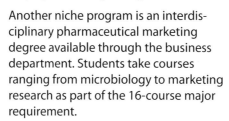

Another niche program is an interdisciplinary pharmaceutical marketing degree available through the business department. Students take courses ranging from microbiology to marketing research as part of the 16-course major requirement.

DeSales has one of the most extensive drama and performing arts programs at any Catholic college. More than 20 percent of undergraduates major in theatre, film, or dance.

The sports management major in the business department prepares students to hold positions in schools and nonprofits. This is one of only 20 such undergraduate programs endorsed by the Sport Management Program Review Council.

The University recently signed exchange agreements with schools in Ireland, Spain, and Greece, and students regularly study in Rome. DeSales is one of only two schools in the world that offers internships at the Pontifical Council for Peace and Justice and the Pontifical Council for Social Communication.

In an effort to integrate Catholic teaching with all areas of life, the University

seeks ways to link academic efforts with student affairs programs. DeSales freshmen participate in Character U, which orients them to several of the

Masses attract a few dozen participants.

There are eight Masses per week at the Connelly Chapel and the Oblates' Wills Hall Chapel: a daily Mass, plus a primarily faculty and staff Mass on Wednesdays, and morning and evening Masses on Sunday.

Confessions are scheduled once a week and by appointment. There are also Eucharistic Adoration on Friday afternoons, scheduled Rosary times, and some retreats.

Residential Life

Seventy percent of undergraduates live on campus, and they are housed in eight residence halls and a townhouse complex. Two of these are female only, one is reserved for men, and the others are co-ed. Aviat Hall has a chapel.

Co-ed residence halls are segregated by gender in separate wings. Guests of the opposite sex are permitted to visit on-campus residences, including the townhouse complex, only during certain hours.

Students of legal age may have alcohol, but in moderation and under campus guidelines. Specialized "substance-free" housing is offered for students who prefer to live with others who forego all alcohol and tobacco use. Smoking is prohibited in all University buildings including residences.

The Lehigh Valley is a vibrant metropolitan area. Nearby Bethlehem has a quaint downtown area that includes art shops, bookshops, and numerous restaurants. With a population of about 106,000, the

"golden counsels" of St. Francis de Sales. Completion is noted on the student's transcript, and some prizes are awarded. An important part of the program is peer mentoring.

Also, each year up to 15 high achieving first-year students are invited to join the Faith and Reason Honors Program that is administered by the Salesian Center. The four-year program includes seminars, cultural events, and a senior thesis. Select students can study executive leadership in the context of Salesian spirituality in the Center's Leadership Institute. The Center also invites students to participate in regular group discussions and lectures, as well as several activities tied to the University's theatre and arts programs, including an acting troupe that focuses on the works of Blessed Pope John Paul II.

Spiritual Life

Campus ministry at DeSales is solidly Catholic, led by a lay minister but supported by about 10 Oblates and a deacon from the Allentown Diocese. They staff campus liturgies as well as student retreats and counseling. The campus ministry sponsors several student groups including a pro-life club, Knights of Columbus, and men's and women's groups for faith development.

One unique initiative is a pen-pal program through which students exchange faith-sharing letters with peers at other colleges, modeling St. Francis de Sales who was famous for his written correspondence with many individuals.

Numerous social service projects are co-sponsored by campus ministry and the Center for Service and Social Justice. Alternative spring break trips are among the outreach activities.

Students will find an active Catholic community, albeit a minority of the student body. Father O'Connor says that both Sunday masses on campus are "just packed with students," but daily

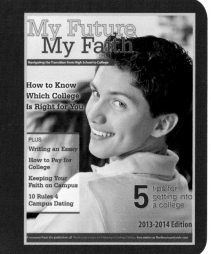

neighboring city of Allentown offers a number of economic, shopping, and cultural opportunities. Among these are the Allentown Art Museum, which contains the works of a number of masters, and the internationally known Bach Choir of Bethlehem.

With a strong industrial heritage associated with Mack Trucks and Bethlehem Steel, the area now has a more diversified economy and a more diverse population, straying far from its one-time Pennsylvania German influence. Crime is at or above the national average in various categories, with a notable problem with drugs and gangs, but the DeSales campus is located in a quiet suburban area and is relatively safe. The University has a student escort program, and campus crime violations seem to be for non-violent offenses.

DeSales is located about one hour north of Philadelphia and 90 minutes from New York. The Lehigh Valley International Airport has eight regional commuter carriers, and major airports are located at Philadelphia and Newark.

Student Activities

DeSales has 36 approved clubs and societies, ranging from the C. S. Lewis book club and The Minstrel campus newspaper to athletic and cultural clubs.

The Pro-Life Club has about 50 members, and many of them travel by bus to the March for Life in Washington, D.C., every year.

There are many clubs and opportunities for volunteer efforts, including the two-day Urban Plunge to serve homeless people in Washington, D.C., Habitat for Humanity, Best Buddies, and tutoring. The Office of Social Outreach encourages volunteer work in the Lehigh Valley. The University also has sponsored a Catholic Volunteer Service Fair for students interested in post-graduate community service.

Among other extracurricular opportunities are intramural and club teams in a variety of sports. For the more competitive athletes, the DeSales Bulldogs compete in eight women's and eight men's sports at the NCAA Division III (non-scholarship) level. These include basketball, baseball, cross country, field

Letter from the President

Dear Parents and Prospective Students:

In the 1600s, St. Francis de Sales tried to debate John Calvin in Geneva so that ordinary citizens could decide between Roman Catholicism or Calvinism. St. Francis de Sales believed that ordinary people were loved by God, as much as monks and clergy. He felt that the common people were called to holiness, and that faith and reason worked together to guide people on their journey.

John Calvin refused to meet De Sales. In fact, De Sales was outlawed from the city and never was able to assume his rightful seat as Bishop of Geneva.

When another duke arrived with an army to forcefully take the city for Francis, he said, "We will take Geneva only by prayer and persuasion." Today, the largest religious denomination in Geneva is Roman Catholic.

DeSales University shares this enthusiasm of the great saint. We like to debate and argue about the great issues of the day, knowing that faith and reason are our guides. Like Francis de Sales, we seek to develop the virtues of gentleness and strength. We like to proclaim the message of the Lord in a loving way and patiently wait for the wonderful activity of God's grace in the world. Come join us.

Yours in Christ,

Fr. Bernie O'Connor, OSFS

hockey, golf, lacrosse, soccer, softball, track and field, and volleyball.

To encourage and to acknowledge student involvement in extracurricular activity, the University issues a co-curricular transcript that identifies involvement in several areas, including campus ministry.

The Bottom Line

Sometimes a name change is just clever marketing, but not so for DeSales University. Since 2001, Salesian spirituality has admirably been at the heart of DeSales University—in its campus ministry, its curriculum, its campus life, even its leadership programs.

DeSales does not serve only faithful Catholics, and its regional reputation and wide variety of majors attracts students for secular reasons. But the University's leadership has ensured a clear Catholic identity that determines its policies and curriculum.

The solid general education program and authentic theology, combined with specialized programs that may not be available at other Catholic liberal arts colleges, will be attractive to many Catholic families seeking a faithful Catholic education.

DeSales University
Frequently Asked Questions

We get questions from Catholic families on a regular basis about the colleges we recommend. Rather than filter the answers, we asked DeSales officials nearly 100 questions in categories such as academics, curriculum, programs of study, campus ministry, residence life, student activities, the make up of the study body, and institutional identity. The answers to some of the most asked questions are provided below and the rest are available on the DeSales profile page at TheNewmanGuide.com.

Majors

List the major, minor and special program areas that students may choose for specialization while pursuing an undergraduate degree:

Majors: Accounting; Accounting – 5-year Master's Degree Program; Biochemistry-Molecular Biology; Biology; Business Administration; Chemistry; Communication; Computer Science; Criminal Justice; Criminal Justice – 5-year Master's Degree Program; Dance; Education: Early Childhood and Elementary Education; English; Finance; History; International Business; Law and Society; Liberal Studies; Management; Marketing; Marriage and Family Studies; Mathematics; Media Studies; Medical Studies (Physician Assistant Program); Nursing; Nursing RN-to-BSN; Pharmaceutical Marketing; Philosophy; Political Science; Psychology; Spanish; Sport and Exercise Science; Sport Management; Theatre; Theology; TV/Film; Undeclared.

Minors: American Studies; Biology; Business; Chemistry; Computer Science; Creative Writing; Criminal Justice; Design/Tech Theatre; Dramatic Literature; English; Forensic Science and Criminalistics; French Studies*; History; Journalism; Law and Society; Management; Marketing; Marriage and Family; Mathematics; Music; Neuroscience; Philosophy; Political Science; Professional Communication; Psychology; Special Education; Sport Management; Theology.

Pre-Professional: Dentistry; High School Teaching; Law; Medicine; Optometry; Pharmacology; Podiatry; Veterinary.

What are the three most popular majors or specialty disciplines for undergraduate students, and about what percentage of undergraduate students specialize in these disciplines?

Nursing, 8.85%

Theatre, 8.66%

Medical Studies, 8.47%

Spiritual Life

Please list the schedule of Masses, noting the following for each Mass: the day and time, the Form or Rite of the Mass, and the style of music, if any (chant, traditional, contemporary, etc.):

Mo 5:00 p.m. (and 12:05 p.m. during Lent)

Tu 5:00 p.m.

We 12:05 p.m. and 5:00 p.m.

Th 5:00 p.m.

Fr 5:00 p.m.

Su 12:30 p.m. and 8:00 p.m.

The Rite of Mass is the Revised Roman Missal, Roman Rite [*Ed. Note*: Ordinary Form]. Music is a mixture of chant and traditional. No Praise and Worship variety of music is used.

List the schedule for Confession by day and time:

Mo

Tu 7:00 p.m

We

Th

Fr

Sa

Su

Other: ANYTIME that is convenient for priest and penitent

List the schedule for Adoration of the Blessed Sacrament by day and time:

Fridays from 9:00 a.m. until 4:00 p.m.

Please identify regularly scheduled devotions on campus for students such as the Rosary and prayer groups:

Stations of the Cross during Lent, Rosary is said weekly.

Devotions depend on student interest and Campus Ministry seeks to accommodate every request.

Residence Life

Please describe options for students to reside on and off campus:

Most DeSales University students live on campus in one of

nine residential communities. Most resident halls have suite-style rooms—two bedrooms that each have two students and a shared bathroom. There are also townhouse style buildings for 8 students who have demonstrated themselves to be both academically and behaviorally successful during their time at DeSales and are traditionally reserved for juniors and seniors.

Community living at DeSales is deeply rooted in the Salesian tradition of the institution and the principles of Christian Humanism. It is also an essential part of the development and education of the whole person. Community members each bring their individual gifts and talents, serve as active and engaged citizens, and promote respect for their peers. Living on campus at DeSales provides the opportunity for students to learn self-awareness, self-advocacy, accountability, communication, trust, cooperation, perseverance, love, patience, hope, and forgiveness.

University policies and residence hall regulations are designed to ensure a high quality of daily life and to prevent behavior that is an infringement on the rights of others, detrimental to personal growth and the common good, or in basic discord with the mission of the University. Because communal living requires self-sacrifice, open-mindedness, maturity, and commitment, it is a truly rewarding experience that often builds students of great integrity and character who are prepared to be engaged citizens on campus and beyond.

By choosing to reside at DeSales University, students actively live the teachings of St. Francis DeSales:

"Let us be who we are and be that well." "Be patient with everyone, but above all with yourself." "Bearing with the imperfections of our neighbor is one of the chief characteristics of our love for him." "Do all by love and nothing by force." "Consider what God is doing and what you are doing." "Don't lose heart, be patient, wait, do all you can to develop a spirit of compassion."

Does your institution offer only single-sex residence halls?

No. Sixty percent of students live in single-sex residence halls.

Are students of the opposite sex permitted to visit students' bedrooms?

Yes. Freshmen residence halls/floors: Sunday through Thursday 10:00 a.m. to 12:00 a.m.; Friday and Saturday 10:00 a.m. to 2:00 a.m.

Upper class residence halls/floors, including the University Heights: Sunday through Thursday 9:00 a.m. to 1:00 a.m.; Friday and Saturday 9:00 a.m. to 3:00 a.m.

How does your institution foster sobriety and respond to substance abuse on campus, particularly in campus residences?

DeSales University does not encourage the use of alcoholic beverages and is concerned about alcohol abuse. It recognizes, however, that individuals of legal age must be given the individual freedom to choose to drink. The University expects that individuals will make responsible decisions about the use of alcoholic beverages.

Responsibility for obeying laws and University regulations concerning alcohol and drugs rests directly with each individual. Any student, faculty, or staff member found in violation of federal, state and/or local law, or who violates the University's alcohol and drug policies, is subject to University disciplinary procedures, as well as criminal arrest and prosecution. Possible disciplinary sanctions include, but are not limited to, residential suspension, expulsion, participation in an alcohol or drug rehabilitation program, and dismissal. Sanctions may also apply to registered student organizations and to off-campus conduct involving activities sponsored or authorized by the University.

In addition to the policy (stated above) the University has many events and programs to promote alcohol awareness as well as the consequences of irresponsible behavior involving alcohol. Before students arrive on campus as freshmen, each student must complete a 1-hour, online alcohol awareness program. At freshman orientation, students hear presentations that discuss destructive decisions, including those involving alcohol. Programs sponsored through the University's Wellness Center raise awareness throughout a student's enrollment. A student presentation, entitled "It's Not an Accident, It's a Choice" described the effects of impaired driving. And if alcohol violations do occur, mandatory counseling is required.

How does your institution foster a student living environment that promotes and supports chastity, particularly in campus residences?

The Campus Ministry Office sponsors and presents a program entitled: "Off the Hook: The Hook-Up Culture and Our Escape from It." This program has been presented to another Catholic college. A follow-up program, also sponsored and presented by Campus Ministry is entitled: "Single and Ready to Mingle: Campus Dating 101." This program is a guide for students to learning about proper dating.

Student Body

Describe the makeup of your institution's undergraduate student body with regard to sex, religion, home state/country and type of high school (public, private, homeschool):

Total number of undergraduates: 1,580
Male: 45% Female: 55%

Catholic: N/A% Other Christian: N/A%
Jewish: N/A% Muslim: N/A% Other: N/A%

Number of states represented: 24
Top three states: Pennsylvania, New Jersey, and Delaware
Students from top three states: 85%

Catholic HS: 33% Homeschool: 2%
Private HS: 5% Public HS: 60%

FRANCISCAN UNIVERSITY OF STEUBENVILLE

Steubenville, Ohio

Overview

Franciscan University was founded in 1946 at the urging of the Diocese of Steubenville, Ohio, which turned to the Third Order Regular of St. Francis of Penance to teach returning war veterans. The University's ownership and the responsibility for its Catholic identity rest with the Franciscan community based in Loretto, Pennsylvania.

The University is located 40 miles west of Pittsburgh, Pennsylvania, on a hill overlooking Steubenville, a small, industrial city with a population of about 19,000. For many Catholics, the term "Steubenville" has come to represent the University, rather than the city. The 2,500 students are 98 percent Catholic, hailing from 50 states and 14 countries.

Franciscan University provides an abundance of opportunities for both academic and spiritual growth, and the role of the friars is at the core of both. Eighteen Franciscan friars and two other priests serve students through counseling, teaching, chaplaincy, or providing Sacramental needs. "Our greatest strength is our Catholic and Franciscan commitment," said current president,

Father Terence Henry, T.O.R. "That keeps us centered and gives us a moral compass in the sea of moral relativity that is higher education in general. Our dominant charism is one of joy."

Father Henry outlines four elements that make Franciscan distinctive. "The academic quality of our school, the quality of our professors and the personal interest they show in our students, our unique Catholic culture, and that sense of evangelism."

A largely lay board of 24 trustees reports to the Order. Traditionally, the minister provincial of the province is chairman of the board. Seven other members of the board are also Franciscans.

The University offers majors in mostly typical liberal arts fields, as well as three religious-oriented majors in humanities and the Catholic culture, catechetics, and theology. It boasts the largest number of students majoring in theology and catechetics of any Catholic university in the United States, and so too the largest number of students majoring in philosophy.

Franciscan's tuition rate is lower than the average for private institutions in Ohio. The undergraduate cost for tuition, room, board, and fees in 2013-14 is $30,420.

Academics

Under the rubrics of the new core curriculum adopted by Franciscan University in 2012, undergraduates at Franciscan complete an integrated liberal arts core curriculum of 45 credits for B.A. majors and 42 credits for B.S. students, based on the Western intellectual tradition and the Franciscan character of education and in accord with the Catholic mission of Franciscan University. The core includes 18 hours of philosophy and theology courses for B.A. students, and 15 hours of philosophy and theology

Quick Facts

Students 2,090

ACTs 25.2

HS GPA 3.81

2013-2014 Academic Year

Majors 41

% Catholic 97%

How Much? $30,420
tuition, room and board

courses for B.S. students. In addition to the core requirements, B.A. students must prove proficiency through the intermediate level of a foreign language, which is satisfied by most students by 12 hours of foreign language instruction.

Students can choose from 41 majors, including a new engineering dual degree program, and 37 minors. The minors include human life studies and Franciscan studies. Franciscan also offers majors including drama, catechetics, international business, legal studies, German, sacred music, and a concentration in bioethics for its Master's in Philosophy. Five of the majors are reserved for associate degree candidates. There also are pre-professional programs including medical fields. Students can pursue an eight-seminar or 32-credit honors program that relies on the Great Books and the Catholic intellectual tradition.

Franciscan now offers an online MBA. It also offers an online Master of Science in Education with a Concentration in Online Instruction, one of the first degrees of its kind, which equips K-12 educators for online education. Sixty percent of Franciscan's graduates pursue advanced degrees. The University offers eight different master's degrees, including an M.A. in theology and Christian ministry.

There also is an impressive study-abroad experience for undergraduates. Approximately 175 students per semester, most in their sophomore year, study for one semester at a former Carthusian monastery in the Alpine town of Gaming, Austria. Coursework is four days a week, allowing students to travel throughout Europe. A 10-day Rome-Assisi trip and a 10-day break are built into the experience. Approximately 50 percent of all graduates participate in this program. There are also several other study-abroad opportunities, including a semester at Oxford.

Ninety-four percent of the faculty is Catholic. Theology department faculty members and all new campus ministers take an Oath of Fidelity.

Spiritual Life

The most prominent building on the 244-acre campus is Christ the King Chapel, a 44-year-old modern-looking structure noted for a large steel cross atop its roof.

Seven or eight priests hear confessions four times a week, and there are 20 Masses celebrated each week. Daily Masses are held Monday through Friday at 6:30 a.m., 12:05 p.m., and 4:45 p.m., and attract more than 700 students each day. All four Sunday Masses are filled to capacity.

The Masses are reverent. Most are charismatic or contemporary. An Extraordinary Form High Mass is offered monthly and Low Mass is offered weekly. The Rosary and other devotions are prayed daily. On Tuesdays, students gather for Praise and Worship and prayer. There are monthly Festivals of Praise and frequent retreats, including silent ones, throughout the school year. Solemn vespers and Benediction are held in the chapel every Sunday evening for students.

The University offers a priestly discernment program that helps about 50 men discern vocations. An annual Vocations Awareness Day showcases nearly 75 religious orders and dioceses. There also is a Franciscan house on-campus where some young men live in a "mitigated program" of scheduled prayer and quiet as part of the spirituality of the Third Order Regular. There are days of discernment for women who might consider religious life as well.

Additional opportunities for prayer exist at the small chapel known as the Portiuncula; it hosts 24-hour Adoration in the spring and fall semesters. There are

Financial Aid Office Info

Offering competitive tuition and a variety of financial aid resources is a priority for us at Franciscan University. Each year, over 80 percent of our students receive financial aid worth more than $10 million. These awards are based upon academic merit, financial need, or both.

We offer nearly 100 endowed and over 50 restricted scholarships. The full-tuition Father Michael Scanlan Scholarship ($22,720 in 2013-2014) is awarded to at least two outstanding students through a scholarship competition held on campus. Attendees are invited to compete based on their SAT/ACT scores and High School GPA. Additionally, the President's Scholarship, Chancellor's Scholarship, Dean's Scholarship and Academic Scholarship are awarded to new students based on GPA and SAT/ACT scores. The application for admission serves as the application for these scholarships.

Additional grants and loans offered include Family Discounts, Institutional Grants, Federal Grants, State Grants, Federal Work Study, and Federal Loans. We will award financial aid to all eligible students. To apply, complete the Free Application for Federal Student Aid (FAFSA).

Our team of financial aid professionals will help make a Franciscan education an affordable reality for you. We even offer an interest-free payment plan. For more information, visit our Web site at www.franciscan.edu/TuitionFinacialAid/ or e-mail us at finaid@franciscan.edu.

also a Marian Grotto, outdoor Stations of the Cross, and a life-sized creche. The campus has Eucharistic chapels in every residence hall.

The Tomb of the Unborn Child is a unique memorial with an eternal flame that pays tribute to aborted babies and reflects the University's strong pro-life commitment. About 750 students attend the March for Life in Washington, D.C., each January.

Residential Life

About 70 percent of the undergraduates live on campus. Franciscan has a three-year residency requirement. There are 12 single-sex residence halls and a nearby apartment complex that houses men and women. Residence halls mix lower and upper classmen together. Each residence hall has a director to ensure that the hall's activities conform to the University's policies and guidelines.

Wireless access is available in the student union, the library, and other places on campus. Access in residence halls is filtered. The student cafeteria is not equipped with wireless access in order to foster conversation between students.

Opposite-sex visitation in student rooms is restricted to Fridays from 6:00 pm to 10:00 pm and Sundays from 1:00 p.m. to 5:00 p.m., and in common areas from noon to 1:00 a.m. Doors must remain open when someone has a guest of the opposite sex. There is a defined and enforced code of conduct, but no dress code at the University.

Students of age are allowed to have alcohol in their rooms, but not in the presence of minors. While some drinking problems have been reported, most occur off-campus. The campus is safe; most crimes committed pertain to petty theft.

Students often congregate in the J. C. Williams Center, the active student center located near the middle of campus, to hear bands and visit the Pub deli. The center includes a lounge, Jazzman's Café and Bakery, student mailboxes, a bookstore, meeting rooms, and a gallery.

A health center staffed by a nurse practitioner treats routine matters. Trinity Health Systems operates two medical centers in Steubenville. There are a number of larger hospitals in nearby Pittsburgh.

Three hotels are located near campus. A variety of restaurants, a mall, and other retail businesses are located slightly farther away. At the bottom of the hill from campus are a coffeehouse and a café.

The city of Steubenville is an old industrial town that has seen better days. The downtown is rather dilapidated and has a higher than average crime index.

Downtown Steubenville is known for its 25 large art murals, and Pittsburgh has a wide variety of sports, cultural, and entertainment opportunities. The Pittsburgh International Airport is a half-hour away.

Student Activities

Students can participate in more than four dozen organizations and student-

From the Career Services Office

Grounded in the belief that students' skills and talents are of immense value to society and the Church, Franciscan University of Steubenville's Career Services Office helps students prepare for internships, graduate school, the job market, or their religious vocation.

Career Services recommends that students read *What Does God Want?* by Father Michael Scanlan, TOR, president emeritus of Franciscan University, as a first step. This practical book guides them to make career and life decisions that conform to God's will for their gifts and their talents and that will lead to ongoing conversion, a Franciscan charism.

Franciscan University offers more than 40 undergraduate majors that can lead to hundreds of career and vocation choices. Career Services provides help early in the academic journey, so students can choose or switch to the academic major best suited to their strengths and goals.

Individual counseling and the Myers-Briggs and other assessment tools may be used to help identify skills, abilities, interests, and values that can lead to success within a particular field.

Among the many ways Career Services helps students: individual help preparing résumés, cover letters, and interview training; workshops on how to conduct a job search, select a graduate program, how to research an employer, transition from college to employment, and more; worldwide job placement through College Network Central as well as long-established relationships with employers including many alumni, dioceses, and Church organizations; assistance locating internships; Career Mentoring Fair connecting students with successful alumni; Lay Vocation Fair that brings over 60 employers to campus; Graduate School Expo that attracts representatives of 40 graduate programs; Etiquette Dinner that teaches proper business etiquette and the opportunity to practice social skills in a professional setting; follow-up support after graduation.

Contact Nancy Ronevich, director, Career Services at 740-284-5251 or nronevich@franciscan.edu.

led programs, including an unusual number of groups engaged in spiritual and Catholic outreach efforts. These include Latinos for Christ; Ut unum sint Society for Christian Unity; Love Revealed, which promotes marriage, family, and sexual integrity; and the Knights of Columbus.

The Students for Life club is very active. In addition to participating in the annual March for Life, they have a prayer ministry outside abortion clinics four days a week, train sidewalk counselors, and host prominent speakers. Annually, a coffeehouse is held to raise money for a pregnancy help center in Steubenville.

Other groups include Excite, which sponsors entertainment and social events, theatre, an equestrian club, student government, and the weekly student newspaper, The Troubadour.

Students participate in community outreach programs such as Project St. Nicholas, which works with needy Steubenville residents. The Works of Mercy outreaches and other programs assist with food kitchens and other ministries, such as ministering to the homeless in Pittsburgh and working with local youth.

Missions of Peace sponsors international mission trips during breaks to places such as Belize, Jamaica, Honduras, and Ecuador. Domestic mission trips have included: Chicago, Fargo, Florida, New Mexico, New York, and Steubenville.

A unique aspect of the University is the "faith household" system. Three or more students of the same sex can come together as a household to support each other spiritually, academically, and in other ways under the guidance of an advisor. Nearly 900 students are involved in a household.

In addition to a wide variety of campus activities, households each sponsor their own events

Homecoming provides the opportunity for the St. Francis Festival on campus.

Letter from the President

Dear Brothers and Sisters in Christ,

I am very excited to assume my new role as president of Franciscan University of Steubenville. Our students pour their hearts into their education and their prayer life; they desire to fall in love with God and the Church, and strive to become saints. Through their witness, they encourage me to become a better friar and priest—and all of us at Franciscan to respond without reservation to the many invitations that God extends.

This year, we are excited to implement our Catholic Core, a newly revised curriculum that immerses our students in the treasures of Western Civilization and the Catholic Intellectual Tradition. They study the best minds of the past 2,000 years from Augustine and Aristotle to John Paul II, Benedict XVI, and Francis. At Franciscan, academic excellence means producing Catholic graduates as ready for their careers as they are for the challenges of a secular culture.

If you desire an academically excellent education rooted in passionate Catholicism, if you want to be prepared to meet the challenges of the secular world, I invite you to learn more about Franciscan University . . . where you will also learn more about yourself and the person God created you to be.

In Christ and Francis,

Rev. Sean O. Sheridan, TOR

The chaplain blesses animals, and some students dress in medieval period costumes. An evening service commemorates the death of St. Francis.

The athletics program intentionally integrates faith and sports. The intercollegiate athletic program includes 16 Division III NCAA teams, an intercollegiate rugby team, and four intramural sports that attract hundreds of student participants. Most head coaches are Catholic, and all support the University's unique mission.

The Bottom Line

There's no place quite like Franciscan University of Steubenville, and its students' enthusiasm for serving God both during and after their college years is most refreshing and exciting.

Few institutions share Franciscan University's reputation for strong Catholic identity, including a powerful witness to the pro-life cause and evangelization, which penetrates everything the institution does. Still a center for charismatic Catholic worship, the University today embraces other orthodox approaches to Catholic spirituality and attracts a diverse population of students, albeit nearly all of them Catholic.

Catholic families will find in Franciscan University a thoroughly Catholic environment that prepares servants of God for every walk of life, while offering a solid education and vibrant campus life.

Franciscan University of Steubenville Frequently Asked Questions

We get questions from Catholic families on a regular basis about the colleges we recommend. Rather than filter the answers, we asked Franciscan officials nearly 100 questions in categories such as academics, curriculum, programs of study, campus ministry, residence life, student activities, the make up of the study body, and institutional identity. The answers to some of the most asked questions are provided below and the rest are available on the college profile page at TheNewmanGuide.com.

Majors

List the major, minor and special program areas that students may choose for specialization while pursuing an undergraduate degree:

Majors: Accounting; Anthropology; Biology (BA); Biology (BS); Business (BS): See Economics, Finance, International Business, Management, Marketing; Catechetics; Chemistry (BA); Chemistry (BS); Classics; Communication Arts: Journalism; Communication Arts: Multimedia; Communication Arts: TV/Radio; Computer Information Science; Computer Science; Drama: Dramatic Literature; Drama: Performance; Economics (BA); Economics (BS); Education; Engineering Dual Degree; English: British and American Literature; English: Western and World Literature; English: Writing; Finance; French; German; History; Humanities and Catholic Culture; International Business; Legal Studies; Management; Marketing; Mathematical Sciences; Music, Sacred: Organ; Music, Sacred: Voice; Nursing; Philosophy; Political Science; Psychology; Sociology; Social Work; Spanish; Theology.

Minor Programs: Exercise Science; Film Studies; Franciscan Studies; Greek; Human Life Studies; Latin—Classical; Latin—Ecclesiastical; Special Programs; MBA 4+1: Five-year program for entering freshmen; Graduate Counseling 4+1;

Special Programs: Priestly Discernment Program: Preparation for major seminary;

Honors Program: Based on the close reading and vigorous discussion of a Great Books curriculum, Franciscan's Honors Program challenges students to engage the canon of western literature, hone their written and oral communication skills, debate the perennial questions, and develop insight into the human experience.

Pre-Professional Programs: Pre-Dentistry; Pre-Engineering Program (this leads to automatic admission, provided sufficient GPA, into a variety of engineering majors at the University of Notre Dame, Dayton University, and Gannon University); Pre-Law; Pre-Medicine; Pre-Optometry; Pre-Pharmacy; Pre-Physical Therapy; Pre-Veterinary Medicine.

What are the three most popular majors or specialty disciplines for undergraduate students, and about what percentage of undergraduate students specialize in these disciplines?

Theology, 23%

Business Administration, 12%

Elementary Education, 11%

Spiritual Life

Please list the schedule of Masses, noting the following for each Mass: the day and time, the Form or Rite of the Mass, and the style of music, if any (chant, traditional, contemporary, etc.):

Mo 6:30 a.m., 12:05 p.m., 4:45 p.m.

Tu 6:30 a.m., 12:05 p.m., 4:45 p.m.

We 6:30 a.m., 12:05 p.m., 4:45 p.m.

Th 6:30 a.m., 12:05 p.m., 4:45 p.m.

Fr 6:30 a.m., 12:05 p.m., 4:45 p.m.

Sa 10:00 a.m.

Su 8:30 a.m., 10:30 a.m., 12:30 p.m., 4:00 p.m.

Most Masses are celebrated in the Ordinary Form of the Roman Rite. There is no music at the 6:30 a.m. Mass; music at the other masses varies from traditional to contemporary and is led by student musicians. On three Saturdays at Noon there is a weekly Latin Extraordinary Form Low Mass; on the fourth weekend the Latin Extraordinary Form High Mass (Missa Cantata) is celebrated on Sunday at 4:00 p.m.

List the schedule for Confession by day and time:

Mo 7:30-8:30 p.m.

Tu 3:30-4:30 p.m.

We 7:30-8:30 p.m.

Th 3:30-4:30 p.m.

Fr

Sa

Su

Or by Appointment

List the schedule for Adoration of the Blessed Sacrament by day and time:

The Portiuncula Chapel has 24/7 Eucharistic Adoration each semester. By the generosity of the Vatican Office of the Apostolic Penitentiary, visitors to the Port can receive plenary indulgences on any of five different occasions through the year.

Please identify regularly scheduled devotions on campus for students such as the Rosary and prayer groups:

Community Rosary, Tuesdays after 12:05 p.m. Mass; Liturgy of the Hours, Sundays, 7:00 p.m.; Sung Vespers; Morning Prayer, weekdays; Divine Mercy Chaplet, 3:00 p.m., weekdays.

Residence Life

Please describe options for students to reside on and off campus:

Students may live in residence halls or apartments on campus. Students may secure their own housing off campus if they meet age and credit requirements, or if they are local commuters living with their parents.

Does your institution offer only single-sex residence halls?

Yes.

Are students of the opposite sex permitted to visit students' bedrooms?

Yes. Students of the opposite sex may visit student bedrooms during Open House hours, which are held from 6:00 p.m.-10:00 p.m. on Fridays and 1:00 p.m.-5:00 p.m. on Sundays. Doors must be propped open when a member of the opposite sex is visiting during Open House hours.

How does your institution foster sobriety and respond to substance abuse on campus, particularly in campus residences?

Through preaching, retreats, households, programs, and personal witness, the University strives to foster a culture of ongoing conversion that encourages students to grow in virtue, holiness, and Christian maturity with respect to alcohol. For example, the Freshman Formation series includes issues related to sobriety and substance abuse. Campus Counseling Services and referrals to AA groups are also available for those struggling with problem drinking.

How does your institution foster a student living environment that promotes and supports chastity, particularly in campus residences?

The residence life culture supports Christian moral behavior. Through preaching, retreats, households, programs, and personal witness, the University strives to foster a culture of ongoing conversion that encourages students to grow in virtue, holiness, and Christian maturity with respect to sexuality. Residence hall visitation policies support chaste habits and decisions.

Student Body

Describe the makeup of your institution's undergraduate student body with regard to sex, religion, home state/country and type of high school (public, private, homeschool):

Total number of undergraduates: 2,090
Male: 39% Female: 61%

Catholic: 97% Other Christian: 3%
Jewish 0% Muslim 0% Other 0%

Number of states represented: 50
Top three states: Ohio, Pennsylvania, California
Students from top three states: 37%

Catholic HS: 39% Homeschool: 17%
Private HS: 9% Public HS: 35%

JOHN PAUL THE GREAT CATHOLIC UNIVERSITY

Escondido, California

Overview

When one thinks of a traditional Catholic college, it's not likely situated in office buildings in a thriving business community in downtown Escondido, California. But no other Catholic college is quite like John Paul the Great Catholic University, and the setting is rather appropriate for this 21st century addition to Catholic higher education.

Students enjoy the mild weather and charm of this San Diego suburb. But look behind the doors, and you will find state-of-the-art technology and software to prepare students for futures in business, filmmaking, and other "new media," with a firm grounding in the liberal arts and faithful Catholic theology. It's a smart combination for the Church in today's culture.

The University has just purchased and moved to its new cluster of academic and administrative buildings in Escondido, more than tripling its former leased space in quiet north San Diego. The campus still features a post-production studio, equipped with software and technology used in Hollywood filmmaking. A sound stage, complete with camera equipment, lighting, and audio equipment allows students to shoot their productions. But also included are a virtual reality lab, acting studio, animation lab and the new "Do. School," which provides basic office infrastructure for student-led startup companies.

And the new campus is strategically located next to the California Performing Arts Center, which provides critical infrastructure for future conferences as well as the University's acting program.

Although it is situated in southern California, the small, specialized University traces its heritage to Franciscan University of Steubenville, Ohio. While visiting there in 2000 with his daughter, President Derry Connolly had the inspiration to develop a college in his hometown.

"While at Franciscan, I saw students incredibly on fire for their faith. That wasn't something I had experienced before," said Connolly, who has worked as a professor and administrator at the University of California-San Diego for more than a decade. "The idea for John Paul the Great came to me while in front of the Blessed Sacrament. I wanted to try to connect the idea of students on fire for their faith with what I did day-to-day, teaching entrepreneurship to students at one of the top 20 schools in the U.S."

The University offers undergraduate degrees in communications media and business, as well as an M.A. in biblical theology and an M.B.A. in film producing. Undergraduates can specialize in film (screenwriting, producing, and production/directing), acting, animation and gaming, fashion business, entrepreneurship, leadership and management, sales and marketing, pre-theology, and New Evangelization—the latter being something of a combination of new media, business, and theology.

But undergraduates also take one course every quarter on some aspect of Catho-

Quick Facts

2013-2014 Academic Year

Students 145

ACTs 23 (SATs 1090)

HS GPA 3.4

Majors 2

% Catholic 99%

How Much? $30,400 *
tuition and room *NOTE: no board costs included

lic philosophy, theology, history, ethics, or culture. And unlike most colleges and universities, John Paul the Great's academic calendar is year-round based on quarters, not semesters.

With nearly 150 undergraduate students, almost all of them Catholic, the University has long-range plans for a traditional campus with up to 1,200 students.

The University is governed by an 11-member board of trustees, chaired by a banker. The others include a priest and several area business leaders. Dr. Connolly, a native of Ireland, has a Ph.D. in applied mechanics from Cal-Tech, 15 years of employment with IBM and Kodak, and eight patents to his name.

JP Catholic is approved to operate by the state of California and is nearing the end of the lengthy eight-year process of seeking accreditation through the Western Association of Schools and Colleges.

A college education in upscale San Diego should be expensive, but JP Catholic is priced far below the average California college. Tuition and room fees for the 2012-13 academic year are $29,700. Financial aid includes merit scholarships, work-study options, and federal grants and loans.

Academics

Although JP Catholic is not a liberal arts institution per se, it requires a 90-credit core curriculum. This includes 24 credits in theology and Scripture, 12 credits in philosophy, 36 in the humanities and science or math, and 18 credits in business.

In many ways, the University combines the best of a college with the hands-on skill learning of a technical school. From their first days in class, many students are able to use cameras and professional post-production software.

The University assumes that most students will be called to work in business, entertainment, and digital media. In their senior year, entrepreneurship students and some others participate in the newly revamped Do. School, which teaches them to create a blueprint for a company and launch it using University facilities. Many students have used these plans to continue their own businesses after graduation.

Not only has JP Catholic established a niche, but the University already has a respectable track record of success with graduates in media, technology, and filmmaking. Students and faculty created a feature film called Red Line and an online television series that attracted more than 125,000 site visitors and a great deal of press coverage. Graduates and employees launched Yellow Line Studios, which is involved in several film projects. The New Evangelization students produced a 13-episode series on the *Catechism* called "Pillars of Catholicism."

JP Catholic is emphatic in ensuring fidelity to the Magisterium:

All teaching faculty will commit to harmony with Catholic Church teachings (the pope and bishops) in speech and action. Faculty, staff, students or volunteers who knowingly in public speech or actions take positions against the Catholic Church compromise their relationship with JP Catholic. JP Catholic expects all trustees, faculty and staff to celebrate the positive spiritual and entrepreneurial components of its mission and eschew cutting down what the institution is striving to build.

Overall, there are 24 faculty members and two visiting faculty. The mandatum is required for all professors of theology. To help keep the University's budget small while also maintaining a practical emphasis, professors must be employed

in part-time work in their field.

JP Catholic offers a brief study abroad program. Over a span of 19 days, students study in Ireland, France, and Italy.

Spiritual Life

The University has transformed a large classroom into a reverent chapel, outfitting it with icons, an altar, and a crucifix. Mass is offered each weekday on campus, including a Chaldean Rite (Iraqi

Catholic) Mass on Fridays.

The campus chaplain is appointed by the San Diego bishop. He and other priests hear confessions four times per week and by appointment. Eucharistic Adoration takes place nearly every afternoon on campus, and students lead evening Rosary and the Chaplet of Divine Mercy at their residence apartments.

The local St. Mary's Catholic Parish has 24-hour Eucharistic Adoration and Latin Mass on Sundays. The pastor, Fr. Rich Perozich, spends well over an hour each day hearing confessions.

Students have become involved in teaching CCD classes, doing pro-life work, helping with homeless people, and attending prayer and Sunday worship services.

Residential Life

About one-third of JP Catholic's students commute from home, and the remainder live in two-bedroom townhomes and apartments leased by the University at the Latitude 33 complex, less than a half-mile from campus. Men and women reside in separate parts of the complex, and no apartment visits are permitted between them.

The townhomes and apartments are located next to a shopping center with a movie theater. There are part-time job opportunities in the shopping center and on historic Grand Avenue, which is home to bistros, bakeries, and gelato and coffee shops. Across the street from the residences is Grape Day Park, with space for sports and short film production.

The University does not offer a meal plan, so students are responsible for their own meals. Students walk or ride bicycles to class.

Households—voluntary groups of students who support each other spiritually and socially, according to the Franciscan University of Steubenville model—are in formation.

Alcohol is not permitted on campus or in apartments, and the University encourages chastity by teaching scripture and writings of St. Francis de Sales. There are weekly get-togethers to talk about spiritual life, including chastity. Student dress can vary with some wearing t-shirts, sandals, and flip-flops, but in theology classes men are expected to wear collared shirts.

With a population of about 1.3 million, nearby San Diego presents a broad array of economic, social, and cultural opportunities. The diversified economy includes military and port facilities, tourism, biotechnology, marine science, and many start-up businesses, particularly in technology. Cultural offerings include the San Diego Museum of Art, the San Diego Zoo, and a wide range of professional sports teams.

San Diego is one of the safest large cities in the nation, but students need to avoid crossing the nearby Mexican border. In addition to the San Diego International Airport, Amtrak and other rail and public bus systems are available.

Students can take the Sprinter train, with a station just two blocks away, to Hollywood for networking events and internships. For $2, students can take the train to the beach.

Student Activities

JP Catholic continues to develop student organizations, with clubs dedicated to anime illustration, animation, pro-life activities, business, and classic movies. There is a writing group and a student

From the Career Services Office

The Career Services Center (CSC) facilitates opportunities for students to build relationships for employment, internships, mentoring, and networking experiences with the professional community.

Guided by the University's commitment to the student's personal success, the Center assists students to discern their future career aspirations and goals. The University strongly encourages all students to start thinking about their future career aspirations from their first day on campus. Career planning is incorporated into the student's Personal Plan for Success. The student, with their academic advisor and the Center, develops a plan for a progression of job experiences from entry level retail, to a career focused internship, to a part-time career focused job, to a full-time job on graduation. By having career aspirations and planning always in mind, the student, on graduation, is better equipped to carry out the University's mission to impact culture for Christ.

Services include: Assessment tools that help identify a student's interests, skills, and work values; assistance finding internships related to one's academic major or career interest; help to build the student's network, resume writing assistance, access to online resources, explore graduate school options, and to meet employers.

choir, and a ballroom dance club and acting club alternate on Friday evenings.

The University has established some sports clubs, such as hiking, climbing, and soccer.

In addition to the local parish-centered activities, there are informal events such as a monthly "open mic" or variety program. Student government sponsors two or three events each quarter, such as dances, movies, and excursions to the Pacific beaches about 20 miles away.

Students also venture into San Diego for the many social, cultural, film festival, and athletic opportunities available there.

The Bottom Line

John Paul the Great Catholic University is part of the new breed of small Catholic institutions that have responded to the crisis in Catholic higher education with a renewed commitment to faithful theology and philosophy.

But JP Catholic is also uniquely modern, preparing students for 21st-century careers in business and media technology while retaining a traditional liberal arts core. The University has found a special niche among Catholic colleges, one that will appeal to a particular student with a love for entrepreneurship, digital media, and evangelization.

The University offers Catholic families three very attractive components: a strong Catholic identity, a complete yet specialized curriculum, and a location in one of the most livable and appealing areas in the country.

Letter from the President

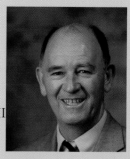

Dear Parents and Prospective Students:

John Paul the Great Catholic University (JP Catholic) welcomes students eager to "Impact Culture for Christ." The University is a response to the call of Pope John Paul II for a new evangelization using media and business. We are committed to Christ and His Church, and seek to transform the world through love and fidelity to Him.

JP Catholic is unique in many ways. We are THE Catholic film school with 6 areas of emphasis within Entertainment Media. Classes run year-round to prepare students for the breakneck pace of business, particularly in the entertainment industry. Our curriculum focuses on action—business students learn to create viable companies; media students make films from short to feature length. Students write, direct, produced, edit, as well as doing cinematography, lighting and sound.

They learn motion graphics, special effects, and animation. Our Video Game students create games for mobile platforms.

All students take a solid liberal arts core in philosophy, theology, literature, art and music. In our campus culture, we are committed to providing the opportunity to encounter Jesus Christ.

May God bless your college decision—and, if you really want to "Impact Culture for Christ," we hope you choose JP Catholic!

In Christ,

Derry Connolly

Dr. Derry Connolly, President

John Paul the Great
Frequently Asked Questions

We get questions from Catholic families on a regular basis about the colleges we recommend. Rather than filter the answers, we asked JP officials nearly 100 questions in categories such as academics, curriculum, programs of study, campus ministry, residence life, student activities, the make up of the study body, and institutional identity. The answers to some of the most asked questions are provided below and the rest are available on the college profile page at TheNewmanGuide.com.

Majors

List the major, minor and special program areas that students may choose for specialization while pursuing an undergraduate degree:

Major: Communications Media

Areas of Emphasis: Screenwriting, Film Producing (Business of Entertainment), Production/Directing, Animation, Video Game Design, New Evangelization, and Pre-Theology

Major: Business

Areas of Emphasis: Entrepreneurship, Business of Fashion, Sales and Marketing, Leadership and Management

What are the three most popular majors or specialty disciplines for undergraduate students, and about what percentage of undergraduate students specialize in these disciplines?

Communications Media, 80%

Business, 20%

Spiritual Life

Please list the schedule of Masses, noting the following for each Mass: the day and time, the Form or Rite of the Mass, and the style of music, if any (chant, traditional, contemporary, etc.):

Mo 11:00 a.m., Ordinary Form

Tu 11:00 a.m., Ordinary Form

We 11:00 a.m., Ordinary Form

Th 11:00 a.m., Ordinary Form

Fr 11:00 a.m., Chaldean Rite

Sa at local parish

Su at local parish – there are varied music styles

List the schedule for Confession by day and time:

Mo After Mass (11:45-finished)

Tu After Mass (11:45-finished)

We After Mass (11:45-finished)

Th After Mass (11:45-finished)

Fr None

Sa Local Parish: 3-4

Su n/a

Other: As needed or at special events (retreats, etc)

List the schedule for Adoration of the Blessed Sacrament by day and time:

Monday -Thursday 11:45 a.m. - 3:20 p.m.

Please identify regularly scheduled devotions on campus for students such as the Rosary and prayer groups:

Nightly Rosary.

Residence Life

Please describe options for students to reside on and off campus:

JP Catholic has acquired a full street of brand new 3 story, 2 bedroom townhomes and 3 bedroom apartments in the Latitude 33 complex, less than a half-mile (5-10 minute walk) from the classrooms and production facilities.

The townhomes and apartments are located right next to a shopping center with a movie theatre. There are an abundance of part-time job opportunities in the shopping center and on historic Grand avenue. Historic Grand Avenue is home to bistros, bakeries, gelato and coffee shops.

Across the street from the student housing is Grape Day Park, which offers plenty of space for sports and short film production.

The Latitude 33 complex includes several workout rooms, a pool, and a cabana area. Students can work and play in either the student center on-campus or in the common town home.

Does your institution offer only single-sex residence halls?

Yes.

Are students of the opposite sex permitted to visit students' bedrooms?
No.

How does your institution foster sobriety and respond to substance abuse on campus, particularly in campus residences?

Alcohol abuse is rare. Abuse has led to expulsion, loss of financial aid, and loss of student work-study positions. To discourage the contemporary fixation on alcohol as a centerpiece of college campus life, alcohol is not allowed in the student residences, even for students of legal drinking age.

How does your institution foster a student living environment that promotes and supports chastity, particularly in campus residences?

Strict policies restrict visitation between students of opposite sexes in student housing and prevent casual sexual "hook-ups" on campus. Men's Nights and Women's Nights are student events that address and promote chastity and purity.

Student Body

Describe the makeup of your institution's undergraduate student body with regard to sex, religion, home state/country and type of high school (public, private, homeschool):

Total number of undergraduates: 145
Male: 55% Female: 45%

Catholic: 99% Other Christian: 1%
Jewish: 0% Muslim: 0% Other: 0%

Number of states represented: 25
Top three states: California (58%), Michigan (5%), Texas (5%)
Students from top three states: 68%

Catholic HS: 33% Homeschool: 33%
Private HS: % Public HS: 34 %

MOUNT ST. MARY'S UNIVERSITY

Emmitsburg, Maryland

Overview

Nestled in the Catoctin Mountains of Maryland, one of the nation's earliest havens for Catholic immigrants, Mount St. Mary's University is the second-oldest Catholic university in America. It was founded in 1808 by the heroic French missionary Father John DuBois and sits on land once frequented by Saint Elizabeth Ann Seton, the first American-born saint and founder of the Sisters of Charity.

What is affectionately called "the Mount" includes the University, a seminary, and a shrine. The University has an under-graduate enrollment of 1,700 students from 34 different states and 14 foreign countries, and a growing number of homeschooled students. The seminary is the largest in the United States and is often referred to as the "Cradle of Bishops," because 51 of its graduates have shepherded dioceses. The National Shrine Grotto of Our Lady of Lourdes, an idyllic shrine for spiritual reflection located on the hill above the University, is the oldest American replica of the shrine in France.

The University's historical Catholic iden-

tity has strengthened under the lead-ership of Dr. Thomas Powell, who is in the 11th year of his presidency, but has announced his retirement at the end of 2013-14. Dr. Powell has heavily empha-sized the University's mission statement, which describes four "pillars" of faith, discovery, leadership, and community. Dr. Powell and his Vice President for Mis-sion, Monsignor Stuart Swetland, have made the University's Catholic identity a priority and have earned support from the faculty.

Several of the Mount's professors have made significant contributions to the Church. Msgr. Swetland leads The Car-dinal Newman Society's Center for the

Advancement of Catholic Higher Educa-tion, that is located at the Mount.

With its variety of majors, large athletics and recreation programming, and di-verse community, the Mount has the feel of a typical private university but with an earnest commitment to authentic Catholic teaching and students' personal development. Students should not expect the degree of uniformity that can be found at some of the smaller *Newman Guide* colleges. Some of the faculty and about a quarter of students are not Catholic, and many come to the Mount for secular reasons.

Tuition, room and board, and fees cost $46,158 in 2013-14. When compared to other private institutions in Maryland, the Mount's actual cost is below the state average. The average freshman financial aid package was more than $25,000 in the 2012-13 school year, and students have the option of a three-year program in any major, which requires summer study but can save on tuition .

Academics

Students at the Mount can pursue more than 40 undergraduate majors, concen-trations, and minors. These include the traditional liberal arts disciplines as well as preparation for careers in business,

Quick Facts

Students 1,747

SATs 1105

HS GPA 3.4

2012-2013 Academic Year

Majors 31

% Catholic 75%

How Much? $46,158
tuition, room, board, and fees

education, law, medicine, and science. An honors program is also available.

The Mount's liberal arts core curriculum, the Veritas Program, requires a sequence of 19 courses over all four years. The common curriculum begins with the new Veritas Symposium "to initiate students into a Catholic liberal arts community;" assigned authors include C.S. Lewis, Cicero, and Jean Vanier. All students receive a solid grounding in Western civilization through a sequence of history, literature, and art courses, as well as five semesters of philosophy and theology, including a "life of virtue" course. Other requirements include courses in science, math, social science, "global encounters," and at least a year of a foreign language.

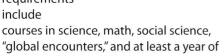

The University's new Institute for Leadership is also implementing a four-credit program which will help integrate students' studies with practical experience. According to Dr. Powell, "Being Catholic is a call to leadership. Yet few colleges require it for graduation." The Mount is now one of the few colleges to require a Leadership experience and portfolio from all undergraduate students before graduating.

Students can take a semester abroad in the Czech Republic, Ecuador, Ireland, Italy, or the United Kingdom. Summer abroad programs are offered in Austria, Costa Rica, France and Spain. Faculty members join students and usually teach courses on location.

The Mount's speakers policy affirms the University's responsibility to support and promote understanding of Catholic teaching, but speakers representing diverse viewpoints are welcome. Controversial topics are handled so as not to cause confusion about Catholic teaching.

Spiritual Life

CrossThe Mount has five chapels on campus, including two in residence halls. There are three Sunday Masses on campus; the 7 p.m. and 9:30 p.m. services are most popular for students. Morning weekday Masses are celebrated at the Chapel of the Immaculate Conception, and daily Masses are also offered at the seminary's St. Bernard's Chapel and chapels in two of the residence halls.

Confessions are available every day and by appointment. Eucharistic adoration is available at various times, and students can enjoy praise and worship music weekly.

The Campus Ministry Organization is the largest student group on campus and presents opportunities for students to serve as lectors, ushers, extraordinary Eucharistic ministers, and in other capacities. There are many retreat weekends, Bible studies, prayer groups, women's and men's vocation discernment groups, and a peer ministry program.

Campus ministry offers numerous opportunities for fellowship and community service activities. A chapter of the Fellowship of Catholic University Students (FOCUS) helps evangelize students.

The Division I athletic department has a unique sports team chaplain program whereby seminarians mentor the teams and help organize opportunities for prayer, team Masses, penance services, weekly face-time during practice, attendance at home games, team dinners, talks on topics such as humility and perseverance, and encouragement for athletes to attend campus ministry events.

Adjacent to campus is the National Shrine Grotto of Our Lady of Lourdes,

Financial Aid Office Info

The Mount is committed to making a private education affordable – in fact, 100% of the class of 2017 freshmen received a merit scholarship from the Mount, and the average financial aid package for 2012-2013 freshmen was $25,611.

Most families at Mount St. Mary's receive a wide variety of financial aid including scholarships, grants, loans, and/or work study options. This aid significantly reduces the cost of attending the Mount.

Merit scholarships are based on GPA, test scores, high school transcripts, recommendations, and other admission file materials. All students are considered for a merit scholarship at the same time they are reviewed for admission.

Need-based financial aid is available, and the Mount requires students to complete the FAFSA form in order to be considered for loans, grants, and/or work study.

an ideal location for student prayer and reflection with a new visitor center and gallery, and nearby is the National Shrine of Saint Elizabeth Ann Seton. Other spiritual opportunities, including Masses, confessions, Benediction, novenas, and Eucharistic Adoration, are available at St. Mary's Chapel on the Hill, affectionately known as the Glass Chapel.

Residential Life

About 85 percent of Mount students live on campus. Residence halls separate men and women by floor, and each floor has a resident advisor. Opposite-gender visitation is prohibited during late-night hours, and individual floor access is locked with check-in security desks in most buildings.

There are traditional residence halls, suite-style rooms, a variety of apartment combinations (for juniors and seniors), themed housing, separate housing for honors students, and a floor in one hall

Mount St. Mary's is located just outside the small town of Emmitsburg, Maryland, which has a population of 2,400. One of the town's landmarks is the National Fire Academy, run by the United States Fire Administration, which provides advanced firefighting training to firemen from across the United States. Serious crime and property crime are well below the national average.

Emmitsburg is one hour northwest of Baltimore and 90 minutes from Washington, D.C. Both major cities offer a large number of cultural, social, and sports opportunities. Students often take day trips on their own to these cities, and the university also offers shuttles to Baltimore and D.C. on weekends.

Three major international airports are located about one hour away: Baltimore-Washington International Thurgood Marshall Airport, Ronald Reagan Washington National Airport, and Washington Dulles International Airport. The university runs shuttles to and from campus during break times for students who need transportation.

Student Activities

Students can choose from more than 80 clubs, ranging from the Knights of Columbus and the Legion of Mary to an Army ROTC Prayerprogram. Intramural

for women in science. There are also a variety of themed housing and living-learning options available for students; these include the Faith Development Community and the Leadership Community.

Many students elect to participate in the Summit Housing initiative. These students adopt as a rule of life a healthy living commitment through outdoor activities, service projects, and abstinence from tobacco, alcohol, and drugs.

In addition to the student dining center with a plethora of food options, the Mount Café is open throughout the day, with earlier and later hours.

Opposite-gender visitors are only allowed in the residences during certain hours, and individual floor access is locked. Buildings where freshmen live also have a check-in security desk where all visitors must register.

In an effort to keep parents and families informed about activities at the Mount, the University sponsors a Mount Family Association, coordinated by Dr. Powell's wife, Irene Quinn Powell. Its activities include a newsletter, the online Mount Family Prayer Memo, orientation, and a fall Family Fest.

The University operates a wellness center, and Gettysburg Hospital is about 15 minutes away.

From the Career Services Office

Starting a career, finding a job or deciding on graduate and professional school is every student's challenge after college. Approximately 94% of Mount St. Mary's University students are employed or in graduate school within the first year after graduation. The Mount offers numerous opportunities for students navigating their way through life-after-graduation plans and for alumni looking to change jobs or careers.

The Mount's Career Center offers guidance and support, programs and services to both students and alumni. The Career Center counselors believe their work is a calling and aid with career exploration, major exploration, career assessments, resumes, job searching, mock interviews, internships, the graduate school process or any aspect of career development. The Center's Career Action Plan is a four-year program that guides students through a systematic career development process.

The Career Center hosts recruiting events throughout the year and an Internship/Job Fair on campus in the spring. Many companies and organizations come to campus to meet and interview students. The Federal Bureau of Investigation, the Secret Service and the National Security Administration actively recruit Mount students Accounting majors and Education majors have active seasons in the Career Center with employers interviewing and hiring many students.

Faculty advisors also pay a key role in helping students take the next step after college. Students are encouraged to get practical work experience through internships, meeting professionals in the workforce and grad-school prep guidance.

The Mount's active alumni serve as an influential guidance and networking tool for students. They serve on advisory boards of the four schools, as well as the pre-law programs. Alumni panels on campus give students a chance to learn more about career fields as well as make contacts to help them in their life beyond the Mount.

sports, Campus Ministry, the Student Government Association, and the Activities Management Program (AMP) are popular organizations on campus.

The Mount Students for Life participates in the annual March for Life in Washington, D.C., and other activities. Nearly 300 students have attended the March in recent years. The group prays a weekly Rosary at an on-campus memorial for the unborn and at a local abortion center on Saturdays.

The Outdoor Adventures program takes advantage of the Mount's location in the Catoctin Mountains, offering weekly excursions in canoeing, caving, backpacking, rock climbing, snowshoeing, and rafting.

The University has a student-run newspaper, The Mountain Echo, which is available in print and online, and students produce a literary magazine, Lighted Corners, and Tolle Lege, a journal of philosophy and theology. There also is a fully functional student-operated campus radio station, WMTB 89.9 FM.

Students are actively involved in a variety of service projects through the Office of Social Justice. These include service trips during breaks and work with Catholic Relief Services, Catholic Charities, the National Coalition for the Homeless, accessible housing organizations, shelters, and food assistance programs.

Athletics are prominent at the Mount, with one of every five undergraduates a Division I athlete. The University fields 16 intercollegiate teams in NCAA Division I that compete in the Northeast Conference. In addition, there are club sports in dance, equestrian, ice hockey, and rugby. Intramural opportunities are available in nearly two dozen sports, from bocce and dodge ball to volleyball and inner tube water polo.

Campus ministry sponsors a group called Allies for students with homosexual inclinations and others who care about them. The group "strives to promote and live the Christian call to healthy relationships, compassion, chastity, and justice," according to the University.

Campus Activities hosts more than 140 entertainment events each year, both on and off campus, such as dances, comedians, and live bands. Many of these events are hosted in the newly renovated Club

Letter from the President

Dear Parents and Prospective Students:

The story of Mount St. Mary's University is a uniquely American one– quite simply, the story of the Catholic Church in America. Father John DuBois, on a voyage filled with courage, faith and determination, settled on our spectacular mountainside and founded Mount St. Mary's in 1808.

Now, more than 200 years later, the Mount's outstanding faculty, staff and students are on a voyage of faith, discovery, leadership and community–a voyage that I invite you to join.

~ Faith: we are proudly a robust and contemporary Catholic university living according to the spirit and letter of Blessed John Paul II's Apostolic Constitution, *Ex corde Ecclesiae* (ECE).

~ Discovery: as a university fully consecrated to the cause of truth (cf. ECE 4), at the Mount you'll not only learn about and encounter the world, but more importantly, you'll learn about yourself.

~ Leadership: we take our charge to prepare leaders for the Church and the nation seriously, and we expect leadership at all levels.

~ Community: you will become part of the Mount family the instant you set foot on campus... and remain part of it long after you graduate.

At the Mount, in addition to Division I Athletics, you will find award-winning student life programs, accentuated by a thriving campus ministry, FOCUS bible studies, retreats, community service, and outdoor adventure excursions helping students to expand and strengthen their faith. We are also proud to be the headquarters of the Cardinal Newman Society's Center for the Advancement of Catholic Higher Education.

I invite you to become more familiar with our campus by coming for a visit. You are certain to find a beautiful, welcoming, faith-filled home here at the Mount.

I look forward to our paths crossing soon!

Sincerely,

Thomas H. Powell

1808 on campus.

The Bottom Line

Mount St. Mary's University is a small private university offering a vibrant athletics, student life, and outdoor recreation program, numerous majors, and a solid common curriculum (the Veritas Program) rooted in the Catholic liberal arts tradition. Students have numerous opportunities to grow socially and spiritually.

"Students who'll thrive at the Mount would be those who are willing to be active and part of a small community," said Michael Post, vice president for enrollment management. "They have

to know that they'll recognize every face and be recognized. Their professors will ask about them if they're missing from class."

Given the University's idyllic setting and deep heritage, its strengthened embrace of Catholic education, a solid core curriculum, and vibrant student life, the Mount is deservedly getting more attention from families nationwide.

Mount St. Mary's University
Frequently Asked Questions

We get questions from Catholic families on a regular basis about the colleges we recommend. Rather than filter the answers, we asked Mount officials nearly 100 questions in categories such as academics, curriculum, programs of study, campus ministry, residence life, student activities, the make up of the study body, and institutional identity. The answers to some of the most asked questions are provided below and the rest are available on the Mount profile page at TheNewmanGuide.com.

Majors

List the major, minor and special program areas that students may choose for specialization while pursuing an undergraduate degree:

Majors and Minors: Accounting; Biochemistry; Biology; Business; Chemistry; Classical Studies; Communication Studies; Computer Science; Criminal Justice; Economics; Education; Elementary Education; Elem. & Special Education; English; Environmental Science; Environmental Studies; Fine Arts - Art, Art Educ., Music, Theater; Foreign Languages;; History; Human Services (anticipated fall 2013), Information Systems; Interdisciplinary Studies; International Studies; Mathematics; Non-Western Studies; Nursing; Occupational or Physical Therapy; Philosophy; Political Science; Pre-Law; Pre-Med Studies; Psychology; Secondary Education; Sociology; Sport Management; Theology.

What are the three most popular majors or specialty disciplines for undergraduate students, and about what percentage of undergraduate students specialize in these disciplines?

Business, 17%

Biology, 8%

Elementary Education, 7%

Spiritual Life

Please list the schedule of Masses, noting the following for each Mass: the day and time, the Form or Rite of the Mass, and the style of music, if any (chant, traditional, contemporary, etc.):

Mo 7:00 a.m. traditional, noon & 10:00 p.m. no music

Tu 7:00 a.m. traditional, noon & 10:00 p.m. no music

We 7:00 a.m. traditional, noon no music, 10:00 p.m. contemporary

Th 7:00 a.m. traditional, noon and 10:00 p.m. no music

Fr 7:00 a.m. traditional, noon no music

Sa 7:30 a.m. traditional, 11:00 a.m.

Su 9:00 a.m. traditional, noon traditional, 7:00 p.m. (Chapel Choir) & 9:00 p.m. mixture of traditional and contemporary

All Ordinary Form. Extraordinary Form – a Low Mass is offered once a month. A Solemn High Mass is celebrated on the Thursday of Easter Week.

List the schedule for Confession by day and time:

Mo 6:15 a.m.

Tu 6:15 a.m., 9:00-10:00 p.m.

We 6:15 a.m., 9:00-10:00 p.m.

Th 6:15 a.m., 7:00 p.m., 9:00-10:00 p.m.

Fr 6:15 a.m.

Sa 6:45 a.m.

Su 6:00-7:00 p.m., 8:25-8:50 p.m.

Other: also by appointment

List the schedule for Adoration of the Blessed Sacrament by day and time:

Monday: 12:30 p.m. - 9:30 p.m.

Tuesday 8:30-9:30 a.m.

Tuesday- Friday 4:00-5:00 p.m.

Thursday: 12:30-4 p.m.

Sunday 4:00-5:00 p.m.

Extended Adoration during Advent and Lent

Please identify regularly scheduled devotions on campus for students such as the Rosary and prayer groups:

Militia Immaculata - Marian group inspired by St. Maximilian Kolbe; Morning Prayer - Liturgy of the Hours - daily; Evening Prayer - Chanted Vespers, Sunday; Eucharistic Adoration; Praise & Worship; Rosary for the Unborn & Pro-life efforts; Spanish Rosary; Marian Procession (annual).

Residence Life

Please describe options for students to reside on and off campus:

Students are able to live in several types of campus housing ranging from traditional residence halls (shared room with a common floor bathroom), to suites and full apartments (with full kitchens).

Several specialty housing areas are available such as Honors Housing, Summit (Wellness) Housing, Senior Success, Women In Science Housing, and the Faith Development Community.

Does your institution offer only single-sex residence halls?

No.

3.4% of students living on campus live in single-sex residence halls. Single-sex housing is open to female students of any year through Summit Living, a holistic, drug and alcohol-free wellness community, and the Women in Science Living and Learning Community, a group of students who are majoring, or have a strong interest in, science and technology fields.

Are students of the opposite sex permitted to visit students' bedrooms?

Yes. 8:00 a.m. - Midnight Sunday - Thursday and 8:00 a.m. - 2:00 a.m. Friday - Sunday .

How does your institution foster sobriety and respond to substance abuse on campus, particularly in campus residences?

Through active education, a plethora of programing options, and strict policy enforcement.

How does your institution foster a student living environment that promotes and supports chastity, particularly in campus residences?

Through a proactive Campus Ministry program, active education which includes a holistic approach to the virtues, including chastity, and strict policy enforcement.

Student Body

Describe the makeup of your institution's undergraduate student body with regard to sex, religion, home state/country and type of high school (public, private, homeschool):

Total number of undergraduates: 1,747
Male: trad UG=45%
Female: trad UG=55%

Catholic: 75% Other Christian: 17%
Jewish: 0% Muslim: 0% Other: 8%

Number of states represented: 35
Top three states: MD, PA, NJ
Students from top three states: 79%

Catholic HS: 41% Homeschool: 2%
Private HS: 4% Public HS: 53%

ST. GREGORY'S UNIVERSITY

Shawnee, Oklahoma

411

For more information on St. Greg's, visit their website at:

www.stgregorys.edu

Admissions contact:

888/STGREGS
admissions@stgregorys.edu

Overview

St. Gregory's University was founded by Benedictine monks in 1875 and is Oklahoma's oldest institution of higher education. With a diverse but close-knit community, the University's strong Benedictine tradition should appeal to a growing number of Catholic families as it becomes better known outside Oklahoma.

The University's impressive, multi-story brick Benedictine Hall rises from the prairie, dominating a 75-acre campus surrounded by miles of farmland at the edge of Shawnee, Oklahoma. With about half its 738 undergraduate students in accelerated working-adult programs at various locations, St. Gregory's is a small university for traditional students.

But given its location in the heart of Indian Territory, the University can boast a higher proportion of Native American students (8 percent) than any other Catholic university in the country. With another 12 percent international students, 13 percent Hispanic, 10 percent African American, and 10 percent multi-racial, the University has one of the most unique and diverse campuses in its region.

Half of St. Gregory's students are Catholic. That of course colors campus life and student relationships in ways that are different from colleges that have primarily Catholic students, but the Benedictine influences and the University's commitment to authentic Catholic education are strong. The University is not shy about integrating its commitment to Catholic teaching in the classroom and in campus life, and the campus ministry is decidedly Catholic.

In recent years, leaders have sought to re-emphasize the University's core values and refocus on campus ministry, the relationship between the University and St. Gregory's Abbey, and Catholic student recruitment. Simply being Catholic in Oklahoma is to stand apart.

"They're building up the Catholic community here and bringing in people who are on fire for Christ," said student Kelly Hogan. The University seems intent on attracting more students who match that description.

Students in the College of Arts and Sciences are provided with a solid foundation in the liberal arts through a common core curriculum, the heart of which is a four-semester "Tradition and Conversation" program that offers students the opportunity to engage some of the greatest minds and discuss some of the most influential texts of the Western and Catholic intellectual traditions.

Students can then choose from more than 30 majors, including several business-related disciplines, social science, natural science, teacher education, health and sports science, and traditional liberal arts majors. A quarter of undergraduates major in life sciences such as pre-medicine, and about 20 percent major in business and behavioral sciences.

The University's primarily lay board of 26 members, including five Benedictines and the Archbishop of Oklahoma City, selected D. Gregory Main to be

Quick Facts

2013-2014 Academic Year

Students 350

SATs 900 (ACT 21.25)

HS GPA 3.27

Majors 32

% Catholic 50%

How Much? $25,723
tuition, room and board

the fourth president in July 2011. Dr. Main came to St. Gregory's after a two-year term as president and CEO of the Michigan Economic Development Corporation. He also served as Oklahoma Secretary of Commerce. The University requires the president to make a public profession of faith and oath of fidelity.

Abbott Lawrence Stasyszen, O.S.B., head of St. Gregory's Abbey, is former president and current chancellor of the University and helps keep focus on the University's Catholic identity. The monks serve in various capacities as administrators, teachers, and staff.

The Archbishop of Oklahoma City and the Bishop of Tulsa have expressed their intention to become sponsors of St. Gregory's University. Archbishop Paul Coakley and Bishop Edward Slattery joined St. Gregory's University Board Chair Rev. Don Wolf and Abbot Stasyszen

in signing a memorandum of agreement and declaration of intent that solidified the Church's involvement in the University's future.

The partnership signifies St. Gregory's commitment to serving the Church of Oklahoma through its academic and student outreach programs, and the Church of Oklahoma's commitment to the advancement of Catholic higher education.

The price is right at St. Gregory's. Total tuition, room, and board in 2011-2012 was $26,379—well below the average for private institutions in Oklahoma, where higher education is offered at a relatively low cost compared to other states. The University offers scholarships, some of which require the recipient to be Catholic or to be discerning a religious vocation.

Academics

St. Gregory's offers a solid 56-credit core curriculum including theology, philosophy, ethics, English composition, communication, fine arts, government, and leadership. The highlight is a four-semester "Tradition and Conversation" seminar program, which offers a modified Great Books curriculum taught in small groups utilizing the Socratic Method. Students read and discuss books of the Bible and works by Homer, Sophocles, Plato, Aristotle, Virgil, Augustine, and a variety of mystics.

Theology courses are explicitly Catholic and are intended primarily to prepare students for pastoral work in parishes, schools, and youth ministries. All theology faculty are required to have the *mandatum*.

The University's successful pre-med graduates have gone on to their first choice of medical school. Housed on campus is the National Institute on Developmental Delays, an international cognitive psychology program founded by Father Paul Zahler, O.S.B., that utilizes various therapies including equine therapy for those with developmental issues. Pre-med, psychology, and pre-veterinary students are able to pursue internships to work with the Institute.

Spiritual Life

Campus spiritual life revolves around the Abbey Church where Mass is celebrated daily. Sunday and Wednesday 9 p.m. Masses are intended especially for students and are preceded by the Rosary, led by the campus pro-life club.

At the beginning of the academic year, all participate in the Opening Mass of the Holy Spirit. A University Community Mass is celebrated on the first Thursday of every month. There are no classes scheduled during the Community Mass, and all offices on campus are closed to allow attendance.

Eucharistic Adoration is held once a

week. Confessions are heard twice weekly. Students are invited to pray morning, midday, or evening prayers in the Abbey Church with the Benedictines.

The Buckley Outreach Team consists of approximately 10 student volunteers who organize and run retreats for Catholic high school students in Oklahoma, Texas, and Arkansas. Established in 1990 from a bequest by the parents of Academic Vice President Father Charles Buckley, O.S.B., the Buckley Team promotes evangelization at about 20 retreats in 50 parishes for 1,000 students each year. Team members are awarded scholarships annually.

Campus ministry frequently hosts coffee house events with speakers on various spiritual topics and special Lent and Advent programs. It also hosts four cycles of courses on Catholic teachings, a catechetical program that is separate from

the academic departments and is open to anyone of any faith. Topics include the Sacraments, the Eucharist, God, moral theology, and the works of mercy.

Residential Life

St. Gregory's features two female residence halls and one male residence hall. There are no coed residence halls. Freshman men are housed in Mark Braun Hall, and have shared community-style bathrooms. Non-freshman females reside in Felix DeGrasse Hall, where two students per room share a private bathroom with two other students. Non-freshman male students reside in Thomas Duperou Hall.

Residence Hall entrances are monitored by camera 24/7 by Security staff. Inter-visitation hours are noon to midnight on Sunday through Thursday, and noon to 2 a.m. on Friday and Saturday.

The residence halls provide free telephone, cable, and wireless Internet access. All full-time students are required to live on campus through their junior year, unless exempt by virtue of age, marriage, or local residency. Beginning in fall 2012, all new student athletes are required to live on-campus as long as they receive an athletic scholarship.

The University is a "dry" campus that is also drug-free and tobacco-free. First-time alcohol violations result in both a fine and a four-hour online education course with follow-up. Additional offenses can result in off-campus counseling and possible suspension.

St. Benedict Chapel is located between the halls. Students utilize the chapel for personal and group prayer and choir practice. Groups of students pray the Liturgy of the Hours and Divine Mercy chaplet there.

The main dining area is Bernard Murphy Hall and features an assortment of home cooking, grilled, or made-to-order items, as well as beverages and desserts.

Although Shawnee's crime rate is generally at or above the U.S. average in most categories, the campus is safe, and crimes that do occur are usually petty violations.

Student Activities

The 14 active campus student organizations include two honor societies, one local fraternity and three local sororities with service components and groups such as Students in Free Enterprise (SIFE), Hispanic Awareness Student Association, and a Student Government Association. The Pro-Life Team is very active and has participated in the 40 Days for Life campaign and annual March for Life.

The SIFE club allows students to create business plans and compete nationally. St. Gregory's has traditionally taken home many prizes in the SIFE competition.

Catholic-oriented groups include Kappa Phi Omega, a Catholic-Christian sorority, the Knights of Columbus, and the Pro-Life Team, which partners with the Shawnee chapter of Project Gabriel to help women facing crisis pregnancies.

The hub of student activity on campus is the Patricia Flanagan Rockwood Center, the student union built in 2000. Students can congregate in the common lounge, play pool, eat at the Cyber Café, use the computer lab, gather in a meeting room or the campus ministry lounge, and purchase books and supplies at the student bookstore.

The on-campus Mabee-Gerrer Museum was founded in 1915 and is one of the oldest museums in the state. It contains artifacts from ancient Egypt, Meso-america, Mesopotamia, Greece, Rome, and China, as well as religious art. Items on display include an Egyptian mummy, shrunken heads, and the official portrait of Pope Pius X, painted by Father Gregory Gerrer, O.S.B.

The Performing Arts Center houses a 250-seat theater that is used for plays, speakers, and other special events. St. Gregory's offers majors in dance, theater, and visual arts.

The Mabee Aerobic Center houses a weight room, indoor pool, racquetball courts, and gymnasium that are used by students and the broader Shawnee community.

St. Gregory's is affiliated with the National Association of Intercollegiate Ath-

From the Career Services Office

Career Services are provided by internship experiences related to students areas of study or interest, and in counseling provided by faculty, Campus Ministry, and by visits to potential employers as part of programs in selected fields. Visits by alumni and community leaders as well as service learning programs are also used to inform students about career opportunities. Tests of aptitude and interest are provided. Graduate study opportunities are provided by faculty advisors in their major. General approaches to application for graduate study are also provided.

letics (NAIA) Division I, and the Cavaliers participate as one of the 12 members of the Sooner Athletic Conference in cross country, track, basketball, soccer, baseball, softball, women's golf, volleyball, and cheerleading/dance. More than half of the campus' students are athletes, for whom some partial scholarship money is available.

There are also outreach activities including the annual March for Life in Washington, D.C., each January (approximately 29 students attended in 2011); the Soles for Souls program that provides shoes to victims of natural disasters and underprivileged persons across the world; spring break mission trips; and Habitat for Humanity. Some have helped with hurricane relief in Louisiana. The student life office hosts a yearly Alternative Spring Break trip in which students give up their Spring Break to serve others.

There is also a student and monk community dinner and the Observation Program for University Students (OPUS), through which young men can live in the monastery and experience monastic life firsthand for a semester.

Nearby Oklahoma City has a population of nearly 550,000 and is home to cultural attractions such as museums, a zoo, sports teams, and the Will Rogers World Airport.

The Bottom Line

St. Gregory's University maintains its identity through its relationship with the Abbey, the presence of Benedictine monks, and its commitment to the Catholic and Benedictine tradition. This carries through to the substantial core curriculum for liberal arts students.

The attractive array of majors includes business-related subjects and the scienc-

Letter from the President

Dear parents and prospective students,

St. Gregory's University seeks students from all walks of life who have a desire to bear witness to Christ's love and faith's light. Truth, goodness, beauty, and unity shape our liberal arts curriculum. Our campus community is home to students, educators, and monks dedicated to lifelong learning.

Students from 14 states and 11 countries help to foster a global perspective on human development and social justice issues. In addition, the university provides many opportunities to engage in community service at the local level. Our mission promotes education of the whole person in which students are encouraged to develop a love of learning and to live lives of balance, generosity and integrity.

Mass is celebrated daily in the Abbey Chapel, and students are both welcome and encouraged to participate in the Divine Office. Those seeking to discern a religious vocation are offered retreats and encouragement throughout the process. Our faculty, staff, and monastic community are committed to providing an excellent education and safe harbor for all students.

We invite you to become part of the St. Gregory's Difference!

Sincerely,

Dr. Gregory Main

es, which are not available at the strictly liberal arts colleges. It is not always easy to marry a strong Catholic identity with career-oriented majors, but St. Gregory's seems to be doing a good job of it, especially in recent years.

Not least important, the price may put St. Gregory's high on the list for Catholic students looking for a solid Catholic education, eager to reap what was sown by the Benedictine monks a century and a half ago. And it just keeps getting better.

St. Gregory's University
Frequently Asked Questions

We get questions from Catholic families on a regular basis about the colleges we recommend. Rather than filter the answers, we asked St. Greg's officials nearly 100 questions in categories such as academics, curriculum, programs of study, campus ministry, residence life, student activities, the make up of the study body, and institutional identity. The answers to some of the most asked questions are provided below and the rest are available on the St. Greg's profile page at TheNewmanGuide.com.

Majors

List the major, minor and special program areas that students may choose for specialization while pursuing an undergraduate degree:

Majors include: General Business, Accounting, Finance, Information Systems, Marketing, Management, Dance, English, Secondary English Language Arts Education, History, Liberal Arts, Philosophy, Theatre, Visual Arts, Biology, Biomedical Science, Exercise Science, Fitness and Health Promotion, Secondary Life Science/Biology Education, Mathematics, Mid-Level Mathematics Education, Secondary Math Education, Communications Studies, Criminal Justice, Elementary Education, Political Science, Psychology, Social Science, Secondary Social Studies Education, Theology, and Pastoral Ministry.

Minors include: Business Administration, Theatre, Visual Arts, Theology, and Political Science.

What are the three most popular majors or specialty disciplines for undergraduate students, and about what percentage of undergraduate students specialize in these disciplines?

Life sciences, 26%

Behavioral sciences, 22%

Business, 18%

Spiritual Life

Please list the schedule of Masses, noting the following for each Mass: the day and time, the Form or Rite of the Mass, and the style of music, if any (chant, traditional, contemporary, etc.):

Mo 5:00 p.m., English Ordinary Form, chant

Tu 5:00 p.m., English Ordinary Form, chant

We 5:00 p.m. and 9:00 p.m., English Ordinary Form, chant

Th 5:00 p.m., English Ordinary Form, chant

Fr 5:00 p.m., English Ordinary Form, chant

Sa 8:00 a.m., English Ordinary Form, chant

Su 10:00 a.m. and 9:00 p.m., English Ordinary Form, chant

List the schedule for Confession by day and time:

Mo

Tu

We 8:15 - 8:45 p.m.

Th

Fr 4:00 - 4:45 p.m.

Sa

Su 8:15 - 8:45 p.m.

List the schedule for Adoration of the Blessed Sacrament by day and time:

Thursday 9:00-10:00 p.m.

Please identify regularly scheduled devotions on campus for students such as the Rosary and prayer groups:

Regularly scheduled devotions on campus include: Adoration of the Blessed Sacrament, Divine Office, Novenas, Rosary, and Stations of the Cross.

Residence Life

Please describe options for students to reside on and off campus:

All full-time enrolled undergraduate students are required to live on campus unless:

- Beginning in the Fall 2013 semester, all new (first-time, transfers, and any student who left SGU and returned after a semester) students are required to live on-campus for the first year of attendance at SGU. Following the first year, students must meet one of the provisions listed below in order to be approved to live off-campus. Exceptions to this requirement may be made at the discretion of the Dean of Students on a case-by-case basis.

- For the entire period in question, the student will continue to live with his/her parents or court appointed legal guardian(s) in the family home where the street address of the home is no more than twenty (20) miles from campus.

- The student is twenty three (23) years of age or older at the time of admittance to the University or if the student turns 23 before degree completion.

- The student is married. Students with plans to marry during the time they are required to live on campus will be required to live on-campus up to the date of the wedding.

- The student is the legal custodial parent or court appointed custodial guardian of a minor, child or children.

- The student is registered with the Student Disability Services program with a documented disability, and is able to provide appropriate documentation to verify the need for a reasonable accommodation in the student residence facility that the University is not able to provide. Students who would like to submit a request for approval to live off-campus consistent with the circumstances listed above should submit a request to the Dean of Students.

- The student obtains senior status, in good academic standing, and is the age of twenty one (21) before the first day of classes for the semester in question. (Note that students applying under this exception must meet ALL criteria listed above.)

Does your institution offer only single-sex residence halls?

Yes.

Are students of the opposite sex permitted to visit students' bedrooms?

Yes. Noon to midnight Sunday - Thursday and noon to 2:00 a.m. Friday and Saturday.

How does your institution foster sobriety and respond to substance abuse on campus, particularly in campus residences?

The University encourages students to abstain from alcohol and other drugs. If students choose to consume alcohol, they should do so responsibly, legally, and not while present on University property. Reporting Alcohol and Drug Related\Other Emergencies: Residents should never hesitate to seek help for their peers' personal welfare in drug or alcohol or other emergencies by contacting the Dean of Students at any time.

Alcohol: Presence of Alcohol (including low point beer) and Consumption
§ On-campus use, consumption, possession, sale, distribution, or the serving of alcoholic beverages is prohibited, no matter the age of the participants.
§ Exceptions to this policy include special events in which faculty and staff are present, all applicable federal, state and local laws are followed, and signed approval has been given in advance by the President.

Alcohol: Drinking Games
§ The presence, possession or use of any bulk or common container of alcohol (i.e., kegs, beer balls, etc.) or any device or activity (i.e., beer bong, beer pong, etc.) used to consume alcohol in a dangerous or unhealthy manner (i.e., competitive drinking games, beer pong, flip cup, etc.), or excessive amounts of alcohol in any residence hall is prohibited, no matter the age of the participants.

Alcohol: Mass Consumption Device
§ The presence, possession or use of any bulk or common container of alcohol (i.e., kegs, beer balls, etc.) or any device or activity (i.e., beer bong, beer pong, etc.) used to consume alcohol in a dangerous or unhealthy manner, or excessive amounts of alcohol in any residence hall is prohibited, no matter the age of the participants.

Alcohol: Public Display
§ Alcohol displays of any kind (posters, lights, signs, etc.) are not permitted in windows or corridors of any residence hall.

Alcohol: Public Intoxication
§ Public intoxication is not permitted, regardless of the age of the individual.

Alcohol: Alcohol and Drug Posters in Student Room
§ No posters, throw rugs, furniture or displays of any kind that advertise alcohol are permitted anywhere in the residence halls.

Alcohol: Policy for Guests to Campus
§ Guests and visitors may not use, consume, possess, sale, distribute, or serve alcoholic beverages, no matter the age of the participants.
§ Guests who are visitors of resident students who violate University policies on alcohol will be removed from campus; a Residence Life official will determine when the visitor can return.
§ The University may contact parents or police in incidents where guests are found violating University policies on alcohol.

How does your institution foster a student living environment that promotes and supports chastity, particularly in campus residences?

Visitation violation results in a follow-up meeting with staff and with the campus chaplain if necessary.

Student Body

Describe the makeup of your institution's undergraduate student body with regard to sex, religion, home state/country and type of high school (public, private, homeschool):

Total number of undergraduates: 350
Male: 48% Female: 52%

Catholic: 50% Other Christian: 20%
Jewish: % Muslim: % Other: 30%

Number of states represented: 17
Top three states: Oklahoma, Texas, Arkansas
Students from top three states: 75%

Catholic HS: 15% Homeschool: 5%
Private HS: 10% Public HS: 70%

THOMAS AQUINAS COLLEGE

Santa Paula, California

411

For more information on TAC, visit their website at:

www.ThomasAquinas.edu

Admissions contact:

800/634-9797
admissions@ThomasAquinas.edu

Overview

Founded in 1971, Thomas Aquinas College (TAC) was the first in a wave of new Catholic colleges born from the crisis of Catholic identity in American Catholic higher education. Although TAC's success has encouraged the emergence of other faithful Catholic colleges, including some that share its emphasis on the Great Books, TAC still has the distinction of being the only Catholic college in America that teaches exclusively from these classic works of Western civilization.

Located six miles from the small town of Santa Paula, CA, about an hour northwest of Los Angeles, TAC is fully committed to its Catholic identity, its Great Books approach, and a discussion-style class format utilizing Socratic dialogue. The College has no departments, no majors, no textbooks, and no lectures. All graduates progress through the same curriculum and receive the same degree: a Bachelor of Arts in Liberal Arts, with roughly the equivalent of a double major in theology and philosophy, and a minor in mathematics.

Despite its small size, the College has

been lauded in both secular and Catholic rankings. Its national student body comes from 42 states and several countries, and 40 percent of its alumni go on to graduate and professional schools. The College has no desire to expand beyond about 350 students. About five percent of the students already come with bachelor's degrees from other institutions, but they are attracted to the unique Great Books education.

TAC was founded by lay Catholics and continues to be led by a lay board of governors. Dr. Michael McLean was appointed president in October 2009, after 31 years on the faculty. Over the years he has served as tutor, assistant dean of student affairs, vice president for development, and academic dean.

"The Catholicity is manifested in the curriculum, the choice of texts, the study of St. Thomas, and the strong devotional life here," says President McLean. The College also believes it important to reject taxpayer support and regulations and therefore does not accept direct government funding. "Every seriously Catholic college trying to maintain its fidelity to the Church has to be vigilant about threats from the contemporary culture and government," explains Dr. McLean.

Tuition, room and board, and books cost students $32,450 in 2012-2013, well below the average for private colleges in California. The College's students participate in federal and state aid programs, and generous financial aid packages are available.

Academics

The Great Books curriculum remains largely unchanged since TAC's founding and is structured around six disciplines: literature, language, mathematics, laboratory, philosophy, and theology. Many of the traditional classical writers are represented, including Plato, Aristotle,

Quick Facts
2013-2014 Academic Year

Students 370

SATs 1280

HS GPA 3.8

Majors 1

% Catholic 98%

How Much? $32,450
tuition, room and board

Descartes, Galileo, Shakespeare, Newton, Tolstoy, Dostoyevski, Einstein, the Federalist Papers, and the debates of Lincoln and Douglas in 1858.

Students read a significant amount of Saint Thomas Aquinas, and in the senior year, they study four landmark papal encyclicals of St. Pius X, Leo XII, Pius XI, and Pius XII.

"We take the teaching authority of the Church very seriously," says Dr. McLean. "We pursue a single academic curriculum in a chronological order. It's done with a distinct ordination to Catholic philosophy and theology, and the study of St. Thomas Aquinas' philosophical and theological works, in obedience to the urging of the Magisterium."

The program is straightforward: All students take required classes each year. There are no electives and no classes that provide "vocational" training. No transfers are accepted, and there are no study-abroad programs to distract from the College's focus.

The circumscribed curriculum causes pre-medical students to need additional coursework before attending medical school. However, any student interested in a broad educational focus can thrive.

The rigor in mathematics and laboratory science is unusual for most liberal arts institutions, with four years required in both subjects. It is one reason TAC tends not to describe itself as a liberal arts college, but rather one that offers a "liberal" or "classical" education.

Freshmen, sophomores, and juniors participate in biannual evaluations with professors in a process known as the "Don Rags," named after a similar system used by Oxford University "dons" or professors. Grades mostly come from class participation.

For non-students the dean's office pub-

lishes a journal, the Aquinas Review, "in the hope of maintaining and enlarging a community of learners that extends beyond the confines" of the TAC campus.

The College has an impressive faculty of "tutors": well-rounded academics who engage students in Socratic dialogue in small classes and must be able to teach in the array of disciplines. The curriculum and the faculty's wide familiarity with it promote a degree of commonality.

New tutors make the Profession of Faith and take the Oath of Fidelity at the College's convocation ceremony. Of 37 teaching faculty, only one is non-Catholic and is exempted from teaching theology. Tutors who teach theology have the *mandatum*.

St. Bernardine of Siena Library houses approximately 70,000 books and includes a humidity-controlled Rare Books Room that features works such as an illuminated Book of Hours (circa 1480), rare Hittite seals (circa 1200 B.C.), religious and decorative carvings in ivory, and pages from early manuscripts of the Bible dating from 1121.

At classes, Mass, weekday meals, and formal events, modesty is emphasized in the dress code. This means slacks, collared shirts, and closed shoes for men and dresses or skirts and tops for women.

To help give prospective students a preview of academic life at TAC, the College runs an annual two-week summer program for rising high school seniors. They are exposed to classmates and tutors in small seminars where they study the Bible, Sophocles, Plato, Kierkegaard, Shakespeare, Euclid, Pascal, and Boethius, and participate in the spiritual life. About half the attendees subsequently enroll as undergraduates.

The TAC environment is stimulating but not intimidating. It is intellectual, yet

Financial Aid Office Info

Thomas Aquinas College is committed to making its unique program of Catholic liberal education available to accepted students, regardless of their financial need. Through the generosity of its donors, the College is able to offer financial assistance to young men and women who would otherwise not be able to attend.

Thomas Aquinas College realizes that in these challenging economic times some families have experienced a dramatic reduction in income and/or assets. The College stands ready and willing to help students and families with their demonstrated financial need as determined by the financial aid application.

We encourage all families who feel they are unable to manage the full cost of tuition, room and board to apply for aid. Visit our website for application materials: www.thomasaquinas.edu/admission/financial-aid.

Sources of financial assistance include Pell Grants, California State Grants, local and national scholarships, Stafford Student Loans, Canada Student Loans, and Veterans Administration benefits. Loan debt is kept to a minimum, with average student loan indebtedness only $16,000 after four years. The College also has its own generous aid program that provides need-based Service Scholarships (work-study) and tuition grants.

So apply for financial aid and let us show you how we can help! Contact: Greg Becher, 800-634-9797, ext. 5936, finaid@thomasaquinas.edu.

relaxed and personal as well. Most of the tutors and chaplains eat lunch with the students.

Spiritual Life

There are four Masses celebrated daily by four non-teaching chaplains: a Dominican, a Jesuit, a Norbertine, and a diocesan priest. There are also two Masses on Saturdays and three on Sundays. The Masses are enhanced by student

participation in a choir that also presents concerts, and by a Gregorian chant ensemble. The Sacrament of Reconciliation is available before and after each Mass. The first Mass of each day is offered in the Extraordinary Form; the others are in Latin in the Ordinary Form.

The $23 million Chapel of Our Lady of the Most Holy Trinity was dedicated in 2009. The Romanesque-style chapel includes a 135-foot bell tower. It also has an eight-foot statue of Our Lady as the Woman of the Apocalypse on top and a limestone cornerstone blessed by Pope Benedict XVI in St. Peter's Square.

The chapel is the result of 12 years of hard effort by the late President Thomas Dillon, who died in a car crash just weeks after it was dedicated. He attended to every detail of the planning and construction and visited artists' workshops throughout Europe.

This new chapel enhances an already vibrant spiritual program. Adoration occurs every First Friday, beginning after the 5 p.m. Thursday Mass and continuing until the Friday 5 p.m. Mass. A daily Holy Hour and Benediction take place at 5:30 p.m. The Rosary is recited and evening prayer generally occurs each night before curfew begins in the residence halls.

A Legion of Mary group leads campus processions and evangelizes door-to-door in town encouraging people to attend Mass.

About 11 percent of TAC alumni have entered religious life, including 59 graduates ordained to the priesthood and 40 professed religious. At least 10 TAC graduates are monks at Clear Creek Monastery in Oklahoma. Others have entered the Norbertines, the Legionaries of Christ, the Archdiocese of Denver, and the Diocese of Lincoln, Nebraska. One is the Superior General of the Priestly Fraternity of St. Peter.

Residential Life

TAC students are housed in six residence halls, three for men and three for women. Each room accommodates two students. There is no visitation at any time in opposite-sex residences. Men and women can gather anywhere else on campus, including St. Joseph Commons, the oldest building and the hub for student activity that houses the cafeteria, a coffee shop, and a game room.

There is an occasional movie night, but there is only one television set on campus, in the chaplain's residence. Chastity is encouraged. Drinking and drugs are no problem at TAC, although there appear to be a number of students who smoke cigarettes.

There is a curfew on weeknights and a later one on weekends. Students who violate curfew either receive an hour of service or they are confined to campus.

A small bookstore on campus carries predominantly Great Books and an assortment of titles by Pope Benedict XVI.

For routine medical attention, the College has a part-time nurse and a medical health specialist. Ten minutes from campus is Santa Paula Hospital, a 49-bed facility, and there are three medical centers within a 20-minute drive.

Student Activities

The academic program is the primary focus of the college, so there are no official student clubs.

"Because the program here is so academically demanding, student activities differ from other colleges," said Steve Cain, assistant dean for student affairs. "Dances, music, sports events rise from the students."

Student-led activities include the journal Demiurgus, study groups for four languages, three dramatic groups,

From the Career Services Office

The administration and faculty of Thomas Aquinas College take an active interest in our student's future. There is a cooperative effort to assist students in choosing a career, in gaining admission to graduate and professional schools, and in securing interviews and opportunities for employment.

The College's Career Center has a library of graduate and professional school information to help in the process. A Career Counselor provides one-on-one counseling with students in their employment and graduate school searches, and arranges career talks and recruiting sessions throughout the year for students to learn about opportunities in various professions. There is also a vibrant network of alumni to whom students can turn for mentoring and counseling as they make their future plans. In addition, chaplains schedule discernment evenings for men and women throughout the year for those considering a vocation to the priesthood or religious life.

various choral and instrumental groups, Schubertiade recitals, the Bushwhackers hiking club, and other informal activities.

The College has an active pro-life group, TACers for Life. The group prays at an abortion business in Ventura. About two-thirds of the student body attends the Walk for Life West Coast in San Francisco each January.

TAC has no formal athletic teams. Rather, the activities director schedules intramural events in softball, soccer, basketball, ultimate Frisbee, volleyball, rugby, or flag football. In the men's residence halls, students put down mats for boxing and wrestling matches.

Surfers take advantage of the beach (approximately 30 minutes away), and hikers take advantage of the surrounding Los Padres National Forest. A Bushwhackers student group maintains and cleans the trails.

There are also non-curriculum book discussions, a Wednesday dance group, and four formal dances per year.

Students have other social service opportunities as well. An annual food drive takes place at Christmas, and there are frequent blood drives on campus. Some students participate in prison ministry; others have volunteered for Santa Paula's annual Clean Up Day.

The college is located six miles from Santa Paula, which has about 29,500 people. The town's stores, restaurants and activities often reflect the primarily Hispanic population.

The Bottom Line

Thomas Aquinas College stands alone as the only Catholic college that exclusive-

Letter from the President

Dear Parents and Prospective Students:

Thomas Aquinas College is unique among American colleges and universities. We hold with confidence that the human mind is capable of knowing the truth about reality, that living according to the truth is necessary for happiness, and that truth is best comprehended through the harmonious work of faith and reason. We understand the intellectual virtues to be essential to the life of reason, and we consider the cultivation of those virtues to be the primary work of student and teacher.

The College offers a single academic program: an integrated, non-elective curriculum rooted in the Western, Catholic intellectual tradition. The greatest books in that tradition, both ancient and modern, replace textbooks; careful inquiry in small tutorials, seminars, and laboratories replaces lectures. The curriculum challenges students and faculty alike to disciplined scholarship in the arts and sciences — indispensable for critical judgment and genuine wisdom.

Thomas Aquinas College also provides a strong Catholic liturgical and sacramental environment conducive to spiritual growth while its rules of residence support the good moral order appropriate for those engaged in the pursuit of truth.

Please visit our website at www.thomasaquinas.edu to learn more about our uniue program of genuine Catholic liberal education.

Sincerely yours,

M. McLean

Michael F. McLean, Ph.D.

ly teaches from the Great Books, with an impressive intellectual rigor that is matched by a commitment to orthodox Catholicism.

There is a certain sense of ongoing immersion in a special adventure at TAC that can last a lifetime—and beyond. "We work hard to attract the right kind of students… who have the intellectual capacity and the willingness to work hard," explains President McLean. "They don't have to be geniuses, but they do

need to have a serious interest in reading and discussing Great Books."

That type of student may not be typical, but for anyone who thinks they have what it takes, a TAC education has much to offer. And TAC's graduates have much to offer the Church and future employers who value critical thinking, analytical reasoning, strong communications skills, and an ethical sense.

Thomas Aquinas College
Frequently Asked Questions

We get questions from Catholic families on a regular basis about the colleges we recommend. Rather than filter the answers, we asked TAC officials nearly 100 questions in categories such as academics, curriculum, programs of study, campus ministry, residence life, student activities, the make up of the study body, and institutional identity. The answers to some of the most asked questions are provided below and the rest are available on the TAC profile page at TheNewmanGuide.com.

Majors

List the major, minor and special program areas that students may choose for specialization while pursuing an undergraduate degree:

We offer only one, fully-integrated curriculum in classical liberal arts. Graduates from our program find themselves well-equipped for a wide variety of pursuits including law, medicine, business, journalism, military service, architecture, education, public policy.

What are the three most popular majors or specialty disciplines for undergraduate students, and about what percentage of undergraduate students specialize in these disciplines?

Liberal arts, 100%

Spiritual Life

Please list the schedule of Masses, noting the following for each Mass: the day and time, the Form or Rite of the Mass, and the style of music, if any (chant, traditional, contemporary, etc.):

Mo 7:00 a.m, 11:30 a.m., 5:00 p.m., 10:00 p.m.

Tu 7:00 a.m, 11:30 a.m., 5:00 p.m., 10:00 p.m.

We 7:00 a.m, 11:30 a.m., 5:00 p.m., 10:00 p.m.

Th 7:00 a.m, 11:30 a.m., 5:00 p.m., 10:00 p.m.

Fr 7:15 a.m., 11:30 a.m., 5:00 p.m.

Sa 7:15 a.m., 11:30 a.m.

Su 7:15 a.m., 9:00 a.m., 11:30 a.m.

The first Mass of each day is offered in the Extraordinary Form; all others are said in the Ordinary Form in Latin and English.

List the schedule for Confession by day and time:

Mo Before and after each of the 4 Masses offered each day

Tu Before and after each of the 4 Masses offered each day

We Before and after each of the 4 Masses offered each day

Th Before and after each of the 4 Masses offered each day

Fr Before and after each of the 4 Masses offered each day

Sa Before and after each of the 4 Masses offered each day

Su Before and after each of the 4 Masses offered each day

Other: Whenever one would like, by appointment with a chaplain.

List the schedule for Adoration of the Blessed Sacrament by day and time:

Monday thru Friday 5:30-6:30 p.m.

Saturday 12:30-2:00 p.m.

Sunday 12:30- 2:00 p.m.

On the eve of First Fridays there is all-night Adoration beginning at 5:30 p.m. Thursday and ending at 5:00 p.m. Friday.

Please identify regularly scheduled devotions on campus for students such as the Rosary and prayer groups:

Rosary daily in the Chapel and in the residence halls; Chaplet of Divine Mercy; Compline; Consecration to the Sacred Heart nightly in residence halls; processions as feast days occur.

Residence Life

Please describe options for students to reside on and off campus:

Students are expected to live on campus unless there is some compelling reason for them not to (e.g., being married, having health issues, or having strong financial need). Any request to live off-campus must be approved by the Dean. Our education is one for life, and we expect the pursuit of wisdom to continue from the classroom into the dining hall, the library, the residence halls. Also, our unique program depends on the development of friendships based on this common pursuit, and friendship requires time spent together. Hence, not living on campus results in a diminished experience of the college.

Does your institution offer only single-sex residence halls?

Yes.

Are students of the opposite sex permitted to visit students' bedrooms?

No.

How does your institution foster sobriety and respond to substance abuse on campus, particularly in campus residences?

Our rules regarding alcohol are stricter than one finds at most institutions: Only at college-sponsored formal dinners and similar social occasions can those over the age of 21 consume alcohol. At all other times students of all ages may not consume alcohol on campus. This rule is well respected; when broken, it normally results in expulsion from the College. The campus atmosphere is more dignified for having this rule in place.

How does your institution foster a student living environment that promotes and supports chastity, particularly in campus residences?

Primarily by having separate residence halls for men and women, with no visitation at any time. In addition, we foster a vibrant spiritual life in a community of friendship that promotes self-control and a sense of dignity and respect among the students.

Student Body

Describe the makeup of your institution's undergraduate student body with regard to sex, religion, home state/country and type of high school (public, private, homeschool):

Total number of undergraduates: 358
Male: 49% Female: 51%

Catholic: 98% Other Christian: 1%
Jewish 0% Muslim 0% Other 0%

Number of states represented: 38
Top three states: CA, MI, OH
Students from top three states: 47%

Catholic HS: 35% Homeschool: 49%
Private HS: 6% Public HS: 10%

THOMAS MORE COLLEGE OF LIBERAL ARTS

Merrimack, New Hampshire

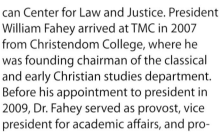

Overview

The traditional charm of most New England colleges, including some of America's oldest universities, has been largely replaced by state-of-the-art buildings, research facilities, and sports complexes. But on a colonial-era farm in Merrimack, New Hampshire, Thomas More College of Liberal Arts (TMC) has preserved both the charm and the essence of traditional American higher education, when thoughtful students studied literature and philosophy beneath the canopy of great maple trees.

TMC's students study Western civilization and Christianity, with an emphasis on the Great Books. The College offers one degree for all students in the liberal arts, with an integrated, four-year core curriculum. Although students come from many states and have beengrowing in number, presently TMC's enrollment is fewer than 100 students.

While the College may seem tiny and quaint to some, for the students and faculty at TMC it represents a much-needed revival of education. Like many of The Newman Guide colleges, this is a post-Vatican II institution, founded by and for Catholic laity in 1978. Its emphasis on student internships and cultural leadership blend with the art and music program, which is designed to imitate medieval guild apprenticeships, and a mandatory Rome semester.

While the trustees and employees of the College all pledge fidelity to the Catholic Faith, the College emphasizes that non-Catholic students are welcome. Accordingly, about 10 to 20 percent of freshmen are not Catholic in any given year.

The college is governed by a 12-member lay board, which includes retired Notre Dame Law professor Charles Rice and attorney Patrick Monaghan of the American Center for Law and Justice. President William Fahey arrived at TMC in 2007 from Christendom College, where he was founding chairman of the classical and early Christian studies department. Before his appointment to president in 2009, Dr. Fahey served as provost, vice president for academic affairs, and professor of humanities.

TMC has a collaborative partnership with Holy Spirit College in Atlanta, Georgia, to operate Sophia Institute Press and the online Crisis Magazine and Catholic Exchange. Dr. Fahey oversees the day-to-day operations and serves as publisher. The College also publishes a semiannual periodical, Second Spring: An International Journal of Faith and Culture.

Currently TMC is located in the New England town of Merrimack, which has about 27,000 residents and is within easy access to Manchester and Nashua. Boston is about 50 miles away. But the College plans to build a new campus closer to Boston in Groton, Massachusetts, and has plans to grow to about 300 undergraduate students with a graduate program in Merrimack.

At $29,200 for tuition, room, and board, costs are well below the average for private colleges in pricey New Hamp-

Quick Facts

2013-2014 Academic Year

Students 92		Majors 1
SATs 1200		% Catholic 87%
HS GPA 3.75		How Much? $29,200
		tuition, room and board

shire. TMC has enhanced its financial aid programs for students, including a scholarship established by the late journalist Robert Novak for underprivileged youth from the District of Columbia and Baltimore.

Academics

TMC's academic program has a number of specific goals, selected as the marks of an educated Catholic. Examples include the ability to read Latin or Greek proficiently; to recognize pattern, harmony, symmetry, and order in works of nature and art; to explain what is meant by happiness and the common good; and to recognize, articulate and defend the deposit of the Faith, drawn from Sacred Scripture and Tradition.

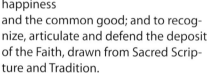

All students take a common humanities core sequenced by year, starting with the Greeks and moving through the Moderns over four years. Also in 2012 TMC added a new course called Traditio, team-taught by Dr. Fahey and British author Joseph Pearce, who has joined the faculty as writer-in-residence. All students of the College meet to discuss texts in common, and the Traditio sequence revolves around great themes such as faith, sacrifice, friendship, pilgrimage, or war and peace.

The core has several other unique aspects. Students take a substantial six semesters of theology and Scripture. In addition to four semesters of Latin or Greek, students learn to communicate according to the principles of classical rhetoric in the three-semester writing tutorial. Students get a healthy dose of mathematics, science, and philosophy.

The curriculum includes a unique emphasis on arts and music, including the "way of beauty" courses in the first year, which introduce students to the philosophical and theological notions

of beauty. All students learn chant and polyphony, including chanting the psalms in the Liturgy of the Hours. They also study the principles of order and harmony in Euclidean geometry, and how it was used in traditional Catholic art and architecture.

The upperclassman core includes a tutorial program. Juniors and seniors work with their classmates and the professors (at TMC called Fellows) to create unique tutorials in areas of interest, which change from semester to semester. In the junior year, the areas of concentration can be particular authors, philosophers, works of literature, theological teachings, etc., culminating in an oral examination. Seniors concentrate in particular disciplines and complete a thesis, which is publicly presented and defended, before graduating.

All full-time sophomores study in Rome for one semester, residing at an historic villa with the Maronite Catholic monks of Saint Anthony Monastery, five miles from St. Peter's Basilica. Students take a full course load and travel throughout the city and to other cities, like Assisi and Siena, as well. Students can also study in England for three weeks at Downside Abbey and Oxford.

TMC supports several internship programs in specific fields including journalism, law, or finance. In Rome, the Vatican Studies Center helps students work temporarily for news agencies including Vatican Radio, Zenit, H2O News, and Aletheia News. Dr. Pearce also teaches a variety of small tutorials and works with students who aspire to be writers.

Students are expected to abide by a code of honor and, with every exam or assignment, pledge that work is their own. Trusting in the honesty of students, Fellows at TMC usually do not proctor exams.

Financial Aid Office Info

The Thomas More College of Liberal Arts offers one of the lowest tuition rates among our peer institutions—and among most private and state schools throughout the country. It is our goal to provide you with an affordable, high-quality education that does not burden you with a lifetime of debt. (Thomas More College alumni have been rated as carrying some of the lowest levels of debt amongst our regional peers.)

We help to reduce your tuition rates even further through various scholarship opportunities, including:

The St. Francis Fund offers scholarships to students based on their demonstrated need for aid.

The St. Thomas More Fund offers scholarship funding based on high test scores, exceptional involvement in the community, and a commitment to learning.

The Faith & Reason Scholarship Essay Contest annually awards over $100,000 in scholarship assistance. Visit www.ThomasMoreCollege.edu for more details.

The St. John Vianney and St. Katharine Drexel Funds provide students who are called to religious life with the opportunity to have any unpaid educational loans absorbed by Thomas More College upon entering a seminary or convent.

Spiritual Life

Three Benedictine monks and two diocesan priests offer daily Mass and confession throughout the week. One Monsignor and several Maronite monks serve the students in Rome.

Thomas More College is consecrated to the Sacred Heart of Jesus every year at Mass. Part-time chaplains celebrate daily Mass, including an Extraordinary Form Mass on Fridays, in a small chapel on campus. The chapel is filled with icons and sacred art produced by the College's artist-in-residence David Clayton.

Typically, about 50 percent of the

students and faculty attend daily Mass. A student schola leads English and Latin chant.

Students also can attend Extraordinary Form Masses on Saturday and Sunday at the local parish, or a Byzantine Catholic Mass at the nearby Melkite Rite church.

Confession is available daily as well as by appointment. Students chant morning prayer (lauds) and evening prayer (vespers) each day. There are also Divine Mercy devotions, nightly recitation of the Rosary, exposition of the Blessed Sacrament, and voluntary retreats for men and women each semester.

Every day since the founding of the College, students have been found reciting the Rosary in the chapel or at the outdoor Marian shrine. They also have access to two local parishes in Merrimack, St. Joseph Cathedral of the Diocese of Manchester is 20 minutes away, and the traditional community of the St. Benedict Center is within a short drive.

The College has two funds to support vocations and absorb student loans accumulated by graduates who are entering a seminary or convent: the Saint John Vianney Fund for future priests and the Saint Mother Katherine Drexel Fund for future nuns.

Residential Life

Thomas More's campus is primarily residential, with 95 percent of the students on campus. There are two residence halls, Kopka Hall for women and Stillman House for men.

Students are not allowed into the residences of the opposite sex. Chastity is encouraged by teaching the Theology of the Body, chastity talks, and peer monitoring. There is a curfew, and students may not leave campus without permission. Alcohol is never permitted except on special occasions monitored by the College.

One student commented that by living on campus, students get to know each other very well. "It's almost like a family. You know 80 people very well. We go to class together, we pray together, and meals are communal."

There are local dinner events in which students sometimes dine with faculty and their families. Typically there is a dinner address by a visiting guest or Fellow of the College.

Crime in Merrimack is very low and as such, it has been recognized as one of the safest small towns in the United States. Students have access to three regional hospitals, each about 10 minutes away.

Student Activities

There is time for informal relaxation, and the Student Social Council meets every week to help direct social functions. Social events include excursions to outdoor locales and to cities such as nearby Nashua and Manchester, as well as Boston. Winters provide opportunities for skiing. There are many hiking options in the mountainous state, and the College's proximity to the sea encourages sailing or whale watching.

TMC's Catholic guilds enable students to gain skills and experience from master craftsmen in areas such as sacred art, music, theater and homesteading. These guilds take their spirit from the associations of men and women who advanced their trades and responded to the needs of their local communities in the Medieval Age. Artist-in-residence David Clayton teaches students to "write" (i.e. paint) sacred icons and composer-in- residence

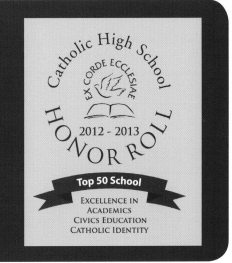

Paul Jernberg teaches the principles and practice of sacred music.

The College has a newspaper, The Smoker's Porch, St. Cecilia's choir and a schola cantorum. In addition, students have access to the Merrimack YMCA next to the college. Students pray in front of an abortion facility and attend the March for Life in Washington, D.C.

The director of student life organizes events including formal banquets and dances, movie nights, talent shows, bonfires, and campus-wide games. TMC also sponsors field trips each weekend to nearby locations such as Boston, the White Mountains, the beaches of Maine, Robert Frost's Farm, and various museums.

All students perform service on campus, including working in the dining hall, participating in snow removal, and assisting with security.

The Bottom Line

The Thomas More College of Liberal Arts provides a rigorous, classical education. Alumni have told us that the College offered a liberating experience that was refreshing and sometimes surprising.

There are several unique aspects of the College, including its humanities sequence, "way of beauty" courses, and traditional spiritual life. In its more than 30 years of existence, the College has lived up to its founders' desire to preserve traditional liberal arts education.

Thomas More College has long emphasized its intellectual offerings and has strengthened its already notable Catholic identity. For students seeking an enriching intellectual experience, TMC has much to offer.

Letter from the President

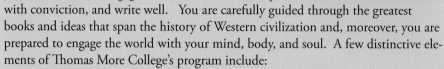

Dear Parents and Prospective Students,

A leading national report recently ranked the Thomas More College of Liberal Arts among the top 2 percent of all colleges and universities nationwide in educational quality. Why?

Because the education at Thomas More genuinely teaches you how to reason, engage in academic discourse, speak with conviction, and write well. You are carefully guided through the greatest books and ideas that span the history of Western civilization and, moreover, you are prepared to engage the world with your mind, body, and soul. A few distinctive elements of Thomas More College's program include:

• No dreary textbooks: You will read the great authors themselves in their original works.

• Experiencing centers of culture: You begin in New England, the birthplace of our country, and then travel to Rome—the living heart of our civilization. Scholarships allow interested students to study British history and literature in Oxford, and teaching internships exclusive to TMC students are available in Spain, Ireland and Poland.

• Ideas in Action: The wisdom of the classroom comes alive in extra-curricular activities such as naturalistic drawing, music, woodworking, icon-painting, life-changing internships, as well as journalism internships with Sophia Institute Press, Vatican Radio, and Aletheia News.

• Creative Focus: Upper-level tutorials enable you and your faculty to partner in the creation of a course of study tailored to your academic interests.

• Catholic: Most importantly, your entire program is joyfully undertaken in a Catholic community, committed to Truth, both natural and revealed.

All of this is offered at one of the lowest tuition rates in the country. I invite you to visit our web site and learn more about Thomas More College. We would be delighted to have you join us in New England.

In Christo Rege,

William Edmund Fahey

William Edmund Fahey, Ph.D.

Thomas More College of Liberal Arts Frequently Asked Questions

We get questions from Catholic families on a regular basis about the colleges we recommend. Rather than filter the answers, we asked Thomas More officials nearly 100 questions in categories such as academics, curriculum, programs of study, campus ministry, residence life, student activities, the make up of the study body, and institutional identity. The answers to some of the most asked questions are provided below and the rest are available on the college profile page at TheNewmanGuide.com.

Majors

List the major, minor and special program areas that students may choose for specialization while pursuing an undergraduate degree:

Thomas More College has a single program of studies for all students, with concentration possible through the upper division tutorial system. (See more on the Thomas More profile page at TheNewmanGuide.com.)

What are the three most popular majors or specialty disciplines for undergraduate students, and about what percentage of undergraduate students specialize in these disciplines?

N/A

Spiritual Life

Please list the schedule of Masses, noting the following for each Mass: the day and time, the Form or Rite of the Mass, and the style of music, if any (chant, traditional, contemporary, etc.):

Mo 11:30 a.m. Latin (Ordinary Form) with chant.

Tu 11:30 a.m. English, without music

We 11:30 a.m. English with Latin chant

Th 11:30 a.m. Latin (Ordinary Form) with Latin chant

Fr 11:30 a.m. Extraordinary Form (Low Mass)

Sa at local parish (Extraordinary and Ordinary Forms)

Su at local parish (Extraordinary and Ordinary Forms)

List the schedule for Confession by day and time:

Mo 11:00 a.m.

Tu 11:00 a.m.

We 11:00 a.m.

Th 11:00 a.m.

Fr 11:00 a.m.

Sa at local parish 30 min prior to mass

Su at local parish 30 min prior to mass

Other: as scheduled personally.

List the schedule for Adoration of the Blessed Sacrament by day and time:

Friday 11:30 a.m. to 3:00 p.m.

Please identify regularly scheduled devotions on campus for students such as the Rosary and prayer groups:

Lauds and Vespers Monday through Friday, Rosary and Compline daily.

Residence Life

Please describe options for students to reside on and off campus:

95% of our students live on campus in one of our two single-sex dormitories, either in New Hampshire or in Rome.

Does your institution offer only single-sex residence halls?

Yes.

Are students of the opposite sex permitted to visit students' bedrooms?

No.

How does your institution foster sobriety and respond to substance abuse on campus, particularly in campus residences?

No alcohol is permitted in the dormitories, however, the College does allow students of age to have a glass of wine or beer during dinners on observed feast days and at College celebrations such as the birthday of St. Thomas More. Alcohol is treated and understood as a created good, which is open to abuse but may be properly enjoyed in moderation under specific conditions. The College has experienced no abuse of drugs or alcohol over the recent years. These difficulties common on larger campuses do not seem prevalent at Thomas More College.

How does your institution foster a student living environment that promotes and supports chastity, particularly in campus residences?

Formal talks on chastity are given during orientation. The students discuss human sexuality within the context of marriage during certain courses in the curriculum. The residential life staff upholds the College rules, which sets the goodness of chastity before the students as a Christian norm expected of Catholic undergraduates.

Talks are given in both semesters for men and women separately on chastity or the theology of the body. The student code and custom encourage exclusive dating only after the first two years. There is a Dean of Men and a Dean of Women who assist the Residence Life Staff in creating a simple, but authentic "culture of life" atmosphere in the halls of residence. The College is not aware of any violations.

Student Body

Describe the makeup of your institution's undergraduate student body with regard to sex, religion, home state/country and type of high school (public, private, homeschool):

Total number of undergraduates: 92
Male: 50%   Female: 50%

Catholic: 85-90%   Other Christian: 10-15%
Jewish: %   Muslim: %   Other: Less than 5%

Number of states represented: 36
Top three states: MA, PA, NY
Students from top three states: 25%

Catholic HS: 30%   Homeschool: 25%
Private HS: 30%   Public HS: 15%

UNIVERSITY OF DALLAS

Irving, Texas

411

For more information on Dallas, visit their website at:

www.udallas.edu

Admissions contact:

800/628-6999
ugadmis@udallas.edu

Overview

Since 1956, the University of Dallas (UD) has earned a national reputation for excellence in both its fidelity to Catholicism and its academics, especially its core curriculum which emphasizes the classics of Western Civilization known as the Great Books.

Although founded by the Sisters of Saint Mary of Namur, UD has always been an independent university governed by a board of trustees, comprised largely of alumni and lay business leaders from the Dallas area. There are a few Catholic religious figures on the board, most notably the bishops of the Dioceses of Dallas and Fort Worth, but no diocesan control.

As part of its mission statement, UD declares: "The University is dedicated to the recovery of the Christian intellectual tradition, and to the renewal of Catholic theology in fidelity to the Church and in constructive dialogue with the modern world."

Located in Irving, 15 miles outside of Dallas, the University draws students from 50 states and 43 countries. Graduate students comprise more than half of the student body, but the undergraduate population is growing rapidly.

There are 29 majors rooted in the typical liberal arts disciplines. Included are classics degrees in Greek or Latin and a studio arts program, and nursing and engineering are available through co-operative degree programs. But unlike most contemporary universities with a range of departments and majors, UD students must take half of their courses in the thorough core curriculum to receive an undergraduate degree.

Class"A quality, rigorous liberal arts education is becoming rarer and rarer in the 21st century, as the vocational, pragmatic, job-oriented approach to education becomes more and more pervasive,"

says Thomas W. Keefe, who became the eighth president of the University in 2010. "I believe that a liberal arts education is integral to humanity and human culture, and it is vitally important to the survival and flourishing of American and Western civilization."

More than 80 percent of UD alumni attend graduate or professional schools. The University also claims seven bishops, 225 priests, and 70 religious brothers and sisters among its alumni.

Along with its Catholic tradition, the University has the distinction of having gained a Phi Beta Kappa chapter faster than any other institution in the 20th century, the largest number of National Merit Finalists per capita of any Catholic college or university in the United States, and 37 Fulbright scholars.

UD reaches out to the broader Catholic community through its School of Ministry, which holds annual ministry conferences that draw nearly 5,500 participants. In addition, UD has benefited from interaction with other Catholic entities. It has had a long relationship with a number of religious orders, including the Cistercians, Franciscans, Dominicans, Sisters of Saint Mary of Namur, and School Sisters of Notre Dame.

Quick Facts   2013-2014 Academic Year

Students 1,356   Majors 29

SATs 1204   % Catholic 83%

HS GPA 3.65   How Much? $41,350
                                        tuition, room and board

Tuition at UD is comparable to other private institutions in the area: $43,510 for tuition, room, board, and fees. The University provides generous financial aid and participates in federal grant and loan programs.

Academics

In addition to its orthodox Catholicism, the University is widely respected for intellectual rigor and quality of teaching. Ninety-three percent of the full-time undergraduate and graduate faculty hold a doctorate or highest degree in their field. An impressive 80 percent of pre-med students are accepted into medical schools, and 90 percent of pre-law students are likewise accepted.

Resisting the nationwide trend of making colleges more like training centers, UD requires a two-year sequence of 60 credit hours as follows: four courses each in English and history, three in philosophy, two in theology (Scripture and Church history/theology), and one each in economics, politics, biological science, physical science, fine arts, and mathematics. Students must also reach an intermediate level in a classical or modern language.

The core courses emphasize critical thinking and fundamental principles of each discipline, drawn from the Great Books. There is a heavy emphasis on Greek thought and Catholic works, but students also read Shakespeare, de Tocqueville, and a significant number of American authors including Thomas Jefferson, Elizabeth Cady Stanton, and Martin Luther King, Jr.

Nearly 80 percent of undergraduate students, most in their sophomore year, participate in the Rome Program. The 15-credit semester is no vacation, and it is widely respected as one of the best in higher education. Students live and study in a 12-acre villa with a vineyard outside of Rome, complete with a 114-student residence hall and athletic facilities. The Pope's summer residence, Castel Gandolfo, is visible from the campus. Students are immersed in the culture and intellectual tradition as they study Western Civilization I, Art and Architecture of Rome, Western Theological Tradition, The Human Person, and Literary Tradition III.

Most of the majors are offered in the College of Liberal Arts, but undergraduates can also earn degrees from the business and ministry schools. UD offers majors and concentrations in several sciences, music, journalism, and other disciplines not found at many of the other *Newman Guide* colleges.

Students benefit from several domestic institutes located at UD. These include the Center for Thomas More Studies, which sponsors courses, conferences, and publications related to the 16th-century English saint.

Spiritual Life

The University invites students to experience an authentically Catholic environment "where faith plays a significant role in every aspect of life." Students have access through campus ministry to daily Mass, reconciliation, retreats, and community service.

Masses are offered daily at the campus Church of the Incarnation where there are four Sunday Masses, including one on Saturday night. Confessions are heard six times a week and by appointment.

The campus ministry has a few programs, such as a weekly Dinner and Discourse faith-based social gathering and pro-life work through the active Crusaders for Life Club (a number of students attend pro-life observances in

Financial Aid Office Info

Approximately 94 percent of University of Dallas undergraduates receive some sort of financial assistance in the form of merit-based and need-based awards and scholarships that are available from federal, state, private, outside and institutional sources. Awards range from scholarships to grants and loans to work study with many packages being made up of a combination. Students interested in need-based aid are required to submit the Free Application for Federal Student Aid (FAFSA).

The application for admission doubles as the application for institutional scholarships. Upon being granted admission to the University of Dallas, students are awarded the merit-based scholarship for which they are eligible. Merit scholarships range from $5,000 per year up to full tuition and are based on GPA and test scores (ACT or SAT). Students may estimate their merit and financial aid award by visiting the university's net price calculator at udallas.edu/scholarcalc.

Furthermore, various departments at the University of Dallas offer departmental scholarships, for which a separate application and interview are required. These scholarships range up to $5,000 per year and reward excellence in a particular subject area. Additional scholarship opportunities exist for high-achieving students, and a comprehensive list may be found at udallas.edu/admissions.

Austin).

Social service activities are particularly strong. Among these is a program that refurbishes inner-city houses and serves meals at homeless shelters. A weekly "Crochet Day" brings students together to create baby blankets for a women's center. Another group volunteers every Friday afternoon at a local St. Vincent de

Student Activities

The University encourages students to take part in the more than 50 clubs and organizations on campus. In addition to typical collegiate groups, there is a Venture Crew for outdoor exploration and camping, a Juggling Club, College Republicans, and a Best Buddies program that works with children with special needs.

UD students can enroll in Army and Air Force ROTC programs, and an ROTC Club helps students keep in top physical shape.

The student government is reported to be strong and typically Catholic-oriented. In addition to an executive council, there is a Student Government Senate and an events programming board known as SPUD.

The weekly student newspaper, The University News, is impressive. The Rotary Club has recently formed a chapter at UD. Language clubs in Italian and Spanish are up and running.

The intramural sports program is one of the most popular activities on campus, including football, volleyball, basketball, soccer, and softball. Recreational classes are offered in dance, yoga, boxing, and more. Past workshops and tournaments have included dodgeball, tennis, chess, and photography.

UD is a member of the Southern Collegiate Athletic Conference (SCAC) and fields 14 athletic teams in NCAA Division III competition. Sports include baseball, basketball, cross country, golf, lacrosse, soccer, softball, track and field, and volleyball.

Every fall the junior class sponsors Charity Week, a major fundraiser for charitable

Paul Thrift Store.

Students can share in the spiritual life of the on-campus Priory of St. Albert the Great, which includes 15 Dominican friars, and the nearby Our Lady of Dallas Abbey, which has 28 Cistercian monks.

Residential Life

All undergraduate students under the age of 21 or with fewer than 90 earned credit hours are required to live on campus. There are seven residence halls and a small number of apartments.

Genders are separated by floor in West Hall, which is reserved to upperclassmen; the other six residence halls are single-sex. UD's handbook specifies visitation times throughout the week, and overnight opposite-sex visitation is not allowed. There are chastity programs promoted in the dorms and by student government.

UD prohibits immoderate and underage drinking, but students of legal age can consume and keep alcohol on campus. An alcohol-awareness week is held each spring.

The health clinic at the Haggar University Center addresses routine medical issues, and there are several hospitals in the area, including the Las Colinas Medical Center and the Baylor Medical Center at Irving.

Nearby Dallas is a world-class city, and the Dallas-Fort Worth Metroplex area includes about 6.4 million people. The region's economy is largely based on health care, aeronautics, communications, and banking. The cultural, sports, and social opportunities in the area are extensive.

Crime in Irving is slightly above the national average, but the UD campus is relatively safe and free of violent crime. Most campus police violations are for alcohol abuse.

UD is easy to reach, especially via the Dallas/Fort Worth International Airport, a key hub for American Airlines. Amtrak is located in Dallas, and there is a new Dallas Area Rapid Transit (DART) Light Rail UD station on its Orange Line, which will provide a direct link to DFW International in 2014.

From the Career Services Office

Career Services at the University of Dallas proactively reaches out to students from the moment they join the UD family, challenging them to pursue opportunities that will help them discern how they can use their talents and education upon graduation. Career Services encourages students to become critical problem solvers and to consider how they will be called upon to contribute.

We help students understand the importance of a tailored cover letter and resume submitted for each unique internship or job opportunity. We reach out to employers on behalf of UD students, and we prepare students for the interview. We run a robust internship program and host professional panels to allow students to learn and network. Ultimately, we personally assist every graduate who has elected to pursue employment with his or her job search.

organizations. Traditional events include Charity Week Jail, Shave-Off, Semi-Formal, Silent Auction, and Air Band.

A program called Dallas Year provides low cost opportunities for undergraduate students to explore amusement parks, entertainment, and cultural events in the Dallas/Fort Worth area. Tickets are generally purchased at a minimal cost with free transportation to events.

The student-led SPUD (Student Programming at UD) provides a variety of social and academic events throughout the year, such as Oktoberfest, Battle of the Bands, the Ruskin Rhetoric Competition, and one of the nation's largest celebrations of Groundhog Day.

The Bottom Line

The University of Dallas is a premier Catholic university in the United States. It combines an extensive core curriculum, often emphasizing classical works, with adherence to the Catholic intellectual tradition. The University prides itself on its quest for knowledge, confident that any inquiry will lead to the Catholic Truth.

UD has an impressive study-abroad semester with its Rome Program; 80 percent of its students take advantage of this opportunity to immerse themselves in the classics in a region steeped in the antecedents of Western and Catholic thought. Many commentators and college rankings give the Rome Programs and the University high marks.

UD has served the Catholic community in Texas and throughout the nation for half a century. It has weathered some storms, expanded, and remained faithful to its mission. A Catholic student interested in a challenging education in the heart of Texas would do well to consider the University of Dallas.

Letter from the President

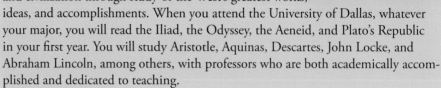

Dear Parents and Prospective Students:

At the University of Dallas we believe that the ends of education are wisdom, truth, and virtue.

Through the University's Core Curriculum students acquire a unified view of the tradition of Western culture and civilization through study of the West's greatest works, ideas, and accomplishments. When you attend the University of Dallas, whatever your major, you will read the Iliad, the Odyssey, the Aeneid, and Plato's Republic in your first year. You will study Aristotle, Aquinas, Descartes, John Locke, and Abraham Lincoln, among others, with professors who are both academically accomplished and dedicated to teaching.

We are extremely proud of our Catholic identity and our Rome program. We are enthusiastically Catholic, meaning that we are proud of our Catholic heritage and we pursue our faith life with passion. The Core is a reflection of Pope John Paul II's charge to "explore courageously the riches of revelation and of nature" in his encyclical on higher education Ex corde Ecclesiae. The beauty of a University of Dallas liberal arts education comes from its ability to weave all of this, from Plato to John Paul II, together to fit into a powerful, compelling continuum.

The Rome Program, which is a cohort to the academic enterprise, brings Western civilization to life by providing students the opportunity to see the most influential places and the greatest art and culture of the West. Rome is one of the birthplaces of Western civilization and the heart of the Roman Catholic Church.

The success of UD graduates shows the value of a liberal arts education in preparing students for life and work in the world. Our students have been awarded 37 Fulbright Awards since our 1956 founding. Eighty percent of pre-med students at UD are accepted to medical school, nearly double the national average of 45 percent. Ninety percent of pre-law students are accepted into law school. But our graduates are prepared for more than just professional success—a UD education aims at engaging students in lasting conversations and study, in a love of learning which endures their whole lives.

God bless,

Thomas W. Keefe, J.D.

University of Dallas
Frequently Asked Questions

We get questions from Catholic families on a regular basis about the colleges we recommend. Rather than filter the answers, we asked UD officials nearly 100 questions in categories such as academics, curriculum, programs of study, campus ministry, residence life, student activities, the make up of the study body, and institutional identity. The answers to some of the most asked questions are provided below and the rest are available on the Dallas profile page at TheNewmanGuide.com.

Majors

List the major, minor and special program areas that students may choose for specialization while pursuing an undergraduate degree:

Majors - Art, Art History, Biochemistry, Biology, Business, Chemistry, Classical Philology, Classics, Comparative Literary Traditions, Computer Science, Drama, Economics, Economics and Finance, Education, English, Modern Languages (French, German and Spanish), History, Human Sciences in the Contemporary World, Mathematics, Philosophy, Physics, Politics, Psychology and Theology

Cooperative Degree Programs – Nursing (Texas Woman's University), Engineering (UT Arlington)

Concentrations - American Politics, Applied Math, Applied Physics, Art History, Art Studio, Biblical Greek, Business, Christian Contemplative Tradition, Computer Science, Environmental Science, Industrial/Organizational Psychology, International Studies, Journalism, Language and Area Studies, Legal Studies, Medieval and Renaissance Studies, Molecular Biology, Music, Political Philosophy and Pure Math

Pre-Professional Programs - Pre-Architecture, Pre-Dentistry, Pre-Engineering, Pre-Law, Pre-Medicine, Pre-Ministerial, Pre-Physical Therapy, Teaching Certification

What are the three most popular majors or specialty disciplines for undergraduate students, and about what percentage of undergraduate students specialize in these disciplines?

Biology, 11%

Business, 10%

English, 8%

Spiritual Life

Please list the schedule of Masses, noting the following for each Mass: the day and time, the Form or Rite of the Mass, and the style of music, if any (chant, traditional, contemporary, etc.):

Mo 12:05 & 5:00 p.m.; no music; Ordinary Form in English

Tu 12:05 & 5:00 p.m.; no music; Ordinary Form in English

We 12:05 & 5:00 p.m.; no music; Ordinary Form in English

Th 12:05 & 5:00 p.m.; no music; Ordinary Form in English

Fr 12:05 p.m.; no music; Ordinary Form in English

Sa 5:00 p.m.; traditional/contemporary music; Ordinary Form in English

Su 9:00 a.m., 11:00 a.m. & 7:00 p.m.; traditional/contemporary music; Ordinary Form in English

List the schedule for Confession by day and time:

Mo 11:00 a.m. & 6:00 p.m.

Tu

We 11:00 a.m. & 6:00 p.m.

Th

Fr 11:00 a.m.

Sa 4:00 p.m.

Su

Other: By appointment with the chaplain

List the schedule for Adoration of the Blessed Sacrament by day and time:

Mo-Fr - 8:00 a.m.-8:00 p.m.

Please identify regularly scheduled devotions on campus for students such as the Rosary and prayer groups:

Praise & Worship - Su 9:00 p.m., Compline - Daily 10:00 p.m., Rosary - Daily 8:00 p.m., Liturgy of the hours - W 6:00 p.m.

Residence Life

Please describe options for students to reside on and off campus:

The university requires matriculated undergraduate students under the age of 21 or with fewer than 90 earned credit hours (senior standing) to live on campus. Students who fall under the residency requirement must actually reside on campus. Married students, veterans and commuter students living with their parents at home do not fall under this requirement.

The university has six 'traditional-style' residence halls and one apartment-style hall for upperclassmen still under the residency requirement.

Does your institution offer only single-sex residence halls?

No. 50% of students living on campus live in single-sex residence halls.

Are students of the opposite sex permitted to visit students' bedrooms?

Yes. Mo-Th 3:00-10:00 p.m.; Fr - 3:00 p.m.-1:00 a.m.; Sa 1:00 p.m.-1:00 a.m.; Su noon-10:00 p.m. Students must follow the university's open-bolt policy, as specified in the Residence Life Handbook. A room's deadbolt must be in the locked position with the door cracked open when a student of the opposite sex is permitted into a student's room.

How does your institution foster sobriety and respond to substance abuse on campus, particularly in campus residences?

Students of legal drinking age are permitted to drink in moderation and store alcoholic beverages in their own residence hall rooms or in their student apartment if all other residents and guests of that room or apartment are of legal drinking age. Students of legal drinking age must store alcohol in an inconspicuous manner (i.e. in the refrigerator or closet). If one roommate is of legal drinking age and the other roommate is not of legal drinking age, no alcohol can be possessed, consumed or stored in the room or apartment. Students of legal drinking age are not permitted to consume alcohol in the rooms of underage students. Underage students may not be present in a room where students who are of age are consuming alcohol.

An alcohol-awareness week is held each spring.

How does your institution foster a student living environment that promotes and supports chastity, particularly in campus residences?

The university handbook specifies visitation times throughout the week, and overnight opposite-sex visitation is not allowed. Students reportedly abide by these rules. There are chastity programs promoted in the residence halls and by certain student organizations.

Student Body

Describe the makeup of your institution's undergraduate student body with regard to sex, religion, home state/country and type of high school (public, private, homeschool):

Total number of undergraduates: 1,356
Male: 48% Female: 52%

Catholic: 83% Other Christian: 7%
Jewish: 0% Muslim: 0% Other: 10%

Number of states represented: 50
Top three states: Texas, California, Virginia
Students from top three states: 59%

Catholic HS: 39% Homeschool: 16%
Private HS: 5% Public HS: 40%

UNIVERSITY OF MARY

Bismarck, North Dakota

411

For more information on the University of Mary, visit their website at:

www.ComeToMary.org

Admissions contact:

800/288-6279
ComeToMary@umary.edu

Overview

The University of Mary (UM) is part of a second generation in the renewal of Catholic higher education. The 53-year-old University has been taking exciting steps to reinforce its academics, student life, and Catholic identity, following the example of *Newman Guide* colleges that have likewise embraced their Catholic mission.

In other ways, UM is unique for *The Newman Guide*. It emphasizes career preparation, with a majority of students majoring in the health sciences or business-related fields. Only about half the students are Catholic, and more than 80 percent attended public high schools. Many of the students do not attend UM primarily for its Catholic identity.

But seriously Catholic students will want to take advantage of the new Catholic Studies Program and the residence halls dedicated to fostering spiritual development and discernment. Exemplary students can also participate in UM's unique program to develop "servant leaders of moral courage" in their chosen fields.

Monsignor James Shea, a diocesan priest who became president of UM in 2009, has led the University's renewal with the support of the founding Benedictine Sisters of the Annunciation, who reside on campus and continue to help govern. The Diocese of Bismarck and the nearby Diocese of Fargo have also taken a strong interest in the University and its growing influence in North Dakota.

Monsignor Shea studied for the priesthood at the Catholic University of America (CUA) and observed the improvements at CUA during the tenure of Father David O'Connell, C.M. (now Bishop of Trenton). Bishop O'Connell helped the young UM president prepare for his position—the very capable Msgr. Shea was an extraordinary 33 years old upon his appointment—and the path of both institutions has been similar.

"Catholic identity in education is the motivating passion of my life," Msgr. Shea said before assuming the presidency. "I am committed to the deepening and the invigoration of the Catholic identity of the University of Mary."

That he seems to be accomplishing much faster than anyone could have anticipated. No doubt that played a part in the decision by Pope Benedict XVI to name him "monsignor" and "Chaplain to His Holiness" in December 2012.

While students from out of state may require some time getting used to North Dakota winters, UM is an attractive choice for students looking for a career-oriented university that is in good Catholic hands, and all at a quite affordable price. Tuition for 2013-14 is just $14,280, not including options for financial aid.

Academics

The general education requirements ensure that even pre-professional students are exposed to the liberal arts. Students take a foundational theology course, choosing from courses ranging from basic Catholic instruction to a study of Pope Emeritus Benedict XVI. Stu-

Quick Facts

2013-2014 Academic Year

Students 1,780

ACTs 23

HS GPA 3.39

Majors 54

% Catholic 52%

How Much? $18,718
tuition, room and board

dents also choose a foundational ethics course, and then one additional course in theology or philosophy.

Every student also studies cultural anthropology, citizenship, composition, oral communication, a science lab, mathematics, and information technology. Following one course in each of these areas, students have substantial flexibility to choose 22 credits from at least two disciplines including the humanities, languages, math, physical sciences, and social and behavioral sciences. The electives allow a student some ability to tailor the general education curriculum to more closely match the student's major.

One of Msgr. Shea's innovations has been a complete restructuring of the University into four distinct schools: Arts and Sciences, Business, Education and Behavioral Sciences, and the popular Health Sciences. Students can choose among 54 majors, ranging from Catholic studies to the liberal arts, social work, marketing, and nursing.

The commitment to health education is particularly impressive. The health sciences building includes large, state-of-the-art labs and workout rooms for physical therapy and athletic training. Students are taught medical ethics and bioethics consistent with Catholic teaching.

The new Catholic Studies program is modeled after the well-respected program at the University of St. Thomas in Minnesota; founding director Dr. Matthew Gerlach formerly studied and taught in the UST program. The courses offer a firm grounding in the Catholic intellectual tradition, especially theology and philosophy. More than an academic program, Catholic Studies students and faculty form a community that meets weekly for Mass and dinner, participates in Eucharistic Adoration and confession,

engages in service activities, attends the March for Life, and comes together for social activities.

Catholic Studies students are especially encouraged to study abroad at UM's campus in Rome, but other students are eligible to participate in the five-week or full-semester programs. The Rome program costs nothing extra—tuition and room and board costs are the same as Bismarck, and financial aid carries over. Students study and explore Rome and the Church, and courses cover several of UM's general education requirements.

Enhancing the relatively small liberal arts faculty, Msgr. Shea hired Dr. Carol Andreini, the longtime director of the Cardinal Muench Seminary's classics program. Priests who studied under Dr. Andreini throughout the Bismarck and Fargo dioceses helped fund the position after the Seminary was closed.

Spiritual Life

Given the diversity of beliefs among students, UM's campus ministry is Catholic but also ecumenical, often taking a non-denominational approach to Christian prayer and social gatherings. Student participation has grown noticeably in recent years.

The University takes a peer ministry approach, with students assisting the full-time staff including two Benedictine chaplains, a lay director, and a young sister from the on-campus Annunciation Monastery.

The four campus chapels are Catholic, and Mass is offered once each weekday and on Sunday. Daily Mass attendance is about 100 students at last count, and the University reports that most of the Catholic undergraduates living on campus attend Sunday Mass. At the beginning of students' freshman year, each residence hall celebrates Mass and

Financial Aid Office Info

As the most affordable, serious Catholic university in the nation, the University of Mary combines reasonable tuition with financial aid opportunities, including the following scholarships:

Academic Scholarships: Every incoming freshman receives a merit-based scholarship based on GPA and ACT/SAT scores. Awards extend to $6,500 per year, renewable for four years.

Catholic Scholars Program: Incoming, first-time freshmen graduating from Catholic high schools are guaranteed a minimum institutional aid commitment of free room and board.

Honors Day Scholarships: Qualifying students can compete in Scholarship Events for additional aid, including a Trustee Scholarship ($14,000), Presidential Scholarships ($10,000), and Benedictine Scholarships ($7,500). Selection is based upon a written essay and professional portfolio.

Music Scholarships: Music scholarships ranging from $800 to $3,500 are available for participation in musical ensembles. An audition is required.(May we insert a line break here, as above?)Athletic Scholarships: As a member of NCAA Division II, the University of Mary also offers athletic scholarships. Coaching staffs determine scholarship eligibility.

students receive a medal of St. Benedict.

The University has significantly expanded opportunities for Eucharistic Adoration and Confession; the latter is scheduled Monday through Wednesday and by appointment, while Adoration is scheduled for one hour each Monday and Tuesday and much of the day on Wednesday through Friday. Students pray the Rosary four days a week. Campus ministry hosts retreats for students every semester in their residence halls. Lecture series and social events occur frequently to foster spiritual develop-

ment and discuss moral issues.

Helping to strengthen students' spirituality is the Catholic evangelization group FOCUS, which recently was invited to campus. FOCUS sponsors several Bible study groups and promotes Eucharistic Adoration.

UM's Collegians for Life group is sponsored by campus ministry, adding a Catholic element to the usual pro-life activities such as a prayer night to honor St. Gianna Beretta Molla, who sacrificed her life for her child. Campus ministry also travels each month to the North Dakota Youth Correctional Center, hosting Mass and holding praise and worship nights.

The University has recently increased its emphasis on vocational discernment. The sponsoring Benedictine Sisters are available to be prayer partners for female students, who are also invited to spend a weekend living at the Annunciation Monastery. And for men, the new St. Joseph's residence hall houses 30

students interested in living a virtuous life and possibly discerning a call to the priesthood. The hall also houses Bishop Paul Zipfel, the recently retired Bishop of Bismarck, and the diocese's new director of vocations, Fr. Joshua Waltz. UM has also launched a similar hall for women, St. Scholastica's, with two Sisters living on the hall with 40 young women.

Residential Life

UM has a mix of single-sex, coed, and apartment-style residence halls—including two new apartment-style buildings for 2013-14—but the respect for privacy and chastity is greater than at many other Catholic colleges. Two halls are for men only (150 beds), and three are for women only (287 beds). Aside from the apartment-style buildings, in which men and women are separated by apartments with private kitchen and bath facilities, the only coed residence is North Hall. The 225-bed facility is large and L-shaped, with the men's and

women's wings separated by doors that are locked at night.

Residence life staff are expected to uphold the University's Benedictine values, encouraging students to pray and to live virtuously. Policies expressly forbid sexual activity outside of marriage, and priests and others talk to students about moral issues including chastity.

We have been told that North Dakota has problems with binge drinking as early as high school, and it carries over with some college students, especially off campus. But UM is a "dry" campus with no alcohol permitted at any age, and the University sponsors alcohol-free activities on weekends and several programs to discourage substance abuse. Students can opt to choose a roommate who is committed to abstaining from alcohol even off campus, and these students are grouped together in the residence halls.

A campus health clinic and a counseling center operate under Catholic ethical guidelines.

The campus is distinctive and quite the opposite of the iconic ivy-covered academic campus or the small, intimate colleges in this Guide. Several of the large stone and concrete structures at UM were designed by famed architect Marcel Breuer, and later construction continued in the Bauhaus style. It carries through to the interiors of the classroom buildings, residence halls, and even the Modernist-styled chapels.

The Bismarck-Mandan area is urban but not large, despite its population of about 80,000. Students can find what they need nearby, and a shopping mall is a

From the Career Services Office

With nearly 60 undergraduate majors, 10 master's degree programs, and one doctoral program, the University of Mary offers a wide range of career opportunities. And with a placement rate of 98%, our graduates succeed in obtaining employment or entering graduate school.

Several of Mary's programs—including business and education—offer "fast-track" options, allowing students to complete both a bachelor's and master's degree in five years or less.

In competitive health science fields such as nursing and physical therapy, qualifying students can apply for early acceptance and secure a place in the program.

The University of Mary strongly emphasizes servant leadership through the Emerging Leaders Academy, which provides experiential learning and professional networking opportunities.

five-minute drive away. Traveling to campus is easy along Interstate Route 94 or through the nearby Bismarck Municipal Airport, less than five miles from campus.

Student Activities

One of the typical benefits of a university is the greater variety of activities outside the classroom, and UM doesn't disappoint. It offers many clubs tied to students' academic interests, as well as a club dedicated to environmental awareness, an international club to celebrate the world's cultures and diverse students at UM, the Student Recreation Program for intramural and fitness activities, and Republican and Democrat groups.

The Knights of Virtue (for men) and Vera Forma (for women) focus on the development of virtue and holiness, studying Scripture and the saints from a clearly Christian but not exclusively Catholic perspective. As noted above, campus ministry sponsors Collegians for Life.

Crowd at gameThe UM Marauders field eight teams for men and eight for women in the NCAA Division II. These include basketball, cross country, soccer, and indoor and outdoor track and field for both men and women; baseball, football, and wrestling for men; and softball, tennis, and volleyball for women. The Fellowship of Christian Athletes works with the varsity athletes to strengthen their relationship with Christ, while also hosting basketball and "powder puff" football events for other students.

In the local area, students can find numerous outdoor bike and walking trails, parks, a zoo, and the Missouri River which runs near campus. Out of the cold, there are many restaurants, museums, performances, and cultural activities.

Letter from the President

Dear Parents and Prospective Students:

Every faithful, college-bound Catholic must weigh carefully two goals: finding an institution committed to fidelity with the Church, but also obtaining an education that prepares them for a meaningful professional career. Our students get both at the University of Mary, the most affordable, serious Catholic university in the nation.

Through our Catholic Studies program, two vocation-based residence halls, and a campus in Rome, Mary offers students an authentic Catholic experience. Yet this unwavering commitment to the Church does not diminish students' professional development. With nearly 60 undergraduate programs in health sciences, education, business and more, Mary produces professionals who contribute to the common good.

Students will also find a complete college experience, with NCAA Division II athletic programs, musical ensembles, and over 60 student organizations.

Come to Mary, and discover a serious, Catholic education at an exceptional value.

Yours in Christ,

Rev. Monsignor James P. Shea K.C.H.S.

The Bottom Line

The University of Mary's renewed vitality as a Catholic university is exciting and pervasive. The faithful curriculum and attention to ethical development, the Catholic Studies Program, the responsible campus residence policies and new halls for seriously Catholic students, the new Rome campus, and other factors combine to make UM a wonderful college for *The Newman Guide*.

But UM is also unique among most *Guide* colleges, with its heavier emphasis on career preparation in health, business, and education. We anticipate that its impressive renewal is not complete, as Msgr. Shea and a number of committed officials and faculty members continue to strengthen the academic program and campus life, so that Catholic students will find a faithful and increasingly fervent atmosphere at UM. The University is seeking students who are eager to take advantage of the current offerings while contributing to UM's development.

University of Mary
Frequently Asked Questions

We get questions from Catholic families on a regular basis about the colleges we recommend. Rather than filter the answers, we asked UMary officials nearly 100 questions in categories such as academics, curriculum, programs of study, campus ministry, residence life, student activities, the make up of the study body, and institutional identity. The answers to some of the most asked questions are provided below and the rest are available on the UMary profile page at TheNewmanGuide.com.

Majors

List the major, minor and special program areas that students may choose for specialization while pursuing an undergraduate degree:

Majors/Minors: Accounting, Addiction Counseling, Athletic Training, Biology, Biology Education, Business, Business Administration, Business Communication, Business Education, Catholic Studies, Chemistry, Coaching, Computer Information Systems, Criminal Justice, Early Childhood Education, Elementary Education, Engineering Science, English, English Education, Environmental Science, Exercise Science, Financial Services and Banking, Government and Political Philosophy, Health Education, Healthcare Administration, History, History Education, Indian Studies, Information Technology Management, Liberal Arts, Liturgy, Marketing, Mass Communications, Mathematics, Mathematics Education, Medical Laboratory Science, Music, Music Education, Music Performance, Music with an Emphasis in Sacred Music, Nursing, Organizational Leadership, Pastoral Ministry, Philosophy, Physical Education, Political Science, Psychology, Public Policy, Public Relations, Radiologic Technology, Religious Education, Respiratory Therapy, Social and Behavioral Sciences, Social Studies Education, Social Work, Sociology, Spanish, Special Education, Speech, Speech Pathology, Sport and Leisure Management, Theater, Theology, Theological Studies, Theology, Web Design, Wellness.

Preprofessional: Chiropractic, Pharmacy, Dentistry, Physician Assistant, Law, Podiatry, Medicine, Veterinary Med, Optometry.

What are the three most popular majors or specialty disciplines for undergraduate students, and about what percentage of undergraduate students specialize in these disciplines?

Management, 30%

Nursing, 12%

Biology, 7%

Spiritual Life

Please list the schedule of Masses, noting the following for each Mass: the day and time, the Form or Rite of the Mass, and the style of music, if any (chant, traditional, contemporary, etc.):

Mo 4:30 p.m., Ordinary Form, Chant

Tu 4:30 p.m., Ordinary Form, Chant

We 10:00 a.m., Ordinary Form, Traditional/Contemporary mix

Th 4:30 p.m., Ordinary Form, Chant

Fr 4:30 p.m., Ordinary Form, Chant

Sa 11:00 a.m., Ordinary form, Monastery, Monastic Chant

Su 8:00 p.m., Ordinary Form, Traditional/Contemporary mix

List the schedule for Confession by day and time:

Mo 3:00 - 4:00 p.m.

Tu 3:00 - 4:00 p.m.

We 7:45 - 9:00 p.m.

Other: By appointment before or after Mass

List the schedule for Adoration of the Blessed Sacrament by day and time:

Monday and Tuesday 3:00 - 4:00 p.m., Wednesday 11:00 a.m. - 9:00 p.m., and Thursday and Friday 9:00 a.m. - 3:00 p.m.

Please identify regularly scheduled devotions on campus for students such as the Rosary and prayer groups:

On Monday, Tuesday, Thursday, Friday Rosary before Mass and during Lent Stations of the Cross.

Residence Life

Please describe options for students to reside on and off campus:

The University of Mary offers both male and female students an opportunity to apply for a faith-based residence life experience where residents make a common commitment to pursuing a virtuous life together as a community while receiving spiritual direction to discern their vocation. Saint Joseph's Hall for Men is a 36-bed facility with a chapel. Spiritual direction is provided by the former Bishop Emeritus of the Diocese of Bismarck and the Diocesan Vocations Director who live in the hall.

Saint Scholastica Hall for women is located in a building that once served as the home of our sponsoring community and features 38 beds. Spiritual direction for the women is provided by two Benedictine sisters (including the Director of Vocations from the Monastery) who live with the residents in apartments located in the hall.

Other residences include traditional residence halls, suite-style residence halls for men and women, and apartment-style facilities. Set to open in the Fall of 2013 are The Cloisters, two twelve-plex apartment style facilities designed for upper-level students that each feature 11 two-bedroom units and a single one-bedroom unit. (More information is available on the UMary profile page at TheNewmanGuide.com.)

Does your institution offer only single-sex residence halls?

No. Most students are placed in single-sex facilities. We have only one co-ed facility remaining, with plans to transition this facility to a single-sex residence soon. 76% of students living on campus live in single-sex residences.

Are students of the opposite sex permitted to visit students' bedrooms?

Yes, Su-Th 10:00 a.m. - 12:00 a.m., Fr-Sa 10:00 a.m. - 2:00 a.m.

How does your institution foster sobriety and respond to substance abuse on campus, particularly in campus residences?

Our approach to address the problem is comprehensive and consists of the following:

1) Prevention Policies: Students of all ages are prohibited from possessing or consuming alcohol on campus and from being intoxicated on campus. Violators are vigorously tracked with the goal of early intervention in the form of education and counseling. Parents, coaches and advisors are notified of violations. First-time violators are required to complete an education program. Second-time violators as well as any student deemed to be heavily intoxicated and any student who gets into other serious problems while under the influence of alcohol are required to undergo an evaluation by a licensed substance abuse counselor and comply with all resulting recommendations.

2) Off-Campus Violations: Through close cooperation with local law enforcement agencies, off-campus violations are also tracked and treated identically to violations that occur on campus.

3) Education: New for the 2013-14 academic year, the University of Mary is working with local experts to develop a comprehensive alcohol education program for its students. In addition, frequent alcohol abuse and substance abuse programming, including alcohol awareness week and programming during key events such as homecoming and winter week celebrations, is offered. Our student health clinic sponsors a peer-education program, Health PRO (Peers Reaching Out), which sponsors numerous programs.

4) Activities: Alcohol-free activities are offered on-campus every Friday and Saturday night.

5) Alcohol-Free Lifestyle: We offer students the option of choosing a roommate who is committed to an alcohol-free lifestyle. We group students who have made this commitment together on a specific wing or floor of a residence hall.

How does your institution foster a student living environment that promotes and supports chastity, particularly in campus residences?

Our approach to foster an environment that promotes and supports chastity includes:

1) Our residence hall policy specifically addresses the issue of pre-marital sex. It states: "…the University of Mary affirms the Catholic belief that human sexuality is a sacred gift from God that should always be treated with the utmost respect and reverence, expressed only within an all-encompassing union of life and love within the context of marriage …. The University of Mary Community Standards for Students expressly prohibits sexual intimacy between persons who are not married to one another in the university's residence halls."

2) Staff are specifically instructed to refrain from treating instances where sexual activity occurs as mere violations of our visitation policy. They are instructed to document all such instances so conduct officers can address the deeper moral issues involved.

3) Educational Programing to Support a Culture of Chastity includes: a) Morals and Mocha, where area priests talk with students about moral issues selected by students. Theology of the Body is one of the topics frequently requested: b) Love and Lattes, featuring faithful Catholic couples who talk to students about topics such as dating and chastity, faith and marriage, and natural family planning.

4) Two new student organizations have been formed, one for men (Knights of Virtue) and one for women (Vera Forma). Each group provides support and fellowship for students who have made a commitment to live a virtuous life.

5) In the past few years, we have opened Saint Joseph's Hall for men and St. Scholastica Hall for women. They facilities are for men and women respectively who have made a commitment to live a virtuous life and support other residents in their commitment to virtue.

Student Body

Describe the makeup of your institution's undergraduate student body with regard to sex, religion, home state/country and type of high school (public, private, homeschool):

Total number of undergraduates: 1,780
Male: 39% Female: 61%

Catholic: 52% Other Christian: 39%
Jewish: 0% Muslim: 0% Other: 9%

Number of states represented: 40
Top three states: North Dakota, Montana, Minnesota
Students from top three states: 71%

Catholic HS: 16% Homeschool: 3%
Private HS: 1% Public HS: 80%

UNIVERSITY OF ST. THOMAS

Houston, Texas

411

For more information on UST, visit their website at:

www.stthom.edu

Admissions contact:

800/856-8565
admissions@stthom.edu

Overview

Located in the heart of Houston, Texas, on a 19-block campus, the University of St. Thomas (UST) has a goal of becoming no less than "one of the great Catholic universities of America." But for decades, this university launched in 1947 by the Basilian Fathers has been something of a secret outside of the Southwest. As it becomes better known, UST's solid Catholic liberal arts education is poised to attract a wider following.

The University has five schools—arts and sciences, business, education, nursing, and theology (offered at nearby St. Mary's Seminary). More than half the students on campus are enrolled in graduate programs.

Among the 38 majors are the interdisciplinary Catholic studies, theology, pastoral studies, international studies, and studio arts programs. Many minors are available, including Irish studies and creative writing. There also are many joint majors, and students have the opportunity to pursue a Western Civilization-oriented honors program.

Forty-six percent of UST undergraduates are Texans, most are commuters, and 63 percent of its alumni have settled in

the Houston area. But the remaining students come from 40 other states and 58 foreign countries.

Over half the students are minorities (Hispanic, African American, Asian American, and Native American), and many of these are first-generation college students. Under Title V of the Federal Elementary and Secondary Education Act, UST is identified as a Hispanic-Serving Institution, reflecting its greater than 25 percent Hispanic student population.

The University is most certainly a college on the move. In 2011, the St. Thomas Cameron School of Business achieved accreditation through the prestigious Association to Advance Collegiate

Schools of Business (AACSB International). UST also reopened its School of Nursing and is running a capital campaign to fund a new 75 million dollar Center for Science and Health Professions. The University partners with the Harris County Hospital District for a nursing preceptor program, which allows students to work and learn one-on-one with expert clinical nurses.

University regulations require the president to be a Catholic. In fact, six of the eight UST presidents have been Basilian priests. The current president is Dr. Robert Ivany, a retired Army major general with tours stretching from Vietnam to Kuwait. He previously headed the U.S. Army War College and holds a Ph.D. in history from the University of Wisconsin in Madison.

The board of trustees is primarily comprised of lay members, although a third of the members are either Basilians or Basilian appointees.

Although 36 percent of the student body is non-Catholic, the Catholic identity of UST is apparent. Seven Basilians reside on the main campus, and the Order permeates the life of the University with its "quiet orthodoxy."

The School's price and financial aid pack-

Quick Facts

Students 1,625

SATs 1128 (ACT 25)

HS GPA 3.61

2013-2014 Academic Year

Majors 38

% Catholic 64%

How Much? $38,190
tuition, room and board

age for the average student are roughly equal to the average for private colleges and universities in Texas. Tuition, room, and board cost $38,190 in the 2013-2014 year.

Academics

While many schools are opting toward curriculums emphasizing vocational education, UST places emphasis on the study of theology and philosophy. In these two disciplines, 21 credits are required for graduation: nine in theology, nine in philosophy, and another three in a synthesis course that brings philosophy or theology into conversations

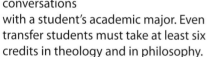

with a student's academic major. Even transfer students must take at least six credits in theology and in philosophy.

These requirements form the basis of the substantial core curriculum, which includes credits distributed among English, foreign languages, history, social and behavioral sciences, natural sciences, mathematics, fine arts, and oral communications. This overall core of 59 hours is unusually large among colleges that offer multiple majors.

The theology courses include two that are required for all students and set a clear tone for the curriculum: Teachings of the Catholic Church and Intro to the Sacred Scriptures. The third course is selected from several options within the field of moral theology.

The philosophy requirement is satisfied by taking three mandatory courses in a systematic sequence (Philosophy of the Human Person, Ethics, and Metaphysics) or in a historical sequence (ancient, medieval, and modern philosophy).

Most unique is the synthesis course, which is selected with the help of an academic advisor. There are a wide variety of options intended to coincide with a student's planned major. All are taught by theology, philosophy, or Catholic

Studies professors.

Incoming freshmen participate in the Freshman Symposium: Educating Leaders of Faith and Character, a program that introduces students to the University by focusing on St. Thomas' mission to educate leaders who can think critically, communicate effectively, lead ethically, and succeed professionally.

Catholic Studies is one of the double majors available. There is also a four-year, seven-course honors program that is heavily weighted toward the heritage of the Christian West. Even the revamped Environmental Sciences and Studies Department incorporates a Catholic moral perspective.

The University also has cooperative agreements for dual-degree programs in engineering and technology with Texas A & M University, the University of Houston, and the University of Notre Dame. There are several other pre-professional programs in dentistry, law, medicine, optometry, and pharmacy.

Students and professorSome departments have few or no Catholics, but faculty members are expected to respect the Catholic identity of UST. Theology professors must be faithful to Church teaching and are required to receive the *mandatum* from the local bishop.

UST offers a study-abroad program in the Czech Republic, Greece, Ireland, Israel and Jamaica. About 10 percent of the students take advantage of these opportunities.

To encourage practical experience in the local community, UST offers a service learning program. Students can ask professors for service placements in the local community, perform service hours for a nonprofit organization, and often write a paper or otherwise reflect on their experiences.

Financial Aid Office Info

At the University of St. Thomas in Houston, 92 percent of first-time freshmen receive financial assistance for their undergraduate education. The University awards nearly $35 million in financial aid annually, including $11.6 million in UST-funded scholarships and grants.

Upon admission to UST, students are automatically considered for a scholarship, ranging from $7,000 to $15,500 using information from the admissions application. Scholarships are based on high school GPA, class ranking, and SAT/ACT scores.

UST participates in federal and applicable state financial aid programs. For more information, visit us online at www.stthom.edu/financialaid. The Office of Financial Aid may also be contacted by calling 713-525-2170 or emailing finaid@stthom.edu. UST's FAFSA code is 003654.

Spiritual Life

Religious life revolves around the small, attractive stucco Chapel of St. Basil. It is at the chapel that most of the 16 weekly Masses are offered and confessions are heard Monday through Saturday. Sunday Masses are well-attended, and there are also Latin, Spanish, and French Masses and Masses for people with special needs. Three times a semester, a student group sings Gregorian chant for a traditional Extraordinary Form Mass.

Adoration and benediction are held every Monday, and adoration is also held on Wednesdays at 8 a.m.

The presence of approximately 10 priests on campus, mostly Basilian Fathers, and the Franciscan Sisters of the Eucharist is important in creating the nurturing spiritual environment that exists. There also is a nearby convent of Vietnamese Dominican Sisters, and these religious participate in campus activities and take classes.

Social service programs are offered through Campus Ministry, but the

Student Activities

Eighty-four campus groups provide students with extracurricular opportunities that include typical clubs as well as several targeted to various ethnic groups. Among the Catholic-oriented groups are the theology club Chi Rho, a Knights of Columbus council, a pro-life club, and the Society of Macrina.

Chi Rho sponsors an annual career and volunteer fair for the Archdiocese of Galveston-Houston and a "Theology at the Lab" series in which professors are invited to give talks to students in a local pub.

The University of St. Thomas Celts for Life Club participates in the Texas Rally for Life in Austin and the March for Life in Washington, D.C. Students also pray weekly at a local Planned Parenthood facility.

UST's young athletics department joined the National Association of Intercollegiate Athletics Red River Conference in 2011. The Celts compete in women's volleyball, men's soccer, men's and women's basketball, and men's and women's golf. There are also 11 sports clubs, ranging from coed fencing to men's rugby, and intramural activities as well.

The monthly *Summa* newspaper reaches 3,000 students. *The Laurels* literary magazine and a new features magazine, *Thoroughfare*, provide additional outlets for student writing. A University committee reviews student publications.

University also has a Center for Social Justice, which offers internships and other opportunities for service.

Residential Life

Only about 20 percent of UST students live on campus, which limits residential life. The coed residence features private bathrooms in student rooms. There is a second residence hall for upperclassmen, and some students live in apartments surrounding the campus.

A Basilian father is in residence. Monday evening Mass and daily night prayers are offered in the Chapel of St. Macrina.

The campus does not have a health center, although UST has a partnership with the University of Texas health services. Students use the world-famous Texas Medical Center, a vast complex of hospitals and health care facilities located a short distance from UST.

Students gravitate to the many cultural, sports, and social offerings that are available in the adjacent museum district and within a short distance from campus. These include the Museum of Fine Arts, the Houston Zoo, and several major shopping areas. The Houston Space Center is the top local tourist attraction.

Houston is a major transportation hub, and students have access to two major airports (George Bush Intercontinental and William P. Hobby), east/west Amtrak service, several major highways, and an extensive bus service. Houston relies heavily on car transportation.

As a large, diverse city with a population of about six million, Houston has a crime index rate of about double the national average. Some of this spills over onto the campus, largely as theft or pranks, but there have been some burglaries reported.

From the Career Services Office

At the University of St. Thomas, students can make plenty of real-world connections early in their college career. Students can present their research findings at the Research Symposium. Undergraduates, including freshmen, have opportunities to conduct research individually or on a team with a professor. Research prepares students for graduate or medical school and for their future career.

Houston is home to the country's second largest number of Fortune 500 companies, and the University of St. Thomas sits in the heart of the city. This means students have ample opportunity for hands-on learning, internships and great careers. At St. Thomas, students study closely with professors and carry their knowledge with them to internships and job opportunities.

Many student clubs host speakers from various professional fields. St. Thomas faculty also help students with recommendations for graduate school and beyond.

The Career Services Center at the University of St. Thomas provides services to both students and alumni. Services include resume and letter-writing assistance, job and internship searches and networking strategy. The Center offers events and programs to help students in building their professional network, and learn about opportunities for their major of study, including a mentor program, career fairs, networking socials, etiquette dinners and employer panels.

Various dramatic and musical performances are offered by the Fine and Performing Arts Department at the campus' Jones Theatre.

Students can volunteer at the nearby John P. McGovern Museum of Health and Medical Science. They assist with Head Start programs there and with other activities.

UST sponsors occasional recreational trips, such as rock climbing, horseback riding, and sailing. There are also several fitness classes available. The Jerabeck Activity and Athletic Center includes a large gym, racquetball courts, a weight room, a fitness room, a dance room, a swimming pool, tennis courts, a volleyball court, and an outdoor basketball court.

The Bottom Line

The University of St. Thomas is an excellent liberal arts-oriented institution. Its extensive core curriculum provides graduates with a well-rounded education. The School continues to place a strong emphasis on its Catholic identity, which is reflected in its faithful theology and philosophy departments and by the way that Catholicism permeates the campus.

UST is unique among most of *The Newman Guide* colleges with its racial diversity and small portion of students living on campus. Students reluctant to attend a small college but wanting a solid Catholic education may be especially attracted to UST.

Hewing to its 66-year-old tradition—and building on it—the University of St. Thomas is poised for growth. Local, first-generation college students from the area will continue to benefit, but so will those from around the country looking for a quality Catholic education at an urban university.

Letter from the President

Dear Parents and Prospective Students:

At the University of St. Thomas in Houston, we are committed to educating leaders of faith and character. Our graduates possess a vibrant spiritual faith, seek to learn more about themselves and the world around them, and have the courage to live their lives in accordance with their faith. We hope that our graduates face the challenges of the world strengthened by the foundation of the Basilian values of goodness, discipline and knowledge. We encourage them to become life long learners who seek every opportunity to continue to grow and give of themselves.

We are proud that our core curriculum provides each student with the ability to think critically and communicate effectively with a world view that is formed by the Catholic intellectual tradition. We are blessed with a faculty that is dedicated to our students and their development as ethical leaders and successful professionals. The university is blessed with the presence of the Basilian fathers who founded our institution in 1947 and the Franciscan Sisters of the Eucharist who joined us in 1999. Our 153 full time faculty look forward to welcoming you to our beautiful campus for a life-changing educational experience.

With best wishes,

Dr. Robert Ivany

University of St. Thomas
Frequently Asked Questions

We get questions from Catholic families on a regular basis about the colleges we recommend. Rather than filter the answers, we asked UST officials nearly 100 questions in categories such as academics, curriculum, programs of study, campus ministry, residence life, student activities, the make up of the study body, and institutional identity. The answers to some of the most asked questions are provided below and the rest are available on the UST profile page at TheNewmanGuide.com.

Majors

List the major, minor and special program areas that students may choose for specialization while pursuing an undergraduate degree:

UST offers 38 programs or majors: Accounting; Archaeology; Applied Mathematics, Art History; Biochemistry; Bioinformatics; Biology; Business (General); Catholic Studies; Chemistry; Classics; Communication; Computer Science, Creative Writing; Drama; Economics; Education; Education (BA/MA); Engineering (Cooperative); English; Environmental Science and Studies; Environmental Science & Studies and International Studies (joint major); Finance; French; General Business; General Studies; History; International Development; International Studies; Irish Studies; Latin; American And Latino Studies; Liberal Arts; Marketing; Mathematics; Medieval Studies; Music; Music Education; Nursing; Pastoral Studies; Philosophy; Philosophy (BA/MA); Physics; Political Science; Pre-Dental; Pre-Law; Pre-Medical; Pre-Nursing; Pre-Optometry; Pre-Pharmacy; Psychology; Russian Studies; Social Justice; Spanish; Studio Arts; Theology; Women, Culture & Society.

What are the three most popular majors or specialty disciplines for undergraduate students, and about what percentage of undergraduate students specialize in these disciplines?

Psychology, 9%

Biology, 7%

Finance, 7%

Spiritual Life

Please list the schedule of Masses, noting the following for each Mass: the day and time, the Form or Rite of the Mass, and the style of music, if any (chant, traditional, contemporary, etc.):

Mo 7:30 a.m., 12:30 p.m.

Tu 7:30 a.m., 12:30 p.m.

We 7:30 a.m., 12:30 p.m.

Th 7:30 a.m., 12:30 p.m.

Fr 7:30 a.m., 8:30 a.m. Latin (Extraordinary Form) , 12:30 p.m.

Sa 12:30 p.m., 5:00 p.m.

Su 10:30 a.m., 7:30 p.m.

Unless otherwise noted, all Masses are Ordinary Form in English. A French Ordinary Form Mass is also celebrated twice a month on Sunday.

All Masses traditional music.

List the schedule for Confession by day and time:

Mo 12:00 p.m.

Tu

We 12:00 p.m.

Th

Fr 12:00 p.m.

Sa

Su

List the schedule for Adoration of the Blessed Sacrament by day and time:

Wednesday 1:00 a.m.- Thursday 11:00 a.m.

Please identify regularly scheduled devotions on campus for students such as the Rosary and prayer groups:

Wednesday Eucharist Adoration, Rosary Tuesday and Thursday afternoons, Augustine Without Walls (group that focuses on the intergrading academic learning and faith convictions) Friday afternoons. Prayer group to end abortions every Friday.

Residence Life

Please describe options for students to reside on and off campus:

UST students have two very exciting and different communities to choose from that serve to meet their spiritual, academic, and social needs on campus. Both Guinan Hall and Young Hall offer students convenience, safety, service, and greater access to classes and campus activities. Living on campus allows UST students to take part in fun planned events; activities that help students meet one another, form friendships, and build a strong respectful community supported by the values of Catholic teaching.

Does your institution offer only single-sex residence halls?

No. 0% of students living on campus live in single-sex residence halls.

Are students of the opposite sex permitted to visit students' bedrooms?

Yes. With the prior approval of their roommate(s)/housemate(s), residents of Guinan and Young Hall may host non-resident guests and guests of the opposite gender in their contracted room/unit during the following designated visitation hours: Sunday-Thursday, 8 a.m.-midnight; Friday and Saturday, 8 a.m.-2 a.m. All guests are required to register with the front desk.

How does your institution foster sobriety and respond to substance abuse on campus, particularly in campus residences?

In coordination with the Drug Free Workplace Act of 1988 and the Drug-Free School and Communities Act of 1989, the University of St. Thomas believes the unlawful use of drugs and the excessive use of alcohol are inconsistent with the behavior expected of the members of a university community. The University is committed to the development and maintenance of a drug free environment on the campus as well as an environment that prohibits abuse of other drugs and alcohol. The University is committed to the expansion of a drug and alcohol abuse prevention program and to the dissemination of drug awareness information to the members of the entire University community. In addition, the University is committed to enforcing the provisions of the Drug Free Workplace Act of 1988 and the Drug-Free School and Communities Act of 1989 and believes that these acts and their implementation regulations provide a proper framework for the drug and alcohol abuse policies of the University.

University Initiated Assistance

Education

a. On-campus speakers presenting programs related to drug and alcohol abuse prevention, recognition or treatment.

b. Brochures describing drug and alcohol abuse prevention.

Information and Referral

a. The University's Office of Health Promotion and Wellness makes available information about drug and alcohol abuse prevention.

b. The Counseling and Disability Services Office makes information available about local community drug and alcohol abuse rehabilitation programs.

Students found to be in possession of drugs may be suspended from the residence hall.

How does your institution foster a student living environment that promotes and supports chastity, particularly in campus residences?

Campus Ministry supports the Theology of the Body (TOB) club on campus. The TOB has equipped several members of the Residences Life program to explain TOB to any residents should the situation arise. We are equipping young people to live chastely and to go out and proclaim that message of true love in the way they dress and live their lives. TOB has and will continue to host lectures for our students on the virtue of chastity.

Student Body

Describe the makeup of your institution's undergraduate student body with regard to sex, religion, home state/country and type of high school (public, private, homeschool):

Total number of undergraduates: 1,625
Male: 38% Female: 62%

Catholic: 64% Other Christian: 16%
Jewish: 1% Muslim: 4% Other: 9%

Number of states represented: 28
Top three states: Texas, Wisconsin, Indiana
Students from top three states: 96%

Catholic HS: 15% Homeschool: 4%
Private HS: 5% Public HS: 69%

WALSH UNIVERSITY

North Canton, Ohio

411

For more information on Walsh, visit their website at:

www.walsh.edu

Admissions contact:

800/362-9846
admissions@walsh.edu

Murry, S.J. President Richard Jusseaume was appointed in 2001. He is a Walsh alumnus, a former student Brother, a former professor and dean of students, and a successful businessman. Committed to Walsh's Catholic identity, he built the University chapel, placed crucifixes in all of the classrooms, and made hiring Catholic professors and staff a priority.

At an average cost of $33,549 in 2013-14 for tuition, fees, and room and board, Walsh is well below the average for private schools in Ohio and nationally. The average financial aid package is $20,962, and scholarships are available ,including some for Catholic high school graduates.

Academics

Walsh's 37-credit general education program—representing about a third of the credits required to graduate—exposes students to the liberal arts and Western thought, and Catholic theology is firmly integrated.

"Scripture and the Catholic Tradition" is the only particular course that every undergraduate student must take. Theology chairman Father Patrick Manning designed the course to ensure "that every student is exposed to the Catholic interpretation of Scripture and the

Overview

Situated in North Canton, Ohio—between a residential neighborhood and farm fields—Walsh University has quietly persevered over the past decade in strengthening its Catholic identity. At the same time, the University's enrollment has climbed 92 percent, and nearly every building on campus has been newly built or renovated. Among the new buildings is the campus' first stand-alone chapel.

Despite serving mostly non-Catholic students, Walsh has demonstrated a sincere commitment to upholding and teaching the Catholic faith, such that we are pleased to include it in *The Newman Guide*.

Named after former Youngstown Bishop Emmett Walsh, the University was founded in 1960 by the Brothers of Christian Instruction. In keeping with the Brothers' charism, Walsh has a special commitment to Ohio's working families.

That commitment extends to students of all faiths, so that the large student body (more than 2,300 undergraduates) is a mix of Catholics and mostly other Christians. Only 20 percent of students come from Catholic schools. The faculty is about half Catholic, although the portion is likely to grow with the University's current direction.

Offering 53 undergraduate majors, seven graduate programs, and five accelerated degrees for 400 working adults, Walsh is particularly known for its education, nursing, physical therapy programs and its unique majors in the medical field of bioinformatics, and museum studies. A quarter of students major in business, and a third in nursing or biology.

Five Brothers serve on the board of directors, which also includes three priests and Youngstown Bishop George

Quick Facts

2013-2014 Academic Year

Students 2,371

SATs 1050 (ACT 22.57)

HS GPA 3.35

Majors 53

% Catholic 43%

How Much? $33,549
tuition, room and board

deposit of faith."

Students choose from a wide range of courses to meet requirements in philosophy, history, literature, science, art or music, and social and behavioral sciences (choosing among government and foreign affairs, economics, psychology, and sociology).

The general education program is completed with a series of "heritage" courses, most of them interdisciplinary. Students choose a course focusing on contemporary challenges such as business ethics, the environment, Nazi Germany, and sexual responsibility; a course in "religious traditions," with some options more explicitly Catholic than others; a course in the development of Western culture; and finally a "capstone" course, pulling together what has been learned about contemporary challenges and exploring solutions by such means as conflict resolution, business policies, bioethics, liturgy and sacraments, etc.

There are additional requirements in mathematics, foreign languages, and reading and writing skills if students do not demonstrate proficiency in those areas upon entering as freshmen.

At least one general education course must qualify as a "diversity course," meaning that it "focuses on how categories of differences are formed, how differences are experienced, and how differences are given meaning through social institutions." Also, at least one general education course must be designated "service learning," involving at least 10 hours of service to a community organization.

Walsh places special emphasis on the Second Vatican Council document Gaudium et Spes, which addresses the Catholic Church's role in the modern world, especially with regard to social justice, culture, science, and ecumenism. All faculty are expected to consider the document and apply it to their teaching.

Walsh's 51 undergraduate majors are provided by schools of liberal arts, education, and nursing. Walsh is one of only three colleges in Ohio to offer a program in the genetics field of bioinformatics. It is also one of the top colleges in the state for nursing and physical therapy. The museum studies program is also unique; students are able to intern with local museums, such as the nearby Hoover Historical Center.

The theology department's Catholic professors are required to have the *mandatum* to teach; two of them are Catholic converts. But also affiliated with the department part-time is Rabbi John Spitzer, who teaches Jewish studies and directs the University's Jewish/Catholic Studies Institute. Several years ago, he publicly offered to perform homosexual "commitment" ceremonies.

Walsh has study abroad programs. Its eight-week Rome Experience allows students to stay in a former monastery that can house 16 students and faculty near the Pope's summer home, Castel Gandolfo, while learning about the Church's history, art, and culture in Rome. A shorter, more concentrated version is offered through Rome Summer. Walsh also offers a four-week Uganda Experience; students examine Ugandan history, traditions, social institutions, and challenges for development.

Spiritual Life

Father Anselm Zupka, O.S.B., began in fall 2011 as the university's full-time chaplain. He serves the University's Catholic and other Christian students together with Director of Campus Ministry Miguel Chavez, a Walsh alumnus, and two other full-time campus ministers.

Financial Aid Office Info

Walsh University understands the financial challenges many families face when investing in college, and is dedicated to providing a quality Catholic education to all who seek it. That is why, our Office of Financial Aid works with every family to make this investment as affordable as possible. This was illustrated this past year, when Walsh awarded nearly $18 million in institutional financial aid to our full-time undergraduate population of 1,922 students.

The $18 million in Walsh institutional funds were awarded over and above any federal or state financial aid programs our students were eligible to receive. Students seeking additional federal and/or state (non-Walsh) financial aid must file the Free Application for Federal Student Aid (FAFSA).

Academic scholarships, ranging from $7,000 to full tuition, are available to new entering freshmen based on a combination of their grade point average and standardized test scores. Students graduating from a Catholic high school will receive an additional $1,000 Catholic High School Grant in recognition of the families commitment to Catholic education.

In addition to the need-based and academic awards, students may also possess the talent to earn an athletic scholarship or chorale or music scholarship. Each of these awards is determined by the coach or director of the program.

"We won't compromise our Catholicism, but a lot of it—like vespers or exposition of the Blessed Sacrament—has to be taught or explained," Chavez said. "It's easy to be Catholic where everyone is Catholic. This is mission territory."

Our Lady of Perpetual Help Chapel serves as the spiritual hub of the campus. Mass is offered twice a day except for Saturday; attendance at daily Mass is

sparse. A Holy Hour and Vespers is held every Sunday evening, and Eucharistic Adoration is available 30 minutes prior to each Mass. The Sacrament of Reconciliation is scheduled seven times each week.

In addition, a mid-week praise and worship service, with Eucharistic Adoration, is held every Wednesday evening. This event is popular with both Catholic and non-Catholic students.

Campus ministry coordinates several retreats throughout the year. Every spring, the staff brings a group of students to the Chrism Mass Chapelat St. Columba Cathedral in Youngstown.

There are weekly Bible study, ancient Greek study, and prayer gatherings including a men's group (League of Extraordinary Gentlemen) and a women's group (Sisters in Christ). In the From Water into Wine group, juniors and seniors can work on discerning their future calling while making wine.

In 2012 Walsh launched the House of St. Andrew, a residence for up to eight men discerning a religious vocation.

In 2008, campus ministry instituted a Peacemaker Program. Four upperclass students receive scholarships to serve as catalysts, living and sharing their faith with students in freshmen residence halls.

Residential Life

Students who do not live locally with their parents must reside on campus. There are nine residence halls, each with its own chapel and access to exercise facilities. Most also have computer labs and wireless Internet.

All first-year, traditional students reside in Alexis Hall, in which opposite-sex students are separated by wing or floor. Most of Walsh's other residence halls are single-sex or apartment-style buildings.

Students who are of legal age can have alcohol in their private residence, but the university does not allow it in public spaces. Records show a significant decline in alcohol-related incidents in recent years.

Privacy hours are between midnight and 8 a.m. during the week—starting at 2 a.m. on the weekends—and there can be no opposite-sex visitation in hallways or rooms during those hours. Visits are always permitted in common areas. Walsh presents several discussions promoting chastity and women's dignity.

Towers Connector is a common area that connects several of the residences and provides a computer lab, classrooms, a fitness center, a 75-seat movie theater, and a convenience store.

Gaetano Cecchini Family Health and Wellness Complex features two gymnasiums, coaches' offices, some classrooms, and a wellness center for fitness activities. Just off campus there are sporting fields, a running track, tennis courts, and Hoover Park.

The University is within minutes of more than 100 restaurants, shopping, recreational, and entertainment options in suburban Canton. Canton is home to the Professional Football Hall of Fame and the William McKinley Presidential Library. Cleveland is about 55 miles north, with additional cultural and sporting events.

Student Activities

Walsh has approximately 60 different official student clubs and other organizations and activities. Student campus ministry is the most popular, working with the University chaplain and other student organizations to provide retreats, prayer, social and service outings, such as an Appalachia immersion experience, Habitat for Humanity service, and more.

The Paul and Carol David Family Campus Center serves as the university's active student union. A game room, on the lower level, features pool, foosball, table tennis, a snack bar, and a piano. Poetry

From the Career Services Office

Through the Walsh University Career Center, students receive one-on-one guidance, whether they are considering entering graduate school upon graduation, or pursuing their career. The Career Center hosts a variety of events geared toward graduate school preparation including an annual graduate school fair, and provides guides and other resources to assist students with making their graduate school selection. The Center also provides individual coaching on how to prepare their graduate school application documents, making sure they have observation hours or whatever other need they have specific to their selected school.

For students pursuing or making a change in their career path, the career center provides a variety of online and in-person resources to students and alumni as they discern careers and apply for internships and career opportunities. From mock interviews to career guidance to networking events, Walsh's commitment to its students and alumni is lifetime. Its national and international network of alumni is available to all who seek support and/or opportunity. Every effort will be made to assist those in need.

readings and other social events take place here.

The University Program Board organizes campus activities such as homecoming, a weekend movie series, bringing national entertainers on-campus, the spring formal, and Little Sibs weekend.

There are a number of academic preparation clubs tied to various majors. There's a student newspaper The Walsh University Spectator, a campus radio station, three choirs, and a marching band. The university recently opened a Center for the Arts to house the student choirs and band.

Walsh offers 20 intercollegiate sports for men and women in baseball, basketball, cross country, football, golf, lacrosse, soccer, Lacrossesoftball, tennis, track and indoor track, and volleyball. The Cavaliers are members of the National Collegiate Athletic Association Division II (NCAA) and the Great Lakes Intercollegiate Athletic Conference for all sports other than men's lacrosse. Men's lacrosse is a member of the Eastern Collegiate Athletic Conference.

In addition, Walsh offers a variety of intramurals. Competitive league play is offered in flag football, dodgeball, softball, soccer, basketball, volleyball, and bowling. Weekend tournaments are held in golf, billiards, table tennis, and corn-hole.

Bottom Line

While Walsh University continues to strengthen its Catholic identity, it is clear to us that the administration, campus ministry, and many faculty are committed to the task. The University is more than doctrinally Catholic; its attention to service and to working families reinforces its mission.

Walsh is not a strictly liberal arts college, like many in The Newman Guide. But today many Catholic students are not interested or prepared for four years of liberal arts studies, and too often they turn to secular and state universities to find particular majors, career preparation, sports, and other programs. For them, Walsh offers an authentic Catholic campus life together with a wide variety of academic disciplines and other services that are typical of contemporary universities.

Letter from the President

Dear Parents and Prospective Students:

Choosing a university may well be the most important decision you make.

Here is what you have a right to expect:

• Effective career preparation and solid academics.

• Competent, communicative faculty.

• A friendly and supportive community.

• Pleasant, well-maintained, comfortable and safe facilities.

Here is what you will find in addition at WALSH UNIVERSITY:

• Guidance and leadership in a Catholic community inspired by Jesus Christ.

• Service experiences here and abroad in preparation for a life of Christian community service.

• Easy access to the sacraments, spiritual guidance, and faith experiences such as retreats, rosary and bible study groups, and adoration.

• Personal transformation that leads to a full and productive life wherever you go.

I invite you to come and see for yourself. Come and experience Walsh University, "A Catholic University of Distinction."

Sincerely,

Richard Jusseaume

Richard Jusseaume

Walsh University
Frequently Asked Questions

We get questions from Catholic families on a regular basis about the colleges we recommend. Rather than filter the answers, we asked Walsh officials nearly 100 questions in categories such as academics, curriculum, programs of study, campus ministry, residence life, student activities, the make up of the study body, and institutional identity. The answers to some of the most asked questions are provided below and the rest are available on the Walsh profile page at TheNewmanGuide.com.

Majors

List the major, minor and special program areas that students may choose for specialization while pursuing an undergraduate degree:

Accounting, Behavioral Sciences/Counseling (B.A./M.A.), Biochemistry, Bioinformatics, Biology, Biology - Accelerated B.S./D.P.T. Physical Therapy Program, Business Management, Chemistry, Clinical Laboratory Science, Communication, Comprehensive Science, Computer Science, Corporate Communication, Counseling (Behavioral Science), Criminal Justice (Sociology), Education - AYA Biology and Life Sciences, Education - AYA Integrated Language Arts, Education - AYA Integrated Mathematics, Education - AYA Integrated Science, Education - AYA Integrated Social Studies, Education - Early Childhood Education Licensure, Education - Early Childhood Intervention Specialist Licensure, Education - Intervention Specialist, Mild/Moderate Licensure, Education - Intervention Specialist, Moderate/Intensive Licensure, Education - Middle Childhood Education Licensure, Education - Multi-Age Physical Education Licensure, Education - Physical Education (not a licensure program), Education (Non-licensure program), English, Environmental Science, Exercise Science, Family Studies (Sociology), French, General Studies, Global Business, Graphic Design, History, International Relations, Marketing, Mathematics, Museum Studies, Nursing, Philosophy, Political Science (Government and Foreign Affairs), Pre-Dental, Pre-Medical and Pre-Optical, Pre-Occupational Therapy (Psychology), Pre-Pharmacy, Pre-Physical Therapy (Biology), Pre-Physical Therapy (Psychology), Pre-Veterinary, Psychology (Community/Clinical), Psychology (Research), Research Methods and Data Analysis (Sociology), Sociology, Spanish, Spanish for Healthcare, Theology.

What are the three most popular majors or specialty disciplines for undergraduate students, and about what percentage of undergraduate students specialize in these disciplines?

Business, 26%

Nursing, 21%

Biology, 14%

Spiritual Life

Please list the schedule of Masses, noting the following for each Mass: the day and time, the Form or Rite of the Mass, and the style of music, if any (chant, traditional, contemporary, etc.):

Mo 6:45 and 11:30 a.m., traditional

Tu 6:45 and 11:30 a.m., traditional

We 6:45 and 11:30 a.m., traditional

Th 6:45 and 11:30 a.m., traditional

Fr 6:45 and 11:30 a.m., traditional

Sa

Su 11:00 a.m., 8:00 p.m., traditional

All Masses are the Ordinary Form of the Mass.

List the schedule for Confession by day and time:

Mo 11:00 a.m.

Tu 11:00 a.m.

We 11:00 a.m.

Th 11:00 a.m.

Fr 11:00 a.m.

Sa

Su 10:30 a.m., 7:30 p.m.

List the schedule for Adoration of the Blessed Sacrament by day and time:

Mon-Fri at 11:00 a.m., Sun at 10:30 a.m. and 7:30 p.m.

Please identify regularly scheduled devotions on campus for students such as the Rosary and prayer groups:

Campus Ministry organizes weekly gatherings with students including: Student-led Bible study called Deliverance, 4-10 students every week; Ancient Greek and Scripture studies, 5-12 people weekly in the fall semester; weekly prayer gatherings including rosary meditations, liturgy of the hours, and meditation prayer experiences for 3-15 people at each session.

Residence Life

Please describe options for students to reside on and off campus:

All students reside on campus unless they live with their parents (if under age 21) within 25 miles of campus or unless they are students taking more than 8 semesters to complete their academic work.

Does your institution offer only single-sex residence halls?

No.

Are students of the opposite sex permitted to visit students' bedrooms?

Yes. 8:00 a.m. - 11:59 p.m.

How does your institution foster sobriety and respond to substance abuse on campus, particularly in campus residences?

The university complies with federal, state, and local laws with regards to alcohol consumption. Furthermore, the university upholds a policy that does not permit students under the age of 21 to be in the presence of alcohol. Students found in violation of this policy participate in a mandatory on-line Alcohol Education course as well as additional educational reflections on the information learned. Repeat violations involve a group counseling program centered on alcohol, its impact and the choices students make. In addition, students may be required to meet with counselors both on and off campus for alcohol and drug assessment and treatment.

Residence Life, in collaboration with other university departments (counseling, wellness, campus police, etc.) provides ongoing programming to educate students about expectations for alcohol consumption as well as the impact of high-risk behaviors.

How does your institution foster a student living environment that promotes and supports chastity, particularly in campus residences?

All of our university residence halls are intentionally single-gender by floor. In collaboration with Campus Ministry, residence hall staff provide expectations and education to students beginning during orientation on upholding the values/teachings of the Catholic faith in regards to human sexuality.

In addition, student staff members (resident assistants) live on each floor to enforce our privacy and cohabitation policies. They conduct nightly rounds to ensure adequate privacy is maintained for both genders. Students found in violation of these policies are referred to the university's judicial system and held accountable.

Student Body

Describe the makeup of your institution's undergraduate student body with regard to sex, religion, home state/country and type of high school (public, private, homeschool):

Total number of undergraduates: 2389
Male: 37% Female: 63%

Catholic: 43% Other Christian: 24%
Jewish: 0% Muslim: 0% Other: 33%

Number of states represented: 19
Top three states: FL, OH, PA
Students from top three states: 98%

Catholic HS: 20% Homeschool: 0%
Private HS: 2% Public HS: 78%

WYOMING CATHOLIC COLLEGE

Lander, Wyoming

411

For more information on Wyoming Catholic, visit their website at:

www.WyomingCatholicCollege.com

Admissions contact:

307/332-2930
Admissions@
WyomingCatholicCollege.com

Overview

Wyoming Catholic College (WCC), only recently founded in 2005, is for pioneers. Nestled in a small town near the Wind River Mountain Range and the Pope Agie River, the Great Books college is perfect for nature and outdoor enthusiasts as well as those who want to stretch themselves intellectually in ways they never dreamed possible.

The founders' statement, "Born in Wonder, Brought to Wisdom: The Philosophical Vision Statement of Wyoming Catholic College," explains that WCC intends to educate the whole person—mind, body, and spirit—emphasizing seven key objectives: Catholic community, spiritual formation, liberal arts education, integrated curriculum, Great Books, immersion in the outdoors, and excellent teaching.

Students study a prescribed four-year program. This includes eight Catholic theology courses and five philosophy courses, as well as logic and rhetoric. Graduates all receive the same Bachelor of Arts degree.

The College eschews the excessive use

of technology in order to foster direct human contact and communication between students and faculty. One of the College's trademarks is its Freshman Leadership Program, a three-week backpacking trip in the pristine Wyoming wilderness in August and a one-week winter adventure in January.

The lay-run, independent college has a strong connection to the local bishop, who ex officio will always be a member of the Board of Directors. The bishop appoints two of the members of the board of directors and can veto any move away from the College's educational mission. The corporate structure requires that at

least two-thirds of the board members be practicing Catholics, and at least two-thirds of the faculty and administrators be practicing Catholics. In reality, the portion is 100 percent.

There are a total of 14 full-time faculty members and two part-time instructors. In June 2013, Dr. Kevin Roberts assumed the mantle of president, succeeding founding president Father Robert Cook. Roberts, a historian by training, founded and led a Cardinal Newman Society-awarded "Top 50 Catholic High School" before returning to his professional "home" of higher education.

Until the College is able to begin a permanent campus capital campaign, it uses buildings in downtown Lander, Wyoming, for classes, library, computer lab space, and student dining. An old hunting lodge adjacent to Lander City Park serves as the administration building, and the College uses Holy Rosary Catholic Church and parish for daily Mass and temporary residence halls.

The College has received pre-accreditation from the American Association for Liberal Education and is also pursuing accreditation with its regional accrediting agency.

Tuition, room and board, and books

Quick Facts

2013-2014 Academic Year

Students 112	**Majors** 1
SATs 1160	**% Catholic** 98%
HS GPA n/a	**How Much?** $25,500
	tuition, room and board

and materials are priced at $26,150 for 2013-14. However, the average student actually pays much less due to generous financial aid packages. Total enrollment is approximately 112 students, with a goal of 400 at the future permanent campus.

Academics

In addition to the theology and philosophy courses, students take nine courses in humanities; eight in trivium or grammar, logic, and written and oral rhetoric; four in Latin; two in art history and two in music; and three each in science and mathematics. Uniquely, students also take two courses in horsemanship. Honors courses in outdoor leadership and in Latin are also available.

The goal is a classical education. According to Dr. Roberts, "Most important to us is that our students learn how to live a balanced life. By that, I mean that we want our students to graduate being able to find joy in learning, to think critically, and to present their thoughts clearly in speech and writing, all the while sustaining a robust list of pursuits that help build up God's Kingdom."

The added outdoor component offers hands-on leadership skills that build self-confidence. "Students learn how to choose a goal, plot how to get there, the food and equipment needed, resolving conflicts, teamwork, and handling things you never dreamed would happen, such as coming to a creek that's too big to cross," explained President Roberts. "Learning all of this is different from the theoretical study of leadership in a classroom."

The 21-day orientation involves all incoming freshmen, split into two male and two female sections with their own chaplain, student leader, and two instructors from Solid Rock Outdoor Ministries (SROM) . SROM also works

with students in risk-management training. All freshmen take a two-and-a-half day wilderness medical training course to learn how to manage injuries in the wild.

Sophomores, juniors, and seniors are expected to go on at least two of four week-long outdoor courses that are offered each year. These consist of everything from white-water rafting and kayaking to canyoneering, to backpacking and mountain climbing and are built into the academic calendar so they do not conflict with class.

Another unique component of the Wyoming Catholic curriculum is a field-based science course during the sophomore year that includes botany, wildlife, astronomy, and geology.

Wyoming Catholic has a distinct conversational Latin program that uses an immersion style of teaching where only Latin is spoken in the classroom. It also offers a Great Books curriculum in which courses are a combination of lecture and Socratic discussion.

All faculty members must agree not to undermine Church teaching or Vatican authority and to support WCC's spiritual vision. At the Convocation Mass each fall, Catholic faculty as well as the president, dean of students, and chaplains profess their faith and recite an Oath of Fidelity in the presence of the Bishop or his delegate. In addition, any faculty who teach theology are required to obtain the canon law *mandatum*.

Spiritual Life

Holy Rosary parish Mass is said at 8 a.m. daily. The College chaplaincy Masses are at noon and 9:15 p.m. An Ordinary Form Mass is celebrated in English with Gregorian chant at noon on Monday, Tuesday, Thursday, Friday, and Sunday. The Extraordinary Form is celebrated on Wednesday at noon, Saturday at 11 a.m., and Sunday at 8 a.m. (a sung

Financial Aid Office Info

Wyoming Catholic College is committed to keeping our tuition and room and board costs affordable and making our program available to all qualified students. In this mission, our costs are significantly lower than most colleges. WCC endeavors to meet the financial requirements of each student through need-based scholarships, work study, and loans. Loan debt is kept to a minimum: the maximum student indebtedness after four years is $19,000. Our most recent class average is $15,750.

Financial aid is distributed on a first-come, first-served basis and all students are encouraged to apply early. Work study arrangements, as well as our merit-based Benedict XVI Fellowship Grants and Presidential Scholarships, further assist some students. Over 80% of our students receive financial aid.

Students are strongly urged to apply for as many outside scholarships as possible. A wide range of opportunities exist for outside aid offered by businesses, service clubs, benevolent organizations, high schools, unions, and other groups.

At many colleges, outside scholarships simply reduce the amount of college financial aid offered to the student. Thus, it is often perceived that outside scholarships provide no cost-reduction to the student and his family. At WCC, the student's financial aid is determined prior to the inclusion of outside scholarships. WCC then shares half of all such aid with students and their families to directly reduce their cost.

For more information visit our website at www.wyomingcatholiccollege.com, or call 877.332.2930.

High Mass). Occasionally, visiting clergy celebrate a fully-sung Byzantine Divine Liturgy of St. John Chrysostom.

Approximately 60 percent of students attend daily Mass, and all attend Sunday Mass. A sizeable number of students have expressed interest in a priestly or

religious vocation.

The campus is served by two full-time chaplains, who celebrate Mass and hear confessions daily, and are available for spiritual direction throughout the week.

Eucharistic adoration is held at the parish Church every weekday afternoon. There are also a number of prayer groups, such as Rosary and Compline, as well as spirituality practicums – small groups of students that meet and discuss various spiritual classics.

Residential Life

Until the permanent campus is built, there are three women's residences and three men's residences located next door to Holy Rosary. In addition, there are two apartment buildings–one male, one female. On weeknights there is a 10:30 p.m. curfew; weekend curfew is midnight. Opposite-sex visitation is prohibited, as are drugs and alcohol. Complimentary laundry facilities are provided in the residence halls.

Because Wyoming Catholic is small, meal service is mandatory. In the dining hall, students get whatever is made that day, with options for allergen-sensitive individuals. A soup and salad bar is available.

The College has a unique technology policy. Cell phones and smart phones are prohibited. If students own cell phones, they are locked up with the prefect. Students traveling long distances are free to check out their phones. Every four students in the residence hall share their own cordless phone and answering machine. Students may not have personal televisions. Electronic devices are not permitted during class. Outside of public spaces, such as the library and computer lab, there is no personal use of the Internet. A number of computers are available for student use in the library and in the mail room.

Frassati Hall houses a student lounge, student-staffed coffee shop, mail room, general assembly hall used primarily as the cafeteria, and dedicated storage

space for the College's Outdoor Leadership Program.

The College has a three-tier dress code: formal, classroom, and casual dress. Classroom dress for men means a collared shirt with slacks or dress jeans. For women it means modest skirts or pants. Formal dress is for Sunday Masses and formal lectures: for men, a jacket and tie; for women, a dress or skirt. Appropriate casual dress is permitted at other times.

Lander is a thriving mid-size town with a population of 8,000. There are a number of hotels, banks and credit unions, restaurants, cafés, a hardware store, theater, Alco, Shopko, and grocery stores all located along the main thoroughfare.

The crime rate is well below the national average and reflects property, rather than violent, crime. However, one statistic that is well above the norm is snowfall; Wyoming winters provide for an abundance of outdoor sports, including skiing.

The town has an 81-bed Lander Valley Medical Center that is supplemented by the Riverton Memorial Hospital, about a half-hour away.

Access to Lander isn't easy. Students typically fly into Salt Lake City or Denver. Riverton, only slightly larger than Lander, has a regional airport with daily flights into and out of Denver International Airport. Salt Lake City International Airport is five hours away. A reasonably priced shuttle service is offered to students at the beginning and end of the academic year.

Student Activities

Student activities are developing, with

From the Career Services Office

Graduate School Seminar (for Juniors and Seniors) - Each year members of the faculty and administration address upperclassmen on the value of graduate school, how to apply, and how to choose the right for them. Breakout sessions afford students the opportunity to seek more detailed information in various fields of study.

Wyoming Career Fair - State industry leaders visit the campus each year to meet and visit with students interested in business-related careers, especially within the state of Wyoming.

Resume Workshop - Each year the College provides a workshop to help students craft a strong resume.

Individual career counseling is provided by the Dean of Student Life to each student to talk about post graduation plans.

significant emphasis on outdoor pursuits.

Students can join the Wyoming Catholic College Choir. Classic movie nights, dances, intramural sports, and informal social activities round out the free-time opportunities. There are four dances each year – in October, at Christmas, at Candlemas, and in the spring. There is a special day of prayer and festivity in honor of Our Lady of the Rosary as well as a special celebration of Our Lady Seat of Wisdom, patroness of the College, in early February.

A variety of clubs have already sprung up on campus, including an Opera Society that makes an annual excursion to a live opera. On Sunday evenings, swing dancing is popular. There are also Latin immersion weekends and backpacking trips.

Students can use a high school gym for basketball and also participate in intramural or pickup games of volleyball, indoor soccer, football, rugby, softball, and ultimate Frisbee. They can also access a swimming pool, a rock climbing gym, and recreational facilities in town.

Students have been involved in various social projects: roadside ditch clean-up work, fasting during lunch on Friday to donate the meal money to Food for the Poor, traveling to a small parish church in Hudson once a month to provide music, and teaching classes to local fifth-graders.

Students participate annually in the March for Life in Cheyenne.

The Bottom Line

The motto of Wyoming Catholic College is "Wisdom in God's Country."

"We intend to do everything we can so that upon graduation, the students will leave stronger in the faith than when they came," said Dr. Roberts.

This College is likely to appeal to students seeking a different kind of undergraduate experience. With its outdoor leadership and equestrian component, its unique immersion Latin program, its

Letter from the President

Dear Parents and Prospective Students:

In a culture filled with despair and disorder, the students and faculty members of Wyoming Catholic College stand out as beacons of hope and authenticity. The supernatural joy that pervades our community is palpable and infectious. Many factors create it—such as living and studying in the midst of the stunning Wind River Mountains—but the foundation is, of course, our collective love for Jesus Christ, His Church, and His Truth. This is the context in which we cultivate our passion for the three great transcendentals—truth, beauty, and goodness.

Truth is nurtured by our unique approach to the Catholic liberal arts tradition. Using a "Great Books" approach that has formed some of the best minds and leaders in Western Civilization, WCC is unparalleled in the degree to which its academic programs are truly integrated, not only with each other, but also with our spiritual formation and outdoor leadership programs. A vibrant, ongoing engagement with the "Great Conversation" ensues, resulting in our students' impressive intellectual breadth and depth.

Facilitating students' quest for Truth is accentuated by WCC's unique approach to forming their minds—by first immersing them in God's "First Book," nature. Beauty captivates our students from their first day on campus, when they prepare for a three-week-long backcountry expedition, where they learn outdoor skills, deepen their faith, and hone their leadership ability. Subsequent trips, both organized by the College and by students themselves, nurture our college community's love for the beauty of Wyoming and the Rocky Mountain West. This is further cultivated by our required freshman course in horsemanship, and by our plans to do our own, tangible cultivation of crops and meat for our own consumption.

Goodness, therefore, permeates every aspect of the WCC community. Rooted in the Holy Eucharist, the most important aspect of our community's goodness is its people. Quite simply, if you are looking for a college experience that will spur your quest to know His Truth, enliven your desire to experience His beauty, and foster in you a goodness that can only be supernatural, then WCC would be an excellent fit.

The formation you receive at Wyoming Catholic College will not only form you intellectually and spiritually, but will also enrich your life by cultivating a deep passion for the wonderment of God's creation. In short, to study at WCC is to know what it means to be fully alive and truly free!

Sincerely yours in Christ,

Kevin Roberts

Dr. Kevin D. Roberts

four-year double focus on humanities and sacred theology, and its strong emphasis on written and oral rhetoric, there's no other Catholic college quite like it.

In the words of one faculty member, "The students who come now and in

the next few years are going to be the co-creators, actively involved in something that is going to make a significant contribution to Catholic colleges in America."

Wyoming Catholic College
Frequently Asked Questions

We get questions from Catholic families on a regular basis about the colleges we recommend. Rather than filter the answers, we asked Wyoming officials nearly 100 questions in categories such as academics, curriculum, programs of study, campus ministry, residence life, student activities, the make up of the study body, and institutional identity. The answers to some of the most asked questions are provided below and the rest are available on the college profile page at TheNewmanGuide.com.

Majors

List the major, minor and special program areas that students may choose for specialization while pursuing an undergraduate degree:

WCC offers a single degree program, the Bachelor of Arts in Liberal Arts—a total of 142 credits comprising imaginative literature, history, philosophy, theology, writing, reasoning, oratory, Latin, art history, music, mathematics, natural science, and outdoor leadership. WCC's liberal arts program comes from a distinguished tradition and is reflected in a carefully designed, chronologically and disciplinarily integrated curriculum.

What are the three most popular majors or specialty disciplines for undergraduate students, and about what percentage of undergraduate students specialize in these disciplines?

Liberal Arts, 100%

Spiritual Life

Please list the schedule of Masses, noting the following for each Mass: the day and time, the Form or Rite of the Mass, and the style of music, if any (chant, traditional, contemporary, etc.):

Mo 8:00 a.m. (Ordinary Form); 12:00 p.m. (Ordinary Form, chant); 9:30 p.m. (Ordinary Form, chant)

Tu 8:00 a.m. (Ordinary Form); 12:00 p.m. (Extraordinary Form Low Mass); 9:30 p.m. (Ordinary Form, chant)

We 12:00 p.m. All-College Mass (Latin Ordinary Form, chant and choral music)

Th 8:00 a.m. (Ordinary Form); 12:00 p.m. (Ordinary Form, chant); 9:30 p.m. (Ordinary Form, chant)

Fr 8:00 a.m. (Ordinary Form); 12:00 p.m. (Ordinary Form, chant)

Sa 8:00 a.m. (Extraordinary Form, Low Mass); 6:00 p.m. (Ordinary Form, traditional music)

Su 7:50 a.m. (Extraordinary Form, High Mass); 10:00 a.m. (Ordinary Form, traditional music); 7:00 p.m. (Ordinary Form)

List the schedule for Confession by day and time:

Mo 4:30-5:30 p.m.

Tu 4:30-5:30 p.m.

We 4:30-5:30 p.m.

Th 4:30-5:30 p.m.

Fr 4:30-5:30 p.m.

Sa 4:00 - 5:30 p.m.

Su 6:00 p.m.-7:00 p.m.

Other: by appointment

List the schedule for Adoration of the Blessed Sacrament by day and time:

Monday through Friday, 12:45 p.m. to 5:45 p.m., concluding with Benediction.

Please identify regularly scheduled devotions on campus for students such as the Rosary and prayer groups:

A regular group of students comes together to sing Compline in Latin (EF) every evening; additional students come to pray the Rosary prior to the 9:30 PM Mass. The recitation of Lauds (Morning Prayer) and Vespers (Evening Prayer) is organized informally by groups of students.

Residence Life

Please describe options for students to reside on and off campus:

Since learning takes place not only in the classroom but in many places on and off campus (including lessons learned through community life), WCC students are required to live in appointed residence halls on or near the interim campus in Lander. All residence halls are single-sex and no intervisitation is allowed. The College employs a full-time Dean of Student Life as well as a Prefect system.

Does your institution offer only single-sex residence halls?

Yes.

Are students of the opposite sex permitted to visit students' bedrooms?

Never. This is an expellable offense.

How does your institution foster sobriety and respond to substance abuse on campus, particularly in campus residences?

The Student Handbook at WCC, which all students are required to read, contains the following section: "The temperate use of alcoholic beverages is in no way opposed to Christian maturity, and can be a good in the service of leisure. At the same time alcohol is a powerful substance that requires sufficient maturity if it is to be used well. For this reason the state of Wyoming prohibits those under the age of twenty-one from consuming alcoholic beverages. In obedience to this law, the College forbids any use of alcoholic beverages by those under legal age. As a result, underage drinking, even when off campus, or the providing of alcoholic beverages to underage persons, is punishable even to the point of expulsion. In addition, the possession or use of alcoholic beverages by any student, regardless of age, is strictly forbidden on campus or on expeditions utilizing college resources (equipment, vouchers, vehicles, etc.), and will normally entail expulsion from the program. The possession or use of illegal drugs is strictly forbidden and will normally entail expulsion from the program."

In pursuance of this clear policy, WCC has expelled students or placed them on disciplinary probation in the few cases where infractions have occurred. The Prefect system and the small size of the campus make infractions of the above policy difficult to hide, and we are happy to report that the campus has a reputation for sobriety.

How does your institution foster a student living environment that promotes and supports chastity, particularly in campus residences?

On campus the rules are strict, and the student body, which is made up almost entirely of seriously practicing Catholic students, are eager to keep the rules in order to reap their moral benefit. Further, no student is allowed to engage in public displays of affection with others, nor are men and women allowed in opposite sex dorms under any circumstances. Lastly the theology practica offer deep spiritual enrichment for students and real world advice on chastity.

Student Body

Describe the makeup of your institution's undergraduate student body with regard to sex, religion, home state/country and type of high school (public, private, homeschool):

Total number of undergraduates: 112
Male: 47% Female: 53%

Catholic: 98% Other Christian: %
Jewish: % Muslim: % Other: 2%

Number of states represented: 39
Top three states: California (18%), Colorado (8%), Wisconsin (7%)
Students from top three states: 31%

Catholic HS: 11% Homeschool: 69%
Private HS: 10% Public HS: 10%

Recommended Non-Residential Catholic Colleges

A Note About the Financial Aid and Career Services Sections

Paying for college and being able to find a job after graduation are two important considerations when choosing a college. In order to help families evaluate these two areas, the editors invited each college to submit information about them. Their submissions are printed in shaded containers within each profile.

About the Quick Facts Box

Quick Facts

Students the number of full-time undergraduate students

Majors the number of academic majors available

SATs the median SATs/ACTs for reading and math for freshmen

% Catholic the percentage of undergraduates who are Catholic

HS GPA the median grade point average for admitted freshmen

How Much? the cost of attendance for one academic year

HOLY APOSTLES
COLLEGE AND SEMINARY

Cromwell, Connecticut

411

For more information on Holy Apostles, visit their website at:

www.HolyApostles.edu

Admissions contact:

860/632-3001
admissions@HolyApostles.edu

Overview

The earliest Catholic universities made no distinction between higher education and preparation for the priesthood. In the same tradition, Holy Apostles College and Seminary offers lay men and women the opportunity to study philosophy and authentic Catholic theology together with seminarians and religious sisters, all of them studying, dining, and praying together daily.

The Seminary was founded in Cromwell, Connecticut, in 1956 by the Very Rev. Eusebe Menard, O.F.M., and entrusted to the Missionaries of the Holy Apostles to provide a college-level program education and formation for men discerning a vocation to the priesthood. Today it serves a large number of dioceses from the Northeast, Midwest, Southwest, Canada, and Vietnam, as well as several small religious orders.

In 1972 Holy Apostles expanded to offer undergraduate degrees for lay men and women, and it has since added an associate's degree, undergraduate and graduate distance-learning, and non-degree programs. Enrollment continues to grow, with an increase in applications over the past several years, to 54 undergraduates, 450 graduate students, and 90 seminarians.

"The lay students appreciate praying with seminarians, studying with seminarians and having lunch with them," said Father Douglas Mosey, C.S.B., the president-rector, but it is also "hugely beneficial" for the seminarians as well. "When you're a totally homogenous group you tend not to think as broadly as perhaps you should. Students at Holy Apostles share the lived experience of communion."

Holy Apostles prides itself on its orthodoxy and is committed to cultivating Catholic leaders for evangelization. "There will be plenty of opportunity for our students to defend the faith and be on the front lines of secular culture when they graduate," said Fr. Mosey.

The College is mostly a commuter school but works collaboratively with local realtors to establish small student nuclei in the surrounding community. It also constructed a convent on campus that is home to several nuns from Vietnam who are pursuing undergraduate degrees. The College is considering expanding residence halls for students in the future.

The core curriculum at Holy Apostles is strong and covers 60 credits or about half of the graduation requirement. Not surprisingly, there is heavy emphasis on theology and philosophy.

Students can major in philosophy, theology, English in the humanities, or history in the social sciences. They can also study bioethics through the College's Bioethics Center and in partnership with the National Catholic Bioethics Center in Philadelphia.

Holy Apostles entices students with a modest but picturesque and peaceful campus. It is also historic; the oldest building was erected in 1751. The campus is heavily wooded, and students and

Quick Facts

	2013-2014 Academic Year
Students 54	Majors 4
SATs not required	% Catholic 100%
HS GPA n/a	How Much? $10,400 tuition only

visitors enjoy a guided trail tour known as the Tree Walk.

Holy Apostles is an independent institution, and its seminary is not controlled by any single diocese. The ex officio chairman and chancellor is the Bishop of Norwich, and the board of directors includes the Archbishop of Hartford, the Bishop of Bridgeport, up to five members of the Missionaries of the Holy Apostles, lay representatives, and the president-rector.

All presidents of Holy Apostles have been priests. Father Mosey, who holds a Ph.D., has been president-rector since 1996.

An education at Holy Apostles is quite affordable. Undergraduate tuition, not including room and board, was $10,080 in 2012-2013, which is considerably less than the average tuition for private institutions in Connecticut. Financial aid is available if needed, including federal loans.

Academics

The College curriculum emphasizes philosophy and the Catholic liberal arts tradition. The College's objective is "to prepare college seminarians for the study of theology and to prepare lay students for graduate study and most especially for life."

The 60-credit core includes six Catholic theology courses, which include catechism, Theology of the Body, apologetics, scripture, moral theology and liturgy. There also are six philosophy courses, including Philosophy of God, only four courses short of a major. Other required courses include two in Latin and several in the traditional liberal arts disciplines, especially in literature and history.

Some of the courses are taught in an interdisciplinary manner, such as the team-taught course on the development of the social sciences. Interdisciplinary electives include religion and law, Catholic approaches to counseling, and bioethics.

Faculty members teaching philosophy and theology make a profession of faith and also promise obedience to the bishop and the Magisterium. Theology professors must have the *mandatum* to teach. All members of the academic and formational faculty of the Seminary are approved by the bishop on the recommendation of the rector of the Seminary.

In the fall of 2011, Holy Apostles added an Online Writing Lab to assist both on campus and distance learning students with specific questions regarding research and composition. The lab is staffed by two degreed professionals who work competently with students who have learning disabilities and students who encounter English as a Second Language.

Holy Apostles has attracted a wide range of students, from traditional recent high school graduates to senior citizens. Some come for two years for personal formation and then move on. Some opt to take the two-year associate of arts degree and return later to Holy Apostles or elsewhere to complete a bachelor's degree.

Lay students may consider vocations and eventually become seminarians, but many students have gone on to graduate studies or to get married and raise a family.

The Bioethics Center was founded in 1982 to articulate authentic Catholic teaching with respect to bioethical issues, from technological reproduction to end-of-life decisions. In addition to

ERUNT SICUT STELLAE
HOLY APOSTLES COLLEGE AND SEMINARY

Financial Aid Office Info

The cost of a college education can be a key factor in choosing which school to attend. Holy Apostles College (HAC) provides quality education at a price that is affordable for all of our students. We actively work with our students to borrow less and thus owe less.

We participate in a variety of programs: New England reciprocal agreements with many of the surrounding states which offer scholarships and/or grants to their residents attending HAC, Title IV participation offering Pell Grants and Direct Loans, and processing of both VA and TA educational benefits.

Parent PLUS loans and private loans have never been necessary for a student to meet their financial needs while attending Holy Apostles College. Financial stewardship is a key focus as our students matriculate through their program.

All potential students wishing to be considered for federal student loans or state grants must fill out the federal application (FAFSA) and the school's application. When the FAFSA has been received by the Holy Apostles Financial Aid Department, the information will be reviewed and inquiries are sent, by request only, an Estimate of Award based on their FAFSA information. However, it is recommended that inquiries contact the Financial Aid Office directly at 860-632-3020 or finaid@holyapostles.edu to receive further personal assistance. We look forward to answering your questions in a clear and timely manner.

other things, the Center offers information to students, scholars, and the general public online, linking to bioethics resources within the Church, the United States Conference of Catholic Bishops, various bioethics organizations, universities, publications, journals, medical associations, and more, providing a broad-based and solid Catholic founda-

tion for research and study.

Holy Apostles also recently initiated a working agreement with the National Catholic Bioethics Center (NCBC) in Philadelphia allowing a student, while earning credits towards a Masters in Theology at Holy Apostles, to also earn a certificate in bioethics from the NCBC.

In the fall of 2012, Holy Apostles added Massive Open Online Courses (MOOCs) to its offerings and allows anyone with an interest in the material to register into them for free via its MOOC registration site.

Spiritual Life

Holy Apostles has two daily Masses at Our Lady Queen of the Apostles chapel. The 7:15 a.m. Mass is primarily attended by the seminarians. The 9:30 a.m. Mass is mainly for staff and students. The 10 a.m. Sunday Mass is mostly for seminarians and local students. Mass in the Extraordi-

nary Form is available twice during the week and on Saturday mornings.

The Sacrament of Confession is available before each 7:15 a.m. Mass and two afternoons a week. There is a daily Holy Hour with exposition of the Blessed Sacrament, as well as 24-hour Adoration on the first Friday of every month.

Students also have the option of participating in Mass and other spiritual activities, including perpetual Adoration, at nearby St. John Church in Cromwell. The parish is staffed by Coventual Franciscan Friars.

Residential Life

Residential facilities for lay students on campus are very limited, but more residential opportunities may arise in the future. Some students share local apartments, but most commute from their homes. To help students with local housing, the admissions director works

with local realtors and homeowners. The college has developed a database of "host families" from local parishes.

Health services are available at Middlesex Hospital and Connecticut Valley Hospital, each located five minutes away in Middletown.

Cromwell is a town of 13,500 people that is 15 minutes from the state capital of Hartford and about 30 minutes from New Haven. The quiet town also is safe, with minimal violent crime and a crime rate only about 40 percent of the national crime index.

Hartford, a long-time center of the insurance industry, has a population of 125,000. It has a number of attractions, including the Mark Twain House and the Hartford Civic Center, which hosts cultural and sports events.

Cromwell can be reached by the north-south Interstate 91. Amtrak serves Hartford, and the city's Bradley International Airport provides non-stop service to several major cities.

Student Activities

As primarily a commuter college, Holy Apostles does not offer a large number of student activities, but it does make an effort to help Studentsstudents join together in fellowship and evangelization activities.

"The social life is very different here than most traditional colleges," said Fr. Mosey. "The social life here is Adoration, study, and pro-life work."

The student-run Holy Apostles Life

League, which coordinates pro-life activities, is quite active. Its activities include a prayer vigil on Saturday mornings at one of the abortion mills in Hartford during the academic year, followed by the Mass of Mercy in the Seminary chapel. In addition, a Holy Hour for Life and Mercy is held at the chapel every Saturday and includes the Divine Mercy Chaplet.

The Life League also coordinates the annual bus trip for students, faculty, and staff in January to the Right to Life March in Washington, D.C., and there is a tomb on campus marking the grave of an unborn victim of abortion where a flame continually burns.

The majority of undergraduate students are involved in campus liturgical life and spiritual activities. Social events are often informal, spontaneous, and student-initiated, and include cookouts, going to movies, playing several sports, as well as several off-campus activities.

With the ability to study and worship alongside seminarians and consecrated students, lay undergraduates readily substitute expanded social activities and residential facilities for the College's commitment to fidelity and evangelization.

The Bottom Line

Holy Apostles College and Seminary, long dedicated to preparing priests, has slowly expanded its lay enrollment since the 1970s. The College's small size and heavy emphasis on philosophy and authentic Catholic theology attract students who seek a quiet, prayerful atmosphere to prepare for evangelization, graduate study, and careers.

Since many courses are relevant both to lay students and to the seminary curric-

Letter from the President

Dear Parents and Prospective Students:

Thank you for your interest in Holy Apostles College & Seminary. Our mission is to cultivate lay, consecrated and ordained Catholic leaders for the purpose of evangelization.

Towards this end, we offer a philosophically-based, Catholic, liberal arts undergraduate degree program to prepare students for what Pope Paul VI called "the greatest drama of our time"—i.e., the split between the Gospel and culture. A degree from Holy Apostles prepares students to be active participants in the culture of life and to succeed in their chosen secular professions.

Holy Apostles is one of the few Catholic colleges in America where lay students, religious and seminarians attend many of the same classes together, worship together and grow intellectually and spiritually together. We are also one of a few Catholic colleges where all members of the faculty must be approved by the bishop in order to ensure fidelity to the magisterium.

Our Catholic identity is very strong and we are committed to providing an affordable education to educate young men and women while forming moral and ethical leaders who know and love God.

I invite you to visit or call to learn more about the exciting opportunities we offer. You are always welcome.

Yours in Christ,

Douglas L. Mosey C.S.B.

The Very Rev. Douglas L. Mosey, C.S.B., Ph.D.

ulum, most classes are open to everyone. That creates a unique interaction among students preparing to serve God in every way. As explained by Fr. Mosey, "Lay graduates often express their gratitude for studying side by side with seminarians and consecrated men and women, as together we form the One, Holy, Catholic and Apostolic Mystical Body of Christ."

Add to that the relatively low cost of education at Holy Apostles, and this is an option well worth considering for anyone who won't miss the trappings of the typical American college campus.

Holy Apostles College & Seminary Frequently Asked Questions

We get questions from Catholic families on a regular basis about the colleges we recommend. Rather than filter the answers, we asked Holy Apostles officials nearly 100 questions in categories such as academics, curriculum, programs of study, campus ministry, residence life, student activities, the make up of the study body, and institutional identity. The answers to some of the most asked questions are provided below and the rest are available on the college profile page at TheNewmanGuide.com.

Majors

List the major, minor and special program areas that students may choose for specialization while pursuing an undergraduate degree:

Philosophy; Theology; English in the Humanities; History in the Social Sciences.

What are the three most popular majors or specialty disciplines for undergraduate students, and about what percentage of undergraduate students specialize in these disciplines?

Philosophy, 45%

Theology, 30%

English in the Humanities, 15%

Spiritual Life

Please list the schedule of Masses, noting the following for each Mass: the day and time, the Form or Rite of the Mass, and the style of music, if any (chant, traditional, contemporary, etc.):

Mo 7:15 a.m. Ordinary Form, sung Mass in English; 9:30 am Extraordinary Form, low Mass

Tu 7:15 a.m. and 9:30 a.m. Both Ordinary Form, 7:15 sung Mass with traditional music

We 7:15 a.m. and 9:30 a.m. Same as Monday

Th 7:15 a.m. Ordinary form in Latin, Gregorian chant; 9:30 a.m. Same as Tuesday

Fr 7:15 a.m. Spanish, contemporary music

Sa 7:15 a.m. Same as Monday; 8:30 a.m. Extraordinary Form and sung once a month

Su 10:15 a.m. Ordinary Form Mass with Gregorian chant

List the schedule for Confession by day and time:

Mo before morning Mass and before evening prayer

Tu before morning Mass and before evening prayer

We before morning Mass and before evening prayer

Th before morning Mass and before evening prayer

Fr before morning Mass and before evening prayer

Sa before morning Mass and before evening prayer

Su before morning Mass and before evening prayer

Or by Appointment

List the schedule for Adoration of the Blessed Sacrament by day and time:

Monday-Thursday 4:00 p.m.

Friday 7:00 p.m.

Saturday 3:00 p.m.

Sunday 7:00 p.m.

Please identify regularly scheduled devotions on campus for students such as the Rosary and prayer groups:

Catholic Underground - 1 meeting per month

Charismatic Renewal - Sunday evening

Contemporary Praise & Worship - Monday evening

International Rosary - Wednesday afternoon

Confraternity of Mary - Thursday afternoon

Student Body

Describe the makeup of your institution's undergraduate student body with regard to sex, religion, home state/country and type of high school (public, private, homeschool):

Total number of undergraduates: 54
Male: 50% Female: 50%

Catholic: 100% Other Christian: %
Jewish: % Muslim: % Other: %

Number of states represented: 13 including Vietnam and Korea
Top three states: CT,NY,KY
Students from top three states: 46%

Catholic HS: 60% Homeschool: 5%
Private HS: % Public HS: 35%

HOLY SPIRIT COLLEGE

Atlanta, Georgia

411

For more information on Holy Spirit, visit their website at:

www.HolySpiritCollege.org

Admissions contact:

678/904-4959
admissions@HolySpiritCollege.org

Overview

Holy Spirit College was founded in 2005 to offer dual credit to the students of Atlanta's Holy Spirit Preparatory School. But the College quickly moved from that role to develop its own specific mission.

Holy Spirit has much going for it: a great location in an archdiocese with a rapidly growing Catholic population, a well-designed liberal arts curriculum, and an achievable growth plan. The College is housed on the 34-acre campus of Holy Spirit Catholic parish, in a peaceful neighborhood on the border of north Atlanta and Sandy Springs. It shares some facilities with the parish and upper school, but it has its own offices, library, chapel, classrooms, and student lounge.

It is also Catholic throughout. Holy Spirit describes itself as an "authentic Catholic" college. Theology is interwoven throughout the program—and it's true to the Magisterium, Scripture, and the teachings of the Church.

That goes for all of the liberal arts courses. According to Chancellor Gareth Genner, "At Holy Spirit, it's not just an English professor standing in front lecturing. A professor is teaching from the great Catholic works, interacting

with students at High Table, mentoring, and influencing students beyond the curriculum."

What the College doesn't yet have is a large number of students—the tiny start-up has just 5 undergraduates with one new student in the 2012-2013 academic year. It no longer offers College-sponsored housing, at least until the enrollment increases.

But Holy Spirit is moving full-steam ahead for 2013-14, welcoming new undergraduates even while its graduate theology programs continue to bring in students. The College looks to grow to 200 undergraduate and graduate students over the next decade. Students

should anticipate very small class sizes and a highly personalized education in the next few years—much different from the typical college experience.

The advantage of such a small school, says Genner, is that "you can create faculty and student relationships that are closer than you could achieve elsewhere." Every student has a faculty mentor who is required to have dinner with them monthly on campus.

Holy Spirit is governed by an independent board of trustees and has strong roots in the Archdiocese of Atlanta. The nine-member board includes Archbishop Wilton Gregory, who serves as College rector; Monsignor Edward Dillon, pastor of Holy Spirit Parish and College president; and Father Paul Burke, chair of the College's theology faculty. Monsignor Dillon has a doctorate in canon law from The Catholic University of America, and he studied for the priesthood at Carlow College, the oldest Catholic college in Ireland.

The College had pursued accreditation from the American Academy for Liberal Education, but because of AALE's disputes with the U.S. Department of Education, Holy Spirit withdrew from the AALE and is seeking accreditation from

Quick Facts

2013-2014 Academic Year

Students 5

SATs 1100

HS GPA 3.4

Majors 1

% Catholic 100%

How Much? $18,626
tuition

the Southern regional agency, which is in progress.

Academics

The 64-credit core curriculum includes the following courses: three history, two Latin, four theology, two philosophy, two literature, two environmental science, one math, a one-credit physical education requirement, and non-credit courses in iconography and Gregorian chant. All students are also required to take a course in Catholic catechetics and a course in rhetoric.

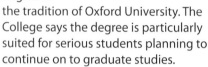

Instead of the usual bachelor of arts degree, Holy Spirit offers a Bachelor of Philosophy degree in the tradition of Oxford University. The College says the degree is particularly suited for serious students planning to continue on to graduate studies.

Students can concentrate in philosophy or theology. But the College also has an agreement with Ave Maria University in Florida, allowing students to transfer their core curriculum credits to Ave Maria and take advantage of a wider array of majors. HSC students also have the option of finishing their B.Phil. (doable in three years) and moving on to complete a Bachelor of Arts at Thomas More College of Liberal Arts (possible with one more year of study).

Holy Spirit College offers study abroad programs each summer, alternating between Rome and Oxford University. The Oxford and Rome programs are offered in partnership with Thomas More College of Liberal Arts in New Hampshire.

Because students are able to carry a 20-credit load and can take study abroad classes over the summer, it is possible to complete a degree within three years.

The College offers a mix of the modern and the Old World. On the one hand, every student is provided an iPad that is pre-loaded with research applications by the College librarian. Wireless access is available throughout the campus, and the College's two classrooms include Smartboards, which faculty routinely utilize for their lectures.

On the other hand, the College borrows some traditions from European education. The professors, for example, wear teaching robes while in class.

Spiritual Life

Located on the parish grounds, Holy Spirit offers numerous opportunities for the sacraments. Daily Masses are offered in the parish's St. Mary's Chapel and in St. Joseph's Oratory, where students may also participate in morning prayer. Weekend Masses are celebrated in the parish church. At the conclusion of Sunday's 11:30 a.m. Mass, a faculty-hosted Fellowship Lunch is offered for the College students.

Five priests serve the parish and schools, including Fr. Nicholas Azar, the chaplain. The Sacrament of Reconciliation is available daily on request. Eucharistic adoration is offered on first Fridays from morning through the night. There is a mandatory retreat each semester, and optional retreats are available through the parish.

Holy Spirit Parish is one of Atlanta's largest, comprised of more than 1,300 families, 4,000 parishioners, and 125 ministries.

Residential Life

Residence halls are not available from the College. Rather, students reside at home or in the local area near to the campus.

The campus is gum-free. The College has general expectations in terms of modesty and appropriate clothing, and formal wear is required during more formal events, such as Mass, matriculation,

Financial Aid Office Info

Data submitted on the Application for Admission is used by the Office of Admissions to award scholarships. Students need not complete additional scholarship applications unless they are seeking a Life Teen scholarship. Catholic students may apply for an Archbishop Donoghue Scholarship covering full tuition and books. Substantial tuition scholarships are available to valedictorians and salutatorians of Catholic high schools. Students who sign a nonbinding letter of intent to pursue postgraduate studies in seminary or to enter religious life will receive a 50% tuition scholarship with 25% of tuition advanced as a noninterest bearing loan to be cancelled upon their entering the seminary or religious life. HSC also offers need-based grants to students with a demonstrated financial need. These grants are funded by HSC and are awarded to students based on family income information provided in the College Scholarship Service Financial Aid Profile.

and graduation.

The College's meal plan is complimentary, with breakfast and lunch offered on days when classes are in session.

The suburban community consists of luxury homes and mansions on Atlanta's northern edge. Nearby to campus are the Galleria Specialty and Cumberland Malls for shopping, banking, and entertainment. The College is within 15 minutes of downtown Atlanta, an exciting and rapidly growing city with the nation's third-largest concentration of Fortune 500 companies and museums, concert halls, restaurants, sporting events, and all of the amenities of city life.

Student Activities

Not surprisingly, students tell us that the College's small size is both its greatest strength and its greatest weakness.

Students enjoy a great deal of individual attention from faculty, but there are fewer social opportunities than might be available on other campuses, especially athletics.

The College does provide for occasional social activities and clubs, varying by agreement between the chaplain and the students, with a mandatory social evening every week. The College partners with the Aquinas Center at nearby Emory University to provide additional activities, events, and lectures.

It also has a relationship with Solidarity School and Mission, a Hispanic outreach program to help those who cannot make it to Church. Students have assisted Moda Real, a virtue and modesty program for the Hispanic mission that culminates in an annual modest fashion show. Students can also participate in social service projects with Catholic Charities and Habitat for Humanity.

The College has plans for organized tennis, basketball, track and field, soccer, and golf when the student body gets a bit larger. There are parish and metro league teams in football and softball, and students with prior experience can volunteer as assistant coaches for the upper and lower schools.

The Bottom Line

Although Holy Spirit is a small start-up college, it has much to offer with its unique combination of parish life and proximity to Atlanta. Most important for Catholic families, it provides a rigorous and thoroughly Catholic education, culminating in the unique bachelor of philosophy degree. The articulation agreements with Ave Maria University and Thomas More College ensure that students have a variety of options for majors.

As Georgia's only Catholic college, Holy Spirit is likely to enjoy much success. Utilizing shared parish and school facilities allows the College to leverage existing

Letter from the President

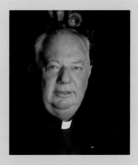

Dear Parents and Prospective Students:

A significant component of the Church's mission focuses on the development and formation of the whole person. This is one of the reasons why there has always been a major emphasis in the Church in Catholic education and the institution of the Catholic school.

We are in the very fortunate position of having a Catholic school, providing an excellent academic education in conjunction with faith formation, from Preschool through the 12th grade. The school has been recognized both as a National Blue Ribbon School of Excellence by the Department of Education & Science and for four years running as one of the Top 50 Catholic High School's in America. A logical extension of this heritage of academic excellence was consideration of the post-secondary years. Since 2005 Holy Spirit College has offered certificate programs in the Liberal Arts and since 2009 we have also offered a professional certificate in Catholic Education.

Holy Spirit College now offers undergraduate and graduate degrees. The undergraduate degrees are ideal for the high school graduate who is not attracted to a large institutional environment or is seeking a more personalized and very rigorous academic experience at an authentically Catholic institution. The graduate degrees and certificate programs will be ideal for the person who already has an undergraduate degree and who wants to continue studying for additional qualifications in a Catholic atmosphere. They are also ideal for the Catholic person who wants to broaden his or her knowledge of the faith to function as a catechist in a parish or perhaps just for personal growth.

Welcome to Holy Spirit College.

Sincerely,

Msgr. Edward J. Dillon J.C.D.
President

space without all of the costs typically associated with beginning a college.

Holy Spirit's commitment to an authentic Catholic education makes it an excellent option—especially for students seeking a high level of individualized attention in the concentration areas of theology and philosophy. College President Msgr. Dillon says, "The most fundamental role of the College is service to the Church, in particular

preparing the leaders of the future – not bishops, priests, and religious, but lay people who are thoroughly grounded in Catholic teaching and know how to fulfill their true vocation as articulated by the Second Vatican Council and the focus on the New Evangelization."

Holy Spirit College
Frequently Asked Questions

We get questions from Catholic families on a regular basis about the colleges we recommend. Rather than filter the answers, we asked Holy Spirit officials nearly 100 questions in categories such as academics, curriculum, programs of study, campus ministry, residence life, student activities, the make up of the study body, and institutional identity. The answers to some of the most asked questions are provided below and the rest are available on the college profile page at TheNewmanGuide.com.

Majors

List the major, minor and special program areas that students may choose for specialization while pursuing an undergraduate degree:

Theology and philosophy.

What are the three most popular majors or specialty disciplines for undergraduate students, and about what percentage of undergraduate students specialize in these disciplines?

N/A

Spiritual Life

Please list the schedule of Masses, noting the following for each Mass: the day and time, the Form or Rite of the Mass, and the style of music, if any (chant, traditional, contemporary, etc.):

Mo 8:30 a.m. and 6:00 p.m., Ordinary Form, traditional music

Tu 8:30 a.m. and 6:00 p.m., Ordinary Form, traditional music

We 8:30 a.m. and 6:00 p.m., Ordinary Form, traditional music

Th 8:30 a.m. and 6:00 p.m., Ordinary Form, traditional music

Fr 8:30 a.m. and 6:00 p.m., Ordinary Form, traditional music

Sa

Su

List the schedule for Confession by day and time:

Mo

Tu

We

Th

Fr

Sa

Su

Other: Daily on request.

List the schedule for Adoration of the Blessed Sacrament by day and time:

First Friday Adoration 9:00 a.m. to Midnight. Other times on student initiative.

Please identify regularly scheduled devotions on campus for students such as the Rosary and prayer groups:

As agreed between the Chaplain and students each semester.

Student Body

Describe the makeup of your institution's undergraduate student body with regard to sex, religion, home state/country and type of high school (public, private, homeschool):

Total number of undergraduates: 5
Male: 20% Female: 80%

Catholic: 100% Other Christian: %
Jewish: % Muslim: % Other: %

Top three states: Georgia, California, Oregon
Students from top three states: 100%

Recommended Online and International Catholic Colleges

CAMPION COLLEGE

Toongabbie East, Australia

Overview

Campion College outside of Sydney, Australia, is a faithfully Catholic liberal arts college established in 2006 under the patronage of the English martyr St. Edmund Campion.

The College welcomes English-speaking students for one or more semesters or to complete a full degree, and it has had several students from the U.S., England, Canada, and New Zealand. They fit well within the close-knit community, which has 92 students in 2013.

The College is governed by a 10-member board of trustees, the Campion Institute. The eight-member Campion Foundation launched the college and provides financial support, but has no direct control over the institution. Since 2012, the college is led by Dr. Ryan Messmore, a native of the United States and a former research fellow in religion and a free society at The Heritage Foundation in Washington, D.C.

Campion College offers a fully-accredited three-year bachelor's degree program in the liberal arts. The College has several credit transfer and recognition agreements with colleges in the U.S. Students planning for graduate studies in the U.S. should check to ensure that a Campion degree is accepted.

The cost of studying at Campion is relatively low. Not only are degrees awarded after three years, but the total cost for tuition, room and board in 2013 (February-November) is about $29,300 in U.S. dollars according to exchange rates in June 2013. Scholarships and need-based grants are available.

Academics

The integrated core curriculum for all students includes 24 required courses in subjects including history, literature, philosophy, and theology. Students also can choose extra courses in Latin, science, mathematics and ethics as electives.

Core subjects are taught in sequence, with some flexibility in choosing courses in the third year. For example, in history, students progress from an overview course to ancient history, the Middle Ages, the Renaissance and Reformation, and beyond. In the third year, students have options such as studying the 20th century or taking the course Australian Politics, Culture and Religion.

Theology courses consider Christian culture, revelation, the Sacraments and contemporary theology. Optional courses include contemporary theology, sexual ethics, bioethics, and Catholic social teaching.

All college lecturers hold doctorates.

Spiritual Life

The chaplaincy team is led by Father Luke Holohan, S.M., who provides daily Mass in the college chapel. To nurture the spiritual life of students and staff, the team provides other sacraments and activities, including confession, Eucharistic Adoration, spiritual retreats, and individual spiritual direction. All-night Adoration occurs every first Friday of the month.

Quick Facts

2013-2014 Academic Year

Students 92

Majors 4

SATs N/A

% Catholic 95%

HS GPA N/A

How Much? AUD$29,300
tuition, room and board

Every fortnight, the College hosts a "Formal Hall," a special dinner held in conjunction with special feast days at which students and staff wear academic gowns. Students and staff also join together for brief times of daily prayer.

Campion students are active leaders in the local Catholic community, including the Australian Catholic Students Association (ACSA), the annual Corpus Christi procession in Sydney, and various Catholic charitable organizations.

Residential Life

Campus housing includes separate men's and women's dorms or houses, with both single and double rooms, with air conditioning and wireless internet access. A linen service is provided for laundry needs.

Students can also rent nearby homes or apartments.

The college is located in Old Toongabbie, one of the oldest suburbs of Sydney, and is located 18 miles from the central business district. It is also near Parramatta, a major business and commercial center.

Three medical clinics, as well as the 975-bed Westmead Hospital, are in the vicinity.

Most travelers to Australia arrive at Sydney International Airport. The 45-minute trip from Sydney to Campion is possible by automobile, bus, and rail service.

Student Activities

Students engage in a number of clubs and activities coordinated by the Campion College Students Association. There is a debating team, chess club, public speaking club, and campus pro-life group that works to support local pro-life organizations.

Favorite events include an annual soccer tournament, talent night, and formal Campion Ball. The annual Campion Olympics is hosted by the classics society. Students enjoy regular poker nights and playing billiards and ping pong in the student common room. Students play the grand piano and a variety of other instruments at Formal Hall every fortnight.

Since the inception of Campion, students have provided assistance to members of the local community and along with staff hold an annual BBQ for the neighbors.

There are many outstanding cultural, shopping and sports opportunities in Sydney, a city of nearly five million people. Residents and tourists enjoy the beaches, including Bondi Beach, about 45 minutes away.

Hiking is a popular activity in the nearby Blue Mountains World Heritage Area.

The Bottom Line

The only liberal arts college in Australia, Campion College was founded to provide students an opportunity to be well-educated and grow in the Catholic Faith. The College's founders carefully studied the renaissance taking place in U.S. Catholic higher education, and they have sought to plant a similar flag of orthodoxy in Australia.

Today Campion is a successful Catholic institution that offers a unique experience to American students seeking a study-abroad option or a full degree. While certain aspects of Australian colleges and universities are unfamiliar to U.S. students—for example, a three-year undergraduate program and a February-to-November academic year—the opportunity to study at Campion with its strong curriculum and Catholic identity could be very appealing to the faithful, adventurous student.

CATHOLIC DISTANCE UNIVERSITY

Online

411

For more information on CDU, visit their website at:

www.cdu.edu

Admissions contact:

888/254-4238 ext. 700
admissions@cdu.edu

Overview

Catholic Distance University offers an associate's degree in Catholic studies and an undergraduate degree completion program exclusively through online study.

The first president and chairman of the board was the late Bishop Thomas Welsh, then of the Diocese of Arlington, Virginia, where the school is located, and who later served as Bishop of the Diocese of Allentown, Pennsylvania.

Originally begun as the Catholic Home Study Institute, the name was changed in 1996 to Catholic Distance University (CDU) to reflect its status as a degree-granting institution. Dr. Marianne Evans Mount, the president, has been with the university in several capacities since its inception.

Although CDU's headquarters is located in Hamilton, Virginia, a small town of about 900 residents one hour west of Washington, D.C., its student body is widely scattered. Every state as well as 60 foreign countries have been represented over the past 30 years.

Students are able to pursue certificate

and degree programs at the noncredit, undergraduate and graduate level and a Vatican-approved Catechetical Diploma at the undergraduate level. But what most interests us, is that students interested in receiving a bachelor's degree in theology can take their final 38 credits at a high-quality, time-flexible institution after completing their general course-work elsewhere. This offers flexibility and cost savings to students who take advantage of a liberal arts core curriculum at another college—preferably one of the solid Catholic institutions in *The Newman Guide*—then complete a theology degree from home. Also, CDU recently introduced a new associate's

degree program in Catholic studies designed to provide a way for students to earn the AA degree first and then move into the bachelor completion program, all at CDU.

The B.A. completion program began in 2004. The first degree was awarded in 2006 and, as of 2013, 49 undergraduate degrees were awarded through this program. CDU's undergraduate enrollment through mid-2013 was 116 students, and graduate enrollment was 149 students. When adding non-credit students, about 900 students take classes each year.

Students are mostly older adults returning to college, but not exclusively. The vast majority, not surprisingly, are Catholics, but there are a few non-Catholics as well. Students come to CDU as a way to increase their knowledge of the Catholic faith, as well as to bring this knowledge to their families and into their professional lives. Some students hope for positions in Catholic schools or other religious education programs.

CDU is governed by an 18-member board of trustees, four of whom are either bishops or priests. The chairman of the board is Bishop Paul Loverde of the Diocese of Arlington. Other board members include Bishop Michael

Quick Facts

2013-2014 Academic Year

Students 119

SATs N/A

HS GPA N/A

Majors 2

% Catholic 98%

How Much? $915/course tuition

Bransfield of the Diocese of Wheeling-Charleston, West Virginia, Archbishop Timothy Broglio of the Archdiocese for Military Services, and retired Auxiliary Bishop John Dougherty of the Diocese of Scranton, Pennsylvania.

Dr. Mount, who helped establish CDU, served as the executive vice president for 12 years before she was named president in 2008. She earned a graduate degree in religious education from the Pontifical University of St. Thomas Aquinas and a doctorate in adult learning and distance education from Virginia Polytechnic Institute and State University.

The graduate dean, Dr. Robert Royal, is a well-known Catholic scholar and author.

In addition to being faithful and flexible, especially for students who have work or family responsibilities, Catholic Distance University is a bargain. The undergraduate tuition for 2013-2014 is $305 per credit.

Academics

The bachelor of arts completion program in theology accepts students either provisionally or fully, depending on previous credits earned. Students need 80 credits from an accredited college to be fully admitted to the program. Forty credits, all in theology, must be taken at CDU; 10 of these credits can be electives.

All courses are taught in conformity with Church teachings. According to Dr. Mount, "All theology professors are reviewed and approved by a board-level Academic Committee. We send their curriculum vitae to his office. The *mandatum* may be obtained in a home diocese or from where a faculty member is working."

CDU has always been a distance institution. From 1983 until 2000, it used a paper correspondence format. Increasingly, it has gone online and describes itself as "an online learning community that is global." But for imprisoned students, instruction is virtually 100% online. Instruction is now approximately 80 percent online and 20 percent paper.

One component of the program includes two half-credit courses "Undergraduate Writing Skills" and "Undergraduate Research Skills," designed to help students develop tools needed for successful online college work such as study skills and time management.

The Associate of Arts in the Liberal Arts program, with a concentration in Catholic studies, emphasizes study of the Catholic intellectual tradition. Upon completion of this degree, students have the option of transferring to another Catholic college or earning a bachelor's degree in theology at CDU. CDU also has arranged for students to have library privileges with Woodstock Theological Center Library, a 190,000-volume library housed on the Georgetown University campus in Washington, D.C.

One special academic outreach is to prisoners. Since its beginning, CDU has provided very low-cost correspondence courses to incarcerated Catholics whose names have been put forward by their chaplains.

Spiritual Life

Catholic Distance University has an online chapel, and the undergraduate dean, Father Bevil Bramwell, O.M.I., celebrates Mass daily at the administrative offices and posts meditations online. He also is the full-time theologian-in-residence and teaches several courses. Students can contact Father Bramwell privately for guidance and post prayer requests.

The Bottom Line

The delivery of education is rapidly changing, and online instruction is a growing and viable alternative to traditional education. Catholic Distance University has been at the forefront of providing quality, faithful Catholic teaching to students seeking flexibility.

The undergraduate completion program, which offers a degree in theology, can be an attractive and low-cost option to students who have completed or are contemplating completing basic, non-major courses elsewhere. Whether for work, location, family or other reasons, more students are likely to view Catholic Distance University as a unique opportunity to receive an education which will enhance an understanding of their Catholic Faith.

IGNATIUS-ANGELICUM LIBERAL STUDIES PROGRAM

Online

411

For more information on Ignatius-Angelicum, visit their website at:

www.angelicum.net

Admissions contact:

719/930-7549
info@angelicum.net

Overview

The Ignatius-Angelicum Liberal Studies Program (LSP) is an online liberal arts program offering courses for all grade levels. At the college level, courses can often be applied toward a bachelor's, master's, or doctoral degree, especially through one of the colleges that have agreements with the LSP.

Since 2010, the LSP has combined a four-year Great Books Program with four theology courses taught by Father Joseph Fessio, S.J. Students can join the LSP as high school or college students.

Launched in the year 2000, the Great Books Program was inspired by the late Dr. Mortimer Adler, who advocated the "great books" approach to education that is used in dozens of liberal arts colleges and universities. But Adler hoped to see the study of these important Western texts begin in high school, so founders Patrick Carmack, J.D., and Dr. Peter Redpath of St. John's University in New York developed an online program. Now partnered with Ignatius Press and its editor Father Fessio—a former student of Pope Benedict XVI and former chancellor of Ave Maria University—the program now has more than 220

students taking its online courses, and students have come from more than 40 countries.

The Great Books curriculum involves reading all or part of a Great Book each week and meeting online for a two-hour Socratic discussion. The discussions are live and conversational, usually including between 15 and 20 students and two moderators, many of them Catholic university professors. Students working for college credit also submit weekly essays and two 1,500-1,800 word essays per semester.

With the addition of Father Fessio's theology courses, the LSP's undergraduate-level courses can count toward a

degree program elsewhere. Graduates have attended numerous colleges and universities, with LSP courses accepted for as many as 59 college credits. The American Council on Education has formally recommended that its more than 2,000 affiliated colleges and universities accept six credit hours per semester of the eight-semester Great Books Program for college level credit.

While there are limitations to an online program, Catholic families may find much to admire in a classical Catholic curriculum that allows students to stay home at a very low cost. The Great Books Program tuition of $1,495 per semester or $2,990 per year for college-level credit has not changed in 13 years, and LSP offers discounts for early enrollment. The theology courses are $250 per credit hour, with the same early enrollment discounts.

Moreover, high school-aged students in Alaska, California, Hawaii, Idaho, Oregon, and Washington may be eligible for state tuition reimbursement.

Fr. Fessio serves as chancellor of the LSP, and the president is attorney Carmack, who participated in Dr. Adler's last several Socratic discussion groups in 1999 and 2000. Carmack's varied background

Quick Facts

2013-2014 Academic Year

Students 221		Majors N/A
SATs N/A		% Catholic 95%
HS GPA N/A		How Much? $2,990 tuition

includes former administrative law Judge at the Oklahoma State Corporation Commission, member of the U.S. Supreme Court Bar, former CEO of an independent petroleum exploration and production company, and founder and former chairman of the International Caspian Horse Society. Dr. Redpath, a respected Thomas philosopher, chairs the Angelicum portion of the program and directs the Great Books Program.

Academics

Adler believed that conversation (the dialectic) aims at teaching students how to think critically and thus attain wisdom, as opposed to a monologue (such as a lecture), which tends to result in indoctrination and mere memorization. In Reforming Education, written in the 1940s, Adler already saw that many Catholic schools were losing their way and following the path of public institutions.

Taking a different path, students in LSP's Great Books Program start with the ancient Greeks the first year, followed by the ancient Romans, the Medievals, and the Moderns. Students are exposed to works including Sacred Scripture, St. Augustine's Confessions and City of God, St. Thomas' Summa Theologiae, Dante's Divine Comedy, Chaucer's Canterbury Tales, Cervantes' Don Quixote, St. Thomas More's Utopia, Shakespeare's great plays, and a short story by Flannery O'Connor. The program also includes exposure to Catholic ascetical and mystical theology, including `a Kempis' The Imitation of Christ, St. Teresa of Avila's autobiography, and St. John of the Cross' Dark Night of the Soul.

The readings are accompanied by more than 2,400 pages of study guides by Dr. Robert and Suzanne Alexander, edited by author Joseph Pearce and Thomist philosophers to provide a Catholic understanding. Carmack estimates that students will read about 45-60 minutes a night for four or five nights a week, depending on the reader.

Identical, live first-year classes are scheduled at different times of day to give students a choice that fits their schedules. Although the program is online, there is opportunity for interaction. Students meet in the online classrooms, may become friends through e-mail exchanges, and sometimes meet during or at the end of the academic year.

The LSP theology courses are asynchronous and so may be taken at any time of year.

Students who complete any portion of the 59 credit hours can earn a degree from an accredited college in an additional one-and-a-half to two-and-a-half years, assuming LSP credits are accepted. LSP has degree-completion agreements with Benedictine College, Campion College in Australia, Catholic Distance University, Bethel University and Harrison Middleton University. Although many colleges accept ACE-recommended credits, not all do; students should inquire with colleges they may be considering.

Students who start LSP's program after high school will need four years to complete the 48 credit hours in the Great Books Program, and two years to complete the theology courses. But some colleges—including Catholic Distance University—allow students to take LSP courses at the same time or even after their own courses. Other students may be content to spread out their studies over time, thereby reducing annual costs and simultaneously getting a head start on a career or exploring a religious vocation.

The Bottom Line

Families considering taking advantage of the Ignatius-Angelicum Liberal Studies Program or any part of it should be prepared to do a little extra homework and study the options and institutions. They should also carefully consider the cost and time implications of distance learning and how to provide for a student's ongoing personal and spiritual development outside of a four-year campus experience.

Having done that, many students will find the Ignatius-Angelicum Liberal Studies Program enticing. It offers something unique in Catholic higher education: worldwide access to a relatively inexpensive, authentically Catholic, high-quality, liberal arts program that can be accessed from home and commenced during high school years.

OUR LADY SEAT OF WISDOM ACADEMY

Barry's Bay, Ontario, Canada

411

For more information on Our Lady Seat of Wisdom, visit their website at:

www.SeatofWisdom.org

Admissions contact:

877/369-6520 ext. 202
admissions@seatofwisdom.org

Overview

Our Lady Seat of Wisdom Academy is faithfully Catholic, offers a strong liberal arts curriculum, and is surprisingly affordable for American students who take advantage of its one-, two- or three-year programs and go on to receive their degree at one of the partnering *Newman Guide* colleges.

The Academy, which grew out of a dream of homeschooling families for faithful and affordable Catholic higher education in Ontario, hopes soon to offer a four-year degree. But the Canadian government has stringent rules for postsecondary institutions, and OLSWA is at least a few years away from final approval.

The Academy has three academic and administrative buildings, located immediately adjacent to St. Hedwig's Parish, which overlooks a scenic lake. It also uses parish space for dining and for an extra classroom. Students live together in small households in three purpose-built residences and in other leased residences in the local community.

With current enrollment at 78 students, the Academy's goal is to have as many as 200 students. More than one-third of the students have been homeschooled, and about 10 percent are American.

Students can earn a Basic Certificate after one year of study, and an Associate Certificate after two years. At the end of three years, students may earn a General Certificate of Christian Humanities or one with a concentration in any of five areas.

A 13-member board of directors governs the Academy, assisted by an academic senate. The episcopal advisory board includes Thomas Cardinal Collins of Toronto, Archbishop J. Michael Miller, C.S.B., of Vancouver, and Archbishop Terrence Prendergast, S.J., of Ottawa. Dr. Keith Cassidy, the president, is an historian who has taught at several Canadian universities and has written on several aspects of American history, most notably about the pro-life movement. .

The very low cost is appealing. Tuition, room and board in 2013-14 cost students C$10,950, or about $10,690 USD as of June 2013. That can be further reduced by scholarships, "bursaries" (grants), and work-study opportunities.

Academics

In the first year, students take courses in Christian doctrine, Scripture, Western civilization, philosophy, essay writing, Latin and chorus. Second-year courses include Scripture and philosophy, including Introduction to St. Thomas, and Survey of Literature.

Students may concentrate in any of five areas: literature, history, philosophy, theology and Church music. They may take electives in these areas as well as in Natural Sciences, Mathematics, Social Sciences and Arts.

The Academy has expanded its music offerings under Maestro Uwe Liefländer, founder of Canada's Sacred Music Society. In addition to directing the choir, he

Quick Facts

2013-2014 Academic Year

Students 78

SATs N/A

HS GPA N/A

Majors 5

% Catholic 100%

How Much? $10,690 USD
tuition, room and board

teaches a wide variety of music courses and offers individual music lessons.

Catholic novelist and artist Michael D. O'Brien and his wife Sheila helped found OLSWA and is its artist- and writer-in-residence.

The Academy has had its credits accepted by Christendom College, the Franciscan University of Steubenville, Ave Maria University, the College of St. Mary Magdalen, and Campion College in Australia. OLSWA credits have also been accepted by colleges not in *The Newman Guide*, including Holy Cross College in Indiana, Redeemer University College in Hamilton, Ontario, and Tyndale University College and Seminary in Toronto. The latter two are nondenominational Christian colleges.

All full-time and part-time faculty members are faithful Catholics.

Spiritual Life

The spiritual life revolves around St. Hedwig's Parish. Most students attend one of the two normally-scheduled daily Masses there. A weekly formal Academy Mass is celebrated by the OLSWA chaplains, with music provided by the Academy choir. There also are two Sunday Masses, one Saturday Vigil Mass, and twice-weekly confessions at the parish. The Extraordinary form is also provided whenever possible based on the availability of celebrants.

Students are active in parish life, serving as readers, altar servers, members of the choir, and participants in Eucharistic Adoration.

Students are invited to join in a daily Rosary with faculty and staff. An annual Consecration to Mary is made every

fall at the campus grotto. There is a men's and a women's retreat each year, two pilgrimages, a Christian formation speaker series, and an annual Day of Recollection held early in the fall semester for the entire OLSWA community.

The Academy's chaplain is Fr. Paul Burchat, a member of the nearby Madonna House lay community, who is assisted by Fr. Joseph Hattie, O.M.I. Students have the opportunity to meet with these priests throughout the week for spiritual direction, counseling and confession.

Residential Life

On-campus students live in single-sex residence houses. Each house has eight to 12 students along with one residence assistant and a proctor, who are older students. Meals are provided at St. Hedwig's parish hall.

The households are an important part of the student life program. The houses have monthly house nights and regular prayer time interwoven into their daily lives.

Chastity is fostered, and there are clear guidelines regarding times for opposite-sex visitations in the houses. Intervisitation in the bedrooms is always forbidden. "Modest" dress is always expected on campus, and a professional dress code applies for classes.

All students are assigned regular chores for three to four hours a week. These include helping with the dinner dishes, sweeping the floors, and cleaning classrooms and common areas.

St. Francis Memorial Hospital is located in the town. There are no significant airports nearby; Americans are likely to use Ottawa International Airport, a two

and one-half-hour drive away, or Toronto Pearson International Airport, which is four hours away. Route 17, known as the Trans-Canada Highway, is an hour's drive from the town.

Student Activities

Campus clubs include the Don Bosco Drama Club, the Frassati Outdoors Club, the Evangelization Club, and the Paul Sanders and Janine Lieu Pro-Life Club, named in memory of two students.

Every year a large number of musically talented students come to campus. There are frequent informal musical events, as well as organized activities such as Schola, which includes members of the wider community.

Students elect a Student Activities Council every year to plan monthly social events such as the Winter Formal and other dances, movie nights, and field trips. New organizations form each year based on interest, and many informal social activities are student-initiated.

Most days there are spontaneous sporting activities. Every week there is a regular sports night at a local gym (which includes soccer, volleyball, basketball, badminton, and weight lifting), followed by a hockey game at the local arena.

The Bottom Line

Our Lady Seat of Wisdom Academy is an affordable yet high-quality option for faithful Catholics. This small institution, committed to its motto of Veritas vos Liberabit ("The Truth will set you free"), provides a wonderful curriculum at a very low cost.

The Academy can help students get acclimated to college life and strengthen their faith before moving on to another solid Catholic college to finish their studies, but we hope the Academy is soon recognized as a full college, able to award bachelor's degrees. The promise of this institution is enhanced by the beauty of studying in the scenic Ontario valley. It's an option worth serious consideration.

PONTIFICAL UNIVERSITY OF ST. THOMAS AQUINAS

Rome, Italy

411

For more information on The Angelicum, visit their website at:

www.pust.it

Admissions contact:

(+39) 06 67 021
angepr@pust.it

Q.ht/WnAkV

Overview

The Dominicans' Pontifical University of St. Thomas Aquinas, more popularly known as "the Angelicum" in honor of the "Angelic Doctor of the Church," is the only pontifical university in Rome that offers a full first-cycle, three-year program (similar to a bachelor's degree program) in English—but some college education before going to Rome is usually necessary.

Students learn Italian during this first cycle and usually continue toward a Vatican-approved license degree (after about five years) or a doctoral degree (after about eight years and a dissertation). The Angelicum recently announced an English-language graduate-level program in ecumenism and interreligious dialogue.

The sponsoring Order of Preachers is known for their orthodoxy and expertise in Thomistic philosophy and theology. Most of the faculty are Dominican priests, and about 80 priests live on campus. The faculty includes Fr. Wojciech Giertych, O.P., Theologian of the Papal Household, and Pope John Paul II fa-

mously was a student of the Angelicum.

The chancellor (Gran Cancelliere) is Fr. Bruno Cadoré, O.P., a French bioethicist and Master of the Order of Preachers since 2010. Fr. Miroslav Konstanc Adam, O.P., became rector (Rector Magnificus) of the Angelicum in May 2012, after serving as dean of the faculty of canon law.

The Angelicum has a broadly international student body, with about 1,010 students from 95 countries—especially the United States, India, Italy, and Poland. In 2012-13, 30 percent of the students were from North America.

Depending on the program, roughly 20 to 25 percent of the students are lay persons.

The 2013-2014 tuition price for the STB degree is a bargain relative to American colleges: €1,830 for the first year, €1,775 for the second year, and €2,290 for the third year. There are some additional fees that may apply. Food and housing are relatively expensive and arranged independently by the student, although the university's student affairs office will make recommendations for housing.

Academics

The Angelicum does not offer an integrated liberal arts curriculum; from the outset, students specialize in particular disciplines. American students will often study at least a couple of years at a college in the United States, and such prior study may be necessary: admission to the first-cycle program requires two years of prior study in philosophy. The Angelicum's philosophy department offers an intensive one-year program that satisfies this requirement, but only students who have at least three years of a college education can take advantage of the one-year course.

Students who have earned a bachelor's

Quick Facts

		2013-2014 Academic Year
Students 1,010		**Majors** 5
SATs N/A		**% Catholic** 90%
HS GPA N/A		**How Much?** €1,830 tuition

degree in the U.S. and want to pursue a graduate-level degree at the Angelicum will often need to take more philosophy or theology courses to obtain a pontifical bachelor's degree.

The philosophy department—and to some extent the entire faculty—concentrates on the writings of Thomas Aquinas and Thomistic philosophers. Students wanting to study a greater variety of philosophical approaches will often complete the first cycle and then transfer elsewhere for advanced studies.

To earn the bachelor's degree, philosophy students complete three years of coursework and must demonstrate mastery of Latin. The courses consider basic philosophical themes—man, God and the world—as well as the history of philosophy, with exposure to philosophers' original works. The program includes courses in psychology and logic. Students attend class for about 15 to 18 hours per week, not including supplemental studies in Latin for students who need it.

First-cycle theology students take introductory courses in fundamental theology, moral theology, spirituality, and even Church archaeology and history. A series of courses study the mystery of salvation according to St. Thomas Aquinas' Summa Theologiae. Specialized courses focus on grace, virtue and contemporary social justice issues. Students begin to learn New Testament Greek and biblical Hebrew.

The Angelicum's other departments are canon law and social sciences. The latter is focused primarily on development in poorer countries, with mostly East European students and some Africans and Americans.

Although the former monastery that houses the Angelicum is quaint, the facilities are older and less well-equipped than American college students are used to. Also, Italian tariffs make books published outside the country extremely expensive, and so students are not permitted to borrow books from the library. Instead, they are encouraged to read in the library, or pages can be photocopied. Many of the books are in Italian and other languages; few are in English. A consortium allows students to access books at all the pontifical universities in Rome.

The school year is somewhat later than the standard American year. Classes begin in mid-October and run through the end of May.

Spiritual Life

With so many priests around, it is not surprising that the Angelicum offers many opportunities for Mass, regular confessions, and spiritual counseling. But because students do not live on the campus, the most popular Masses are at midday during the week. Most students attend daily and Sunday Mass elsewhere.

Residential Life

The University also offers little by way of student activities and culture. There is no residential campus, and only the Dominicans live on campus.

Most lay students rent or lease apartments in the historical district of Rome; the quaint Trastevere district is increasingly popular among university students for housing and nightlife. Some students prefer the beach towns about an hour away, which offer low-cost rental housing during the off-season. The university's Office of Student Affairs helps students with information on affordable and available housing.

The Angelicum lies just on the eastern edge of the historic district of Rome, a safe area of the city with restaurants and shops nearby. The campus is easily accessible by subway and buses. Leonardo da Vinci-Fiumicino Airport is about an hour's drive from the Angelicum.

The Bottom Line

The appeal of studying in Rome is undeniable—at the Dominicans' pontifical university, no less. The Angelicum offers an impressive and rigorous English-language curriculum for students who are prepared to specialize in philosophy or theology, and to enjoy living independently in one of Europe's most magnificent cities. And the price is right.

American students will need to carefully consider the substantial courses required before beginning the first-cycle program, the lack of a residential campus, and the absence of a liberal arts core outside of theology and philosophy. But if study at the Angelicum seems appropriate, students will find a faithful Catholic program awaiting them in the heart of the Eternal City.

REDEEMER PACIFIC COLLEGE

Langley, British Columbia, Canada

411

For more information on Redeemer Pacific, visit their website at:

www.redeemerpacific.ca

Admissions contact:

877/477-7212
info@redeemerpacific.ca

Overview

Redeemer Pacific College is a one-of-a-kind Catholic college embedded within Trinity Western University (TWU), an evangelical Christian institution that offers undergraduate degrees in 45 majors.

Located less than a half hour north of the American border in British Columbia, the University draws about 21 percent of its 2,200 undergraduates from the United States. Aside from the expected theological differences, Catholic families will be pleased with the emphasis of Trinity Western on authentic Christian identity and students' moral development.

The embedded Redeemer Pacific College (RPC), founded in 1999, offers more than 25 courses in Catholic studies for about 120 students dually enrolled at the College and University. The College building includes a classroom, faculty offices, student lounge, supplemental library, and chapel.

RPC does not offer its own degree, but courses can be applied to a TWU degree. The College does offer three certificates—liberal arts, theology and education—and its courses can be used to

satisfy a Catholic studies minor through the University's religious studies department.

The College's nine-member board of governors includes Father John McCarthy, representative for the Archdiocese of Vancouver. Reflecting RPC's "associate college" partnership with the Franciscan University of Steubenville, one FUS faculty member, Dr. Andrew Minto, serves on the College's board of governors.

RPC's president is Dr. Christine Jones, who earned her M.A. and Ph.D. from McGill University and a Canada-Research Chair post-doctorate in religion and culture from the University of British Columbia. New additions to the faculty

include theologian Dr. Christophe Potworowski, the former chair of Catholic studies at McGill, and Sister Gabriella Yi, O.P., who has a doctoral degree in theology from Rome's Angelicum.

Depending on the exchange rate with Canada, RPC's price can be very attractive to Americans. Total tuition, room, and board in 2013-14 is C$26,920. Students receive generous financial aid from TWU and from the College. Vancouver's Archbishop J. Michael Miller, C.S.B., former secretary to the Vatican's Congregation for Catholic Education, recently provided the College an endowed scholarship fund, and two other scholarships are available to students. Other financial aid is available.

Academics

Students can take four RPC courses each semester of the freshman year to meet the core requirements for a TWU degree. These courses emphasize "the Catholic heritage of faith and culture."

To qualify for a minor in Catholic studies, students need to take 24 credits in religious studies courses such as those on the Old and New Testament, Catholic spirituality, and Theology of the Body, as well as philosophy courses, including

Quick Facts

2013-2014 Academic Year

Students 130

SATs N/A

HS GPA N/A

Majors 45

% Catholic 100%

How Much? $26,920 CDN
tuition, room and board

those on St. Thomas Aquinas. The College consults with Franciscan University on the Catholic content of its courses.

Beyond the Catholic formation provided by Redeemer Pacific College, students complete their studies in TWU courses. TWU offers a wide range of majors in schools of the humanities and social sciences, natural and applied sciences, professional studies and performing arts, business, education and human kinetics (focused on physical fitness and coaching). The University has a semester-long program at its Laurentian Leadership Centre in Ottawa for students studying Canadian government, and a variety of study abroad programs.

All RPC professors make an annual oath of loyalty to the Magisterium of the Catholic Church. Three of the five faculty members teach theology, and they have the *mandatum*.

Spiritual Life

Redeemer Pacific has a chaplain who offers Mass from Monday to Thursday, hears confession, and gives spiritual guidance. Adoration and Benediction take place on Wednesdays. Masses are also available at two area parishes. Students attend retreats each semester at the Seminary of Christ the King in Mission, British Columbia.

TWU has a nondenominational chapel and active Christian ministry, including a variety of guest speakers and musicians.

Residential Life

RPC students live in the larger University's housing. Fewer than a third of TWU students (about 850) live on campus, although the university encourages it. One residence hall is set aside for first- and second-year female students; the remaining halls are co-ed, with men and women separated by floor or in suites with separate bathrooms.

Policies are consistent with Catholic moral teachings. TWU requires all students to sign a statement pledging to forego premarital sex, alcohol, and other detriments to academic and spiritual life.

The nearby town of Langley, with a population of 115,000, is less than one hour from the city of Vancouver and about 20 minutes from the Pacific Ocean. Among sites of local interest are the Canadian Museum of Flight and Transportation, Fort Langley National Historical Site, and the Langley Centennial Museum.

Major roads connect Langley with Vancouver, and the Vancouver International Airport is a large and modern facility.

Student Activities

RPC has a newly-formed Student Association which organizes many social events for students, including Bowling with the Profs, Thanksgiving and Advent dinners. Overall, there is an attempt made to foster a sense of community

for the RPC students as a supplement to student activities at Trinity Western.

Students are also able to participate in university-wide activities, including a variety of clubs that are mostly related to academic disciplines, student government, and campus media. The Spartans field men's and women's basketball, soccer and volleyball teams. There are also the typical diversions such as those reflected in Theatre at TWU, Jazz Night, and intramural sports.

The campus is set in the shadow of the North Shore Mountains, offering opportunities for skiing and hiking. The 157-acre campus includes 60 acres of protected natural forest and a lake circled by hiking trails.

The Bottom Line

Redeemer Pacific College is guided by dedicated Catholics who seek to provide intellectual ballast to young men and women who want to live and share their faith in the world. It certainly helps that they draw inspiration and advice from the Franciscan University of Steubenville.

The location within a larger Christian university is not a problem, and in fact ensures a morally appropriate campus life that is hard to find at most Catholic universities. Catholic students should be secure in their faith and prepared to address theological differences.

The personal attention that RPC students receive is uncommon and refreshing. For all these reasons, Redeemer Pacific College is yet another affordable and attractive option for Americans seeking a solid Catholic education.

THE CARDINAL NEWMAN SOCIETY

HAS BEEN PROMOTING AND DEFENDING
FAITHFUL CATHOLIC EDUCATION FOR 20 YEARS!

WHAT ARE WE
DOING TO CELEBRATE?

GIVING AWAY 40,000 COPIES OF MY FUTURE,
MY FAITH MAGAZINE TO HELP CATHOLIC FAMILIES
NAVIGATE THE TRANSITION TO COLLEGE

HELPING FAITHFUL CATHOLIC HIGH SCHOOLS ACHIEVE
EXCELLENCE THROUGH OUR EXPANDED CATHOLIC HIGH
SCHOOL HONOR ROLL PROGRAM

PUBLISHING THE 4TH EDITION OF THE NEWMAN GUIDE TO
CHOOSING A CATHOLIC COLLEGE, WHICH RECOMMENDS
COLLEGES THAT EMBRACE FAITHFUL EDUCATION

WORKING DIRECTLY WITH PRESIDENTS AND SENIOR FACULTY
AND STAFF AT FAITHFUL CATHOLIC COLLEGES TO TACKLE
TOUGH PROBLEMS AND PROMOTE BEST PRACTICES

THE CARDINAL
NEWMAN SOCIETY
Promoting and Defending
Faithful Catholic Education

1993 **20**th 2013
ANNIVERSARY

CARDINALNEWMANSOCIETY.ORG • 703.367.0333

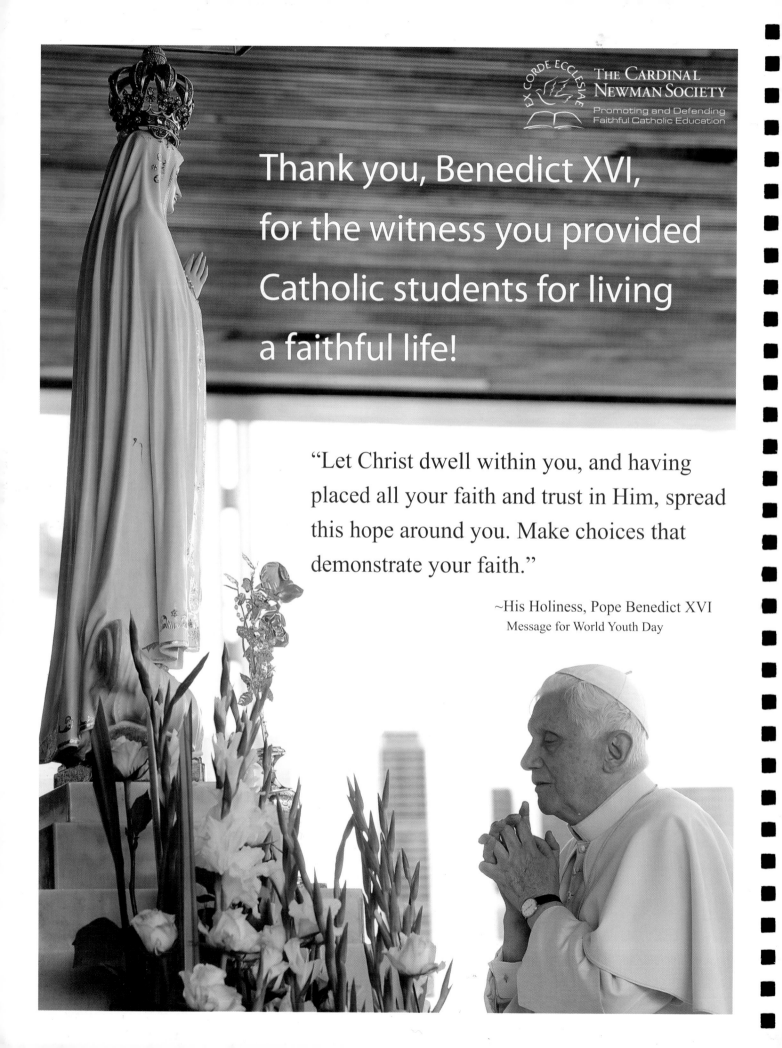